University Futures
and the Politics of Reform
in New Zealand

University Futures
and the Politics of Reform
in New Zealand

by
Michael Peters and Peter Roberts

d
p

Dunmore Press

©1999 Michael Peters and Peter Roberts
©1999 Dunmore Press Limited

First Published in 1999
by
Dunmore Press Limited
P.O. Box 5115
Palmerston North
New Zealand

Australian Supplier:
Federation Press
P.O. Box 45
Annandale 2038 NSW
Australia
Ph: (02) 9552-2200
Fax: (02) 9552-1681

ISBN 0 86469 350 8

Text: Times New Roman 11/13
Printer: The Dunmore Printing Company Ltd
               Palmerston North
Cover design: Murray Lock

Contents

Preface

This book has emerged from our joint interest in the politics of university
reform and the future of tertiary education in New Zealand. We believe
the tertiary sector is currently at a critical moment in its development in
this čountry. Over the past two years, far-reaching changes in systems
of governance and accountability, tuition fees, the funding of research,
and quality assurance mechanisms have been enacted or proposed.
These build on more than a decade of neoliberal economic and social
reform, and give evidence of a pivotal shift in prevailing conceptions of
education. Indeed, at the heart of the reforms is a particular construction
of the human subject from which a new view of the role of the state –
and the *market* – in social and educational policy has been formed.
After such a sustained period of significant change, key words in the
language of neoliberalism have become familiar to many New Zealanders.
Terms such as 'consumer', 'provider', 'input', 'output', 'competition'
and 'choice' have become part of everyday discourse in New Zealand
society. This book aims to problematise this language, the philosophical
assumptions behind it, and the institutional transformations associated
with it. We try to avoid the temptation to call for a nostalgic (but

impossible) return to the university of the past, yet also defend those features of higher educational life worthy and capable of preservation in a globalised, postmodern world.

While questions of timing are always important in the publication of a book, they acquired special relevance in this case. Much of the writing for this volume was completed during 1997 and the first few months of 1998. Our intention in addressing key policy documents was to integrate an analysis of the white paper on tertiary education with comments on the various green papers released in the latter half of 1997. The white paper, however, seemed to take forever to arrive. In one of the most tumultuous periods in New Zealand's political history, tertiary education appeared to be a relatively low priority: throughout 1998 observers in the tertiary education community waited – and waited – for the white paper to appear. The messages issued from the government to the tertiary sector were unclear: at one point, it seemed several white papers dealing with different aspects of the reform process would be published, but this plan was subsequently dropped. Finally, in November 1998, *Tertiary Education in New Zealand: Policy Directions for the 21st Century* was released by the Ministry of Education and we were able to proceed with ithe remaining writing and editing.

We have organised the book thematically rather than chronologically. Our goal is to offer a series of reflections on related topics; we do not claim to provide a systematic historical account of post-1984 changes in tertiary education in New Zealand. While there is now an extensive critical literature on educational policy in this country, the number of book-length studies on the politics of university reform is still relatively small. The literature on university *futures* is even smaller. Given the potential breadth of our subject, we see plenty of scope for further work and hope others will be able to flesh out areas examined in brief detail here.

Acknowledgements

We wish to thank colleagues and friends in the School of Education at the University of Auckland for their dialogue and encouragement over recent years. Our conversations with Jim Marshall and Patrick Fitzsimons have been especially helpful. We have also valued the opportunity to discuss some of the ideas in this book with students in our educational policy and philosophy of education courses. At Dunmore Press, Sharmian Firth's enthusiasm for this project was very important in getting it off the ground and seeing it through to completion. Murray Gatenby's attention to the manuscript in its later stages was also significant. We would like to express our sincere gratitude to Tina and Linda for their continuing support of our academic work. Finally, thanks are due to the editors of the following journals and books for their permission to reproduce material accepted for publication elsewhere: the *Oxford Review of Education* (Roberts, 1996a); *Access: Critical Perspectives on Cultural and Policy Studies in Education* (Roberts, 1997a); the *New Zealand Annual Review of Education* (Peters and Roberts, 1998a; Roberts and Peters, 1999); the *Electronic Journal of Sociology* (Roberts, 1998a); the *Journal of Education Policy* (Peters, 1998); *First Monday: The*

Peer-Reviewed Journal on the Internet (Roberts and Peters, 1998); *Laboring in Academe*, edited by Harry Smaller and David Cooke (Roberts, 1999b); *Australian Universities Review* (Peters and Roberts, 1999); the *International Review of Education* (Roberts, 1999a); and *Discourse: Studies in the Cultural Politics of Education* (Peters and Roberts, 2000). Full details are provided in the bibliography.

Michael Peters and Peter Roberts
March 1999

introduction

The Transformation of Tertiary Education in New Zealand

This book addresses the transformation of tertiary education in New Zealand under the policies and practices of neoliberalism, and considers possible futures for universities here and elsewhere. The changes in New Zealand are not dissimilar to those enacted in a number of other Western democracies over the last two decades, and concerns expressed by critics here resonate with those advanced by scholars in Canada, Britain and Australia, among other countries. The terms used to describe the processes vary in the different countries – Australians speak of 'economic rationalism' instead of 'neoliberalism', for example – but the underlying principles are essentially the same in each case: higher education has been reconfigured along market lines, with a heavy emphasis on 'student choice', competition between different 'providers', new 'accountability' mechanisms, and a favouring of corporate models of governance and ownership. While our prime focus is the New Zealand context, this book also draws extensively on the wider international literature. In this Introduction we identify some of the key features of neoliberal social policy reform in New Zealand, provide brief comments on the current political scene in this country, and analyse the reconfiguration of 'education' following the New Right revolution. Pivotal elements in the restructuring of New Zealand universities during the period 1984–1998 are noted here and given more extended critical treatment in later chapters.

Neoliberal Social Policy Reform in New Zealand

Changes in New Zealand universities need to be understood in relation to wider shifts in economic and social policy introduced from 1984 to the present day. As has been well documented in a number of studies (e.g. Kelsey, 1993, 1995; Boston, 1995; Boston *et al.*, 1991; Sharp, 1994; Peters and Marshall, 1996), New Zealand has been subject to a massive programme of restructuring following the election of the fourth Labour government in 1984. To the dismay of many traditional Labour supporters, key members in the Lange government – particularly the newly appointed Minister of Finance, Roger Douglas – began to systematically implement a radical new economic strategy while simultaneously dismantling key components of the welfare state in New Zealand. Douglas, together with Richard Prebble and a number of other senior members of Cabinet, planned to drastically reduce the entire state sector, ostensibly with the intention of diminishing governmental and bureaucratic intrusion into individual lives.

An ambitious blueprint for managerialist reform – involving the related neoliberal processes of corporatisation, marketisation and privatisation (Easton, 1995; Fitzsimons, 1995; Gordon, 1995; Peters, Marshall and Parr, 1993; Peters, 1997a, 1997b) – was enacted. Public services and institutions became 'state-owned enterprises', and thousands of workers in the state sector lost their jobs. State subsidies to farmers were scrapped and tariff barriers to trade were withdrawn. In the latter half of the 1980s interest rates soared to new heights, average house prices rose steeply, and skyscrapers began popping up in the major centres. A new class of young, aggressive, urbane entrepreneurs – the 'yuppies' of the 1980s – emerged. Fortunes were won – and subsequently lost (following the 1987 sharemarket 'crash') – through speculative investments on the stock exchange. The rapidity of the changes stunned even the most seasoned political observers, including some within the Labour Cabinet. Roger Douglas's proposal for a flat tax was the final straw for many, and in 1988 Prime Minister Lange shifted control over the Finance portfolio from Douglas to (the somewhat more moderate) David Caygill.

By 1990 dissatisfaction with the Labour government was such that the National Party was returned to power with a record majority. The process of reform initiated by Douglas and others was, however, keenly pursued by incoming Minister of Finance Ruth Richardson and given strong endorsement by the new Prime Minister, Jim Bolger, and other Cabinet ministers in pivotal portfolios. Shortly after assuming responsibility for social welfare, Jenny Shipley sanctioned wide-ranging cuts to benefits. 'User pays' charges were initiated in health and education, contributing to the unpopularity of ministers Simon Upton and Lockwood Smith. The former was relieved of the health portfolio when he failed to 'sell' neoliberal reforms in the health sector to an increasingly cynical public, and later Lockwood Smith was to relinquish the education portfolio in favour of lower-key responsibilities in agriculture and other areas. The boom years of the 1980s were replaced by a deep recession in the early 1990s, and public opinion of politicians reached an all-time low.

Poverty was by this stage becoming an increasingly prominent feature of the social landscape in New Zealand, and the emergence of food banks and other emergency assistance centres stood out in sharp relief against the relative prosperity of earlier decades. The introduction of the Employment Contracts Act served to further alienate the government from thousands of people whose conditions of work were ruthlessly undermined in the new labour relations environment. Real wages had declined, unemployment and underemployment reached record highs, and the bargaining power of unions had been systematically reduced. Interest rates were low, but fewer people had money to spend. The gap between the rich and the poor grew glaringly larger, and the National Party came perilously close to losing the 1993 election.

With National's grip on power remaining tenuous throughout the period from 1993–1996, voters waited with eager anticipation for the inauguration of a new electoral system: Mixed Member Proportional representation. Many hoped MMP would encourage the incoming government of 1996 to adopt a more democratic and dialogical style. The likelihood of coalitions between political parties would, some felt, make governments more subject to constraints against economic and social extremes than had been the case in the past. The extent to which these constraints would operate was always going to be dependent on the portion of the vote granted to parties other than National – principally Labour (by now avowedly centre left), the Alliance (always clearly to the left), and New Zealand First (ostensibly centrist) – in the 1996 election. As it turned out, New Zealand First held the balance of power, and kept the country waiting for several weeks as it negotiated with *both* Labour and National over possible coalition agreements. In eventually siding with National, New Zealand First leader Winston Peters made at least a partial return to his Tory roots, and the parties of the left – Labour and the Alliance – retreated to reassess their political futures.

The inability of Labour and the Alliance to put their differences behind them in building a cohesive opposition persisted in the lead-up to, and beyond, the 1996 election. This chill in relations has only recently thawed. Jim Bolger's replacement as Prime Minister by Jenny Shipley signalled a clear move (further) to the right by National. With Shipley at the helm, tensions between the coalition partners and within New Zealand First were heightened. In August of 1998 the coalition collapsed. The collapse was triggered by differences between the two parties over the sale of government shares in Wellington airport. This was, however, only the final step in a series of crises. Disagreements between Peters and Shipley had become more visible, and some weeks earlier Tau Henare had been sacked as the New Zealand First deputy leader. The New Zealand First caucus ruptured in several directions, with some of its MPs remaining loyal to Peters and staying with the party, some signalling their intentions of building new political organisations (while pledging allegiance to National in the meantime), and others declaring themselves independents. In early 1999 the National Party was clinging to power as a minority government, with support from the right-wing Association of Consumers and Taxpayers (ACT) Party and several independents.

The sweeping economic and social changes of the past fourteen years have been premised on a set of neoliberal philosophical assumptions. The primacy of the market as the organising principle for all human activity has been advanced with ruthless efficiency as the years have passed, to the point where many of the assumptions underpinning this change are no longer questioned. The marketisation process in New Zealand, as elsewhere, has proceeded from the presupposition that society is nothing more than the aggregate of self-interested individuals. Neoliberalism introduces a new ontological category: *homo economicus*, the self-contained, rational, autonomous, utility-maximising chooser (see Peters, 1993; Marshall, 1996). For over a decade, older communitarian ideals have been forced into the background as an ethic of competitive individualism has swept (almost) all in its path. Of course, communitarian *practices* have not been entirely stamped out; indeed, the ruthlessness of the reforms has arguably contributed to the emergence of a new collectivism among certain groups. The mainstream churches, for example, have joined other community groups in rallying against the injustices of poverty and unemployment. An active, organised, collective form of struggle against cuts to health funding has emerged with new vigour and depth of conviction among some previously divided and relatively inactive groups. Many Māori have also reasserted traditional collective values (in, for example, arguments over property rights), and a number of small rural and coastal communities have (re)discovered a shared sense of responsibility toward each other in the face of genuine hardship. Such examples have, however, been very much against the grain of the prevailing ideology of market liberalism. Almost every official document produced in the reform period bears at least some traces of this ideology, from the explicit endorsement of neoliberal economic principles in Treasury reports on education (e.g. Treasury, 1987) to the infusion of ideas on skills, competition and the world economy in curriculum guides and training support policies (e.g. Ministry of Education, 1993; Education and Training Support Agency, 1993).

With this shift in official rhetoric comes a new language. Citizens are now *consumers*, whether buying vegetables in a produce market or 'purchasing' education in a tertiary institution. Universities, colleges of education and polytechnics are *providers*, and are expected to actively compete with each other in attempting to attract enrolments and research monies. For a period, nurses and doctors were told they worked with clients (not patients) and hospitals were known as Crown Health Enterprises. The population has recently been instructed to return to the old terminology, but the effects of the linguistic transformation linger and 'Treasury speak' has, for many, become the norm. All complex social processes, for those who endorse the Treasury line (a line supported by a range of other government departments, including the State Services Commission: see Dale and Jesson, 1992), can be reduced to a series of 'inputs', 'outputs' and 'throughputs'. Education becomes a commodity to be bought, sold, traded and consumed in a competitive marketplace; it is a private rather than public good. Students (consumers) exercise their rights as individuals in *choosing* which qualifications (if any) to pursue, and, since they are the ones who are presumed to benefit from their education, they should be expected to pay for it. 'User pays' policies, requiring students to cover an increasing proportion (or the full amount) of their tuition costs, are the logical extension of this form of thinking.

While the 'New Zealand experiment' (Kelsey, 1995) was being conducted, changes of enormous import were taking place in the world economy. A number of theorists have discussed the significance of the shift from 'Fordist' to 'Post-Fordist' systems of production, the former being characterised by the mass production of manufactured goods, the latter placing greater emphasis on 'flexible' regimes of production, export-driven manufacturing growth, and niche marketing (cf., Gee, Hull and Lankshear, 1996). Service industries have become a key component of contemporary economies, and information is increasingly becoming the principal commodity of 'New Times' capitalism. Multinational corporations have assumed an imposing presence on the world stage over the past decade. Nations have been 'resited' and states have been 'reshaped' (Dale and Robertson, 1997). The economic successes and subsequent failures of Asian countries have seen politicians rapidly realigning socio-geographical boundaries in their positioning of New Zealand relative to other competitors on the world stage. Some years ago, in a move that would have been unthinkable for earlier generations, former Prime Minister Jim Bolger started declaring that New Zealand was part of Asia. Now politicians are rushing to distance themselves from the troubled economies of our Asian neighbours.

As Western countries across the globe have moved away from the smokestack capitalism of the earlier industrial age, repeated references (principally, but not exclusively, by politicians and corporate élites) have been made to a 'skills crisis'. This claim – in its various guises – is intimately related to the notion of retaining a competitive (economic) edge in a rapidly changing world. Our wellbeing as a nation, it has frequently been asserted, depends on our ability to compete with other countries in an increasingly sophisticated technological environment (cf. O'Rourke, 1993; Creech, 1997a). Education, it is almost always noted, ought to be much more explicitly geared toward the 'needs of the economy' and in particular the need for more skilled workers in industries reliant upon advanced technologies. Public educational institutions have allegedly suffered from 'provider capture' in the past and now need to be forced to adjust their priorities to fall more into line with changes in the global marketplace.

Reconstructing Tertiary Education

All institutions in the New Zealand tertiary education system have been affected by the neoliberal reform process. Some emergent educational groups – those involved in private training establishments, for example – have relished fresh opportunities for gaining government and student dollars. The new language of the market provides precisely the kind of framework such organisations need to compete with older, traditional offerings in other institutions. Others have been somewhat ambivalent about the marketisation of education; the polytechnics might perhaps be placed in this category. On the one hand, the provision for mounting degree-level qualifications in the new tertiary environment, hitherto the almost exclusive preserve of the universities, has been welcomed by many administrators and teachers in polytechnics. On the other hand, the fostering of competition among multiple 'providers' – a kind of educational 'open warfare', if you like – has, under conditions in which funds are always strictly limited, put pressure on polytechnics to deliver programmes that will not only attract (or retain) students but also begin to generate international academic reputations.

Teachers colleges have enjoyed mixed fortunes over the past decade. The belief that there were too many stand-alone teacher training institutions for a country with a population of little more than three million people has been shared by a number of government officials over the years, and threats of potential job losses have loomed large in the minds of (some) college principals for much of this time. Amalgamations with universities emerged as a realistic and financially expedient possibility following the publication of the *Learning for Life I and II* policy documents (Department of Education, 1989a, 1989b) in the second term of the fourth Labour government. The University of Waikato and Hamilton Teachers College were the first to go down this route. Massey University and Palmerston North Teachers College have subsequently followed suit. In more recent times, as part of an aggressive campaign to become the biggest 'provider' of tertiary education in New Zealand, Massey has been successful in gaining support for mergers with Auckland College of Education and Wellington Polytechnic. In the early 1990s Colleges of Education endured a situation in which teachers could not find jobs but have lately gained ground as the problem of serious teacher shortages has become glaringly apparent to government officials – with a corresponding, if rather belated, push to encourage more students into teaching as a career.

The universities have, in some ways, encountered more far-reaching challenges to their status, role and character in the last ten years than ever before. They no longer enjoy a monopoly over degree courses, and competition between (and within) institutions has become more intense. Vice-chancellors have become 'chief executives' and serve as 'the employer' for staff in their institutions. A new logic of performativity has emerged, with continuous appraisal and review of individuals, departments and programmes now the norm (cf. Lyotard, 1984; Peters, 1994a). The authority of the universities to manage their own affairs has been routinely questioned and the traditional composition of university councils has been threatened. The university's role (currently protected in legislation) of acting as the 'critic and conscience' of society has been systematically undermined in some quarters (Peters, 1994b). A determined attempt has been made (eventually without complete success) to force university qualifications into a framework based on 'unit standards' (Fitzsimons, 1995; Roberts, 1997a, 1997b; Codd, 1996; Hall, 1995a, 1995b; Elley, 1996). Those who wish to retain a distinction between 'academic' and 'vocational' learning are now labelled as élitist, misguided or out of step with the times. University programmes have frequently been attacked as 'irrelevant' to the 'needs' of students, industry and employers, and courses in the humanities have been ridiculed for their alleged emphasis on bizarre theoretical fads and political correctness (see Kerr, 1997).

This storm has been weathered in the face of unprecedented financial pressure. Figures provided in a recent OECD review of tertiary education in New Zealand provide clear evidence of decreasing government support for staff and students in universities over the past decade. The number of students in the tertiary education sector increased substantially in the late 1980s and early 1990s (with a particularly dramatic leap in total enrolments of 10.2 per cent in the 1990–1993 period). Universities experienced strong growth in numbers from 1985 to 1994, although the number of part-time students fell back slightly in 1995 (OECD, 1997a: 39–40). The surge in total enrolments has not, however, been met by a level of government funding commensurate with the increase. Funding per effective full-time student has declined every year from 1992 to 1996, and tuition fees have grown steadily in the same period (p. 42).

With the National government's decision some years ago to make institutions set their own fees (in a climate of declining government support), the battle over tuition costs has often been played out on university campuses, with Registry occupations grabbing headlines as much as protests on the streets or the steps of the Beehive. Classes have grown dramatically in size, but there has been little money available for funding new buildings and developing the necessary infrastructure to cope with increases in the student population. Student–staff ratios in universities have grown from a figure of 14.1:1 in 1988 to an average of 18.5:1 in 1993, 1994 and 1995 (OECD, 1997a: 43). As averages across all departments, such figures mask the fact that some staff in the university – particularly in the humanities and social sciences – have been forced to carry even heavier loads (ratios of 21:1 or 22:1 are not uncommon) in order to allow more intensive teaching in areas such as medicine. Despite claims (by politicians and some business leaders) of inefficiency and 'ivory tower' detachment from the 'real' world, universities have, year after year, had to 'do more with less'. This pressure-cooker situation had stretched resources almost to breaking point, added significantly to workloads for academics and other university employees, and brought morale for many staff down to an all-time low.

Some of these tensions could be detected by the team responsible for preparing the OECD report:

In their institutional visits and meetings, the reviewers became aware of rather higher levels of dissonance and tension than in some other countries, although the reform measures everywhere are generating anxiety in some sectors and can be expected to stimulate opposition. While it is normal for the academic community, in exercising its role as 'social conscience' and intellectual critic (important roles that need to be recognised within as well as outside of tertiary education), to take an oppositional line to major policy changes that directly affect its own way of life, the nature of the opposition was such that we believe there is cause for greater efforts to be made by government, Ministry of Education and institutional leadership both to broaden and strengthen the dialogue (p. 22).

If it was hoped that the multifaceted review of tertiary education under the National–New Zealand First Coalition government would put an end to university woes, many will have been disappointed. The green paper on tertiary education, *A Future Tertiary Education Policy for New Zealand* (Ministry of Education, 1997a), released in September of 1997, needs to be read alongside several other major policy statements. Green papers on qualifications policies (Ministry of Education, 1997b) and teacher education (Ministry of Education, 1997c) were issued in the same year. A proper assessment of the context for and agenda behind the tertiary education review green paper must also take the widely circulated leaked version of the document, 'Tertiary education review: Proposals and key decisions' (Ministry of Education, 1997d), into account. Representing a compromise between an extreme form of consumer-driven, fully-marketised education and what we have now (a less extreme consumer-driven marketised system), the tertiary education review green paper left the way open for vouchers (entitlements), an escalation of competition between institutions, the separation of 'teaching' from 'research', new modes of governance (where a business model might prevail), and substantial cuts to state subsidies on student fees. The apparent 'toning down' of the most radical elements in the proposed reform package was in part a response to the timely release of the leaked version of the document, where the full extent of the marketisation agenda was laid out in chillingly clear detail. The tertiary education review green paper, as we argue in Chapter 7, did not prevent the leaked version from coming into being; it simply wove extreme and less-extreme variants of further marketisation into the one document, leaving either route open.

The publication of the white paper, *Tertiary Education in New Zealand: Policy Directions for the 21st Century* (Ministry of Education, 1998), was a protracted process. At different times during the year after September 1997, there was uncertainty over both the question of when the paper would be ready and whether there would be more than one document. The initial intention, it seems, was to publish one white paper. Some months later, the prospect of releasing several papers (separating, for example, issues such as tuition from matters of ownership and governance) was seriously considered. In the end, officials returned to the idea of one paper while giving early notice (via the 1998 Budget announcements) of some forthcoming changes. Given the extraordinary delays, the eventual publication of the white paper in November 1998 was greeted with disappointment as well as disapproval by many. As the culmination of a process that had started almost two years ago, the white paper was an insubstantial document, similar in scope and content to the tertiary education review green paper. Despite claims to the contrary in the document, the white paper appeared to many critics to be clearly driven by a privatisation agenda, as evidenced by the favouring of new government subsides for private training establishments, the decline in EFTS-based research support for public institutions, the introduction of new capital charges, and significant changes in the composition and nature of university councils. Most worrying of all was the potential for undermining academic freedom and institutional autonomy with the granting of important new powers to the Minister of Education.

It is possible to see the white paper as one of the final steps in a process of incremental neoliberal reform, paving the way, via a far-reaching set of policy and legislative changes, to a fully privatised tertiary education system. The beginnings of this process date back to the mid-1980s. There has been a determined effort on the part of influential ministers in successive New Zealand governments from 1984 to give the universities a good 'shake-up' (Butterworth and Tarling, 1994). This attitude is partly revealed in some of the key policy documents produced during this period: the Hawke Report (Department of Education, 1988a), *Learning for Life I and II* (Department of Education, 1989a,

1989b), the Todd Report (Ministry of Education, 1994), and the recent green and white papers on tertiary education (Ministry of Education, 1997a, 1998). To get to the heart of the reform process, however, it is necessary to understand the context within which such documents have been generated. The ascendancy of neoliberal thought within key policy-making circles from 1984 to the present day was, when combined with both the wealth and power of corporates eager to shake off years of Muldoonism and the opening up of (so-called) 'free trade' across the globe, pivotal in setting the stage for the reconstruction of the educational sphere. Corporate giants played a crucial role not just in giving certain policies their financial backing (and in endorsing Roger Douglas) but, more explicitly, in *creating* or overseeing policy changes in key social areas. The appointment of people who had been successful in business as chairs of major policy reviews – e.g. Alan Gibbs in the health sector and Brian Picot in the educational arena – was an overt manifestation of a new mode of policy development and implementation. Indeed, this phenomenon reflected a fundamental shift in government thinking. Deciding what was best for hospitals or schools should not, it was felt, be left to those with professional expertise in these areas (e.g. doctors or nurses in the case of the former; teachers or university lecturers in the case of the latter). Individuals with professional ties would, it was believed, be encumbered with the same interest-serving biases that had led to what Treasury (in)famously called 'provider capture' in public institutions. Experts from the business world would, given their managerial success and separation from the daily life of the institutions they were evaluating, be ideally placed – so right-wing Cabinet ministers, Treasury officials and like-minded bureaucrats argued – to make the best decisions in the interests of all.

Butterworth and Tarling's *A Shakeup Anyway: Government and the Universities in New Zealand in a Decade of Reform* (1994) provides both a succinct historical account of the evolution of New Zealand universities and a detailed analysis of changes in tertiary education in the decade following the election of the Labour government in 1984. Many of the observations in this insightful book are based on the direct involvement of the authors (Butterworth through the Association of University Staff, Tarling in his role as Deputy Vice-Chancellor of the University of Auckland) in some of the negotiations with politicians and bureaucrats during this period. Another comprehensive account of the recent history of New Zealand universities (addressing the period 1984–1996) is provided by Glenys Patterson (1996). Patterson has also published a book on the history of the university from ancient Greece to the twentieth century (Patterson, 1997). A rich critical literature on more specific features of the tertiary reform process has also emerged. Jonathan Boston (1988) has completed an excellent critical analysis of the Watts Committee Report and the Treasury's briefing papers for the incoming government of 1987. The Combined Chaplaincies at Victoria University of Wellington (1995) have published an edited collection on the university, ethics and society. There has been discussion of the 'cultural politics' of the university in New Zealand (Peters, 1997c), and the significance of virtual technologies in tertiary education (Peters and Roberts, 1998b) has been explored. A volume on the economics of higher education (Maani, 1997) has also appeared. There is a sizeable body of work on the relationship between the NZQA and the universities. (Of the many studies pertinent to this theme, compare: Elley, 1996; Hall, 1995a, 1995b; Fitzsimons, 1995; Codd, 1995, 1996, 1997; Roberts, 1997a, 1997b). The universities – represented by both the AUS and the New Zealand Vice-Chancellors Committee – have consistently opposed the move to make 'unit standards' the basis for acquiring and comparing educational qualifications. Such an approach has been seen as either an entirely unsuitable or an unnecessarily restrictive means for making evaluative judgements within many university subject areas. The attempt to break down distinctions between 'vocational' and 'academic' education, a move instituted with enthusiasm by senior NZQA officials (e.g. Barker, 1995; Hood, 1995) and some politicians, has been viewed with suspicion by some in university circles. Proponents of the blurring of these traditional boundaries have countered with accusations of élitism on the part of the universities. Several critics in the university sector have argued that the NZQA reforms have been premised on technocratic (Roberts, 1996a), instrumentalist (Tuck, 1994) or behaviourist (New Zealand Vice-Chancellors Committee, 1994) assumptions about learning and assessment. (We address the relationship between the universities and the NZQA in Chapter 6.)

Following the legislative reforms introduced under *Learning for Life* policies and the changes inaugurated by the NZQA, the door was opened for institutions other than universities to offer degrees. Some of the polytechnics have seized the opportunity to reposition themselves in the tertiary marketplace and have succeeded in not only securing degree status for a number of programmes, but are now actively seeking to rename themselves as universities. Colleges of education have taken and are continuing to take similar steps to change the titles of their offerings. A genuine attempt to rethink institutional cultures and break down past disciplinary and professional barriers lies behind some of these reforms. Many staff in polytechnics and colleges of education have sought higher qualifications, undertaken rigorous programmes of research and changed the nature of their teaching in recent years. The universities, too, have made an effort to improve measures for ensuring greater fairness and consistency in assessment and course workloads. Dialogue between institutions, while inimical to the imperative for competition, has by no means disappeared; indeed, in some cases it has been significantly enhanced, as new strategic alliances – some justified in academic terms, others more obviously products of financial expediency – have formed. Massey University has taken a lead in the entrepreneurial reconstruction of the tertiary sector, but other institutions are also working hard to 'position' themselves in the educational 'marketplace'. 'Branding' strategies (e.g. the endorsement of the documentary series 'The Human Body' by the University of Otago, and the University of Auckland's sponsorship of 'The New Zealand Wars' and 'Dancing in the Street') give one indication of where the tertiary sector is heading.

   It is also interesting to see how others have viewed the reform process. In the Executive Summary of the OECD report mentioned earlier, 'the need for change to bring tertiary education into the mainstream of national development' in New Zealand is noted (OECD, 1997a). The report writers admit that there has been some disquiet in the tertiary sector over the nature of the reform process, but suggest there is 'no going back' and urge 'all stakeholders – learners, providers, employers, government departments and agencies among them – to seize the new opportunities and build on the progress achieved thus far'. Those involved in the reform process should, it is argued, now concentrate on maintaining and strengthening 'both the quality and the relevance' of initial tertiary education (p. 5). The OECD reviewers draw attention to the dramatic and rapid transformation of New Zealand society under successive governments in the 1980s and 1990s, and observe that both the overall direction and specific policies have been the subject of intense debate in the tertiary education sector. Following a brief overview of some of the major policy changes over the past decade, the reviewers conclude that the New Zealand education system has been transformed from 'a protected and highly regulated domestic market to a more open, strategically directed, de-regulated and internationally-attuned sector'. There has, it is claimed, been a shift from a 'centrally-administered and rule-bound educational system into a devolved, largely self-managing one ... challenged by government and marketplace alike to deliver the new products and services' (p. 11).

With this shift in the balance of control in matters of governance and management, increasing pressure has been placed on universities to cut internal costs and generate revenue from external sources. This has left some sections of the university community in a very vulnerable position. When times are tight, as recent examples here and elsewhere (in Australia and the UK, among other places) have reminded us, the axe invariably falls on the least 'entrepreneurial' departments – classics, languages and art history are all prime candidates – in the first instance. If current trends continue, it might be predicted that research and scholarship will – despite vigorous claims to the contrary by policy-makers, politicians, and bureaucrats – be successively pushed into the background as the drive for student dollars gains momentum. The universities in New Zealand have fought a continuous battle in recent years over this issue. If the process of marketisation is not halted, new systems of legitimation will begin to come into play in the tertiary sector. Traditional canons of scholarly rigour could be placed under increasing threat, not just because 'standards' will have been lowered in an environment where any organisation can set itself up as a university, but also because they will no longer *matter* for many people. What will count, if the marketisation agenda is pushed to its limit, will be the logic of revenue generation (cf. Soley, 1995; Symes and Hopkins, 1994).

Australia has, since the election of the Howard Government in 1996, had to confront the prospect of several thousand job losses in universities as this century draws to a close. Some Canadian academics suffered pay cuts in recent years but have been told, in effect, that they should be thankful for retaining their jobs at all. In the United States, a growing underclass of younger academics, clutching recently acquired PhDs but unable to find anything other than perpetual short-term 'teaching assistant' work, has emerged. In New Zealand similar patterns are evident, although some of the most severe staffing cuts may be yet to come. The University of Auckland (which promotes itself, on not unreasonable grounds, as the pre-eminent research university in the country) has been subject to periodic financial difficulties – with continuing cuts to departmental budgets – over the last three years. Some even more serious problems have arisen at other New Zealand universities. The Humanities division at the University of Otago, for example, has been forced to make wide-ranging cuts with inevitable losses in staffing and the disappearance of a number of domains of study. The cuts have also had an impact *within* fields of study. At Otago, students wanting to study Education will, if the recommendations of the Maling Report (1998) are enacted, encounter only staff whose primary interests relate to classrooms, schooling and teacher training. Staff with expertise in other domains of educational inquiry have, in effect, been told they are no longer wanted or needed.

It is clear that universities the world over have been under enormous pressure over the past decade. With the spectre (or promise, depending on one's point of view) of the tertiary education review hanging over their heads all year during 1997, New Zealand university administrators struggled with ongoing budgetary concerns and mounting internal dissatisfaction from staff and students. The subsequent green and white papers on tertiary education have heightened rather than relieved these tensions. Operating in a mode of 'financial crisis' has, for several years, become the norm rather than the exception. This point often finds its most practical expression in the gestures of utter frustration – sometimes anger (certainly no longer mere bewilderment) – among academics who discover that the excessive teaching loads carried in the previous year, justified at the time as an exceptional response to the a crisis situation, now become 'standard practice' on top of which additional duties for the new year (inevitably also one of crisis) must be piled. Mutterings about ever-diminishing time for research and writing draw, at best, mildly sympathetic replies and, at times, vigorous attacks on the lack of 'efficiency' within university departments.

A Cautionary Tale

The changes in economic, social and educational life in New Zealand over the last fourteen years have been momentous. It is instructive to reflect on the manner in which such changes have occurred. We shall finish this discussion with a brief description of one event in New Zealand's tertiary education history which, for us, captures the essence of the neoliberal transformative process in this country. In early August of 1997 a draft version of a Ministry of Education policy paper on tertiary education (Ministry of Education, 1997d) was leaked to the media and universities. The paper, entitled 'Tertiary Education Review: Proposals and Key Decisions', was dated 17 July 1997. On 18 July Fiona Ross, a Senior Policy Analyst with the Ministry of Education, faxed a copy to officials in the Department of the Prime Minister and Cabinet, Treasury, the State Services Commission, Te Puni Kokiri, the NZQA, the Education and Training Support Agency, the Ministry of Research, Science and Technology, the Department of Labour, and the Ministry of Women's Affairs. In her covering letter, she noted that the Minister of Education and the Minister of Finance would be meeting on 22 July to discuss the tertiary education review green paper. The draft paper was intended to cover 'the fundamental aspects of the tertiary review package' and to seek 'broad agreement on the direction of the proposals'. Comments were required by 9.00 a.m. on 21 July to allow the paper to be sent to Ministers that afternoon (for consideration prior to the meeting the next day). Ross apologised for the 'short timeframe' but said the paper could be considered in more detail on 22 July. She concluded by noting: 'This early briefing paper would form the basis of Cabinet papers which we expect to be considered by EEP on 20 August'. The individuals consulted were invited to telephone with their comments if they felt they did not have time to put their ideas on paper.

Given the far-reaching implications of the changes proposed in the paper, the nature and speed of this policy consultation process could be seen as remarkable – indeed, frightening. The briefing paper was, admittedly, merely a draft version of a document (the tertiary education review green paper) which was itself to be released for discussion and debate prior to the policy implementation stage. Yet, with such a quick turn-around time for comments from the various associated ministries and organisations, it is not clear why these groups were consulted at all. Certainly there was not time for a thorough consideration of the issues at stake in the document. The history of policy making (particularly in relation to the tertiary education sector) in New Zealand over the last fourteen years is littered with examples of significant changes – many requiring legislative amendments – being pushed through with great rapidity (see Butterworth and Tarling, 1994). Indeed, former Labour Minister of Finance Roger Douglas (1993) explicitly advocated the implementation of economic and social reforms in quantum leaps and at great speed. This, he claimed, would prevent interest groups from mobilising. The same sort of thinking, not always expressed in such brazen terms, has underpinned many of the policy changes initiated by Cabinet ministers – under Labour, National, and National–New Zealand First governments – eager to keep the momentum of earlier neoliberal changes going.

The white paper on tertiary education is consistent with the proposals set out in the leaked document, although the extent to which further privatisation measures will be implemented over the next few years will depend on scheduled reviews of new systems. (The contestable research funding regime is one example.) What, it might be wondered, are university staff and students doing about this? *Should* they be doing anything about it? It would be unfair to assume that academics are simply accepting such radical changes – built on policies formed in haste and deeply embedded in an entrenched ideology – without question or opposition. To the contrary, university staff have, often in solidarity with students, vigorously resisted the commercialisation, marketisation and privatisation of tertiary education and the anti-democratic manner in which the changes have been made. There have been outcries from students, staff, unions, and opposition political parties over the more draconian features of the reform process. But, precisely because the neoliberal transformation of academic life has been so effective and far-reaching, people working in universities have had less and less time for active and well organised resistance. There has simply been too much to do: too much pressure, too many essays to mark, too many urgent (*always* urgent) administrative tasks to attend to, too many financial crises to address. Time, in some respects the most precious element of a reflective academic life, is these days in perpetually short supply. After a decade of neoliberal reform in the social sector many tertiary education workers have limited energy for fighting further battles.

Part of the problem, we believe, lies in the very manner in which tertiary education reform is framed. Many of our politicians and government officials would have us believe there *is* no problem. Universities must, we are frequently told, adapt to the changing nature of economic and social life across the globe if they are to survive at all. Yet, it is possible to acknowledge the need for certain forms of change while nonetheless upholding elements of traditional university life. To be an academic, as opposed to being a business woman or man, is, among other things, to engage in a lifelong quest to *know*, to search and investigate, to discuss and debate ideas, and to teach. Once these features of academic life have been lost and the university has become just another corporation – hustling for dollars to improve the bottom line – the battle will have been lost. Those working in universities must convince themselves as much as their detaractors that even in the face of overwhelming pressures to the contrary, living a scholarly life is still an important part of contributing to a democratic and just society.

The Purpose and Structure of This Book

This book does not offer 'solutions' to these difficulties, but it does attempt to 'rub against' the prevailing neoliberal discourses on universities. While our principal subject is tertiary education in New Zealand, the reforms in this country cannot be understood in isolation from changes occurring elsewhere. The book thus attempts, where appropriate, to compare policies, events and ideas in New Zealand with other international developments. Similarly, although our prime focus is the university (rather than other tertiary education institutions and organisations), the definition of a university is now very much 'up for grabs'. The blurring of boundaries between universities and other institutions is simultaneously recognised and *promoted* by the New Zealand government. Policy developers tend to talk of 'tertiary education institutions' and 'post-compulsory education', rather than dealing in a comprehensive way with policy questions pertaining to each domain within the sector (universities, polytechnics, colleges of education, wānanga and private training establishments). For many politicians, bureaucrats and business leaders the universities no longer have a distinctive role to play in New Zealand society. Our overall purpose in this book is to outline, analyse and question key elements of neoliberal tertiary education reform in New Zealand, with a particular but not exclusive focus on changes in the function, status and character of universities. The book is dominated by a concern with the future, as well as the present (and, to a lesser extent, the past), and depicts a tertiary education system in turmoil. The challenges facing the universities, as we see them, are momentus, but not insurmountable.

Chapter 1 sets the scene for the rest of the book with an overview and critical commentary on the tertiary education white paper (Ministry of Education 1998). The first part of the chapter provides a summary of the major policy proposals in the document under the following headings: 'Tuition and Funding', 'Quality Assurance', 'Protected Terms', 'Financial Viability', 'Research', 'Tertiary Education Information', 'Governance', 'Monitoring and Accountability' and 'Capital Assets'. Brief reference is made to the Minister's Foreword and the section on Māori participation in tertiary education. The remainder of the chapter analyses some key areas for concern. It is suggested that the developments signalled in the white paper are an extension of neoliberal political thought and form part of a wider process of privatisation in the public sector. Problems with the proliferation of references to 'needs' are noted, and attention is drawn to the lack of consideration of information technology issues in the document. The shift from collegial and representative systems of governance to a business model is discussed, and the move to a contestable research funding regime tied more closely to government-defined strategic objectives is problematised. We make reference to the changing role of the NZQA and raise questions about the wide-ranging and extensive new powers granted to the Minister of Education under the indicative legislation. The chapter concludes with brief comments on the appeal to 'social cohesion' in the white paper and other recent policy documents. The key issues raised in this chapter provide the focus for more detailed discussion in the rest of the book.

Chapter 2 addresses the crisis in the idea of the modern university in the light of broader changes in the global economy. We identify some of the major pressures currently being confronted by tertiary education institutions, problematise recent claims about the emergence of 'knowledge societies', and situate discourses of 'futurology' in their wider social and historical contexts. The chapter investigates possible university futures (defined in the plural) and stresses the importance of considering what we call 'alternative globalisations'.

These ideas are further developed in Chapter 3, where we assess Bill Readings' arguments about the shift in contemporary universities to a technical ideal of performance couched within a discourse of 'excellence'. While we are sympathetic to Readings' depiction of the contemporary university as a 'ruined' institution, we believe his account is tied too closely to a European (German idealist) conception of higher education. In our view, Readings conflates the Kantian and Humboltian ideas of the university (while remaining committed to a variant of the Kantian idea of reason) and dispenses with the idea of culture rather too quickly. We also argue that Readings does not draw a sufficiently sharp distinction between two kinds of market liberalism: national economic neoliberal reform on the one hand, and neoliberal economic globalisation on the other. We maintain that the latter form presents new problems – legal, ethical and epistemological – for the university. The remainder of the chapter addresses these issues in some detail, concentrating on the status and function of science, the emergence of the research-based university, and its harnessing by the liberal nation-state.

Another theorist whose work has been pivotal in rethinking the role of university, Jean-Francois Lyotard, is the focus in Chapter 4. Nearly two decades have passed since Lyotard first published *The Postmodern Condition*. Following the release of an English translation of the text in 1984, *The Postmodern Condition* has been widely cited, and now no major work on postmodernism is 'complete' without reference to it. This chapter returns to Lyotard's concise account of the changing nature of knowledge in late capitalist societies and reassesses his claims about performativity, commodification and the future of the university. An appraisal of the New Zealand policy scene suggests Lyotard was stunningly accurate in his predictions about many features of the changing higher educational landscape. While some commentators, following Lyotard, have announced the 'death of the professor' in computerised societies, others believe academics might play a vitally important role in postmodern universities. The chapter provides an overview of this debate and considers its relevance in the New Zealand context. The chapter analyses the views of A.T. Nuyen – a theorist who takes the latter position – in the light of the New Zealand context and assesses prospects for pedagogical resistance against the dominant metanarrative of our time.

Chapter 5 addresses recent debates over the governance and ownership of New Zealand universities. After brief comments on programmes of structural adjustment New Zealand's model of public management, we move to a consideration of two opposing models of devolution. The shift from 'state control' to 'state supervision' provides the background for an analysis of governance in New Zealand universities. The establishment of a government taskforce on capital charging some years ago prompted the New Zealand Vice-Chancellors' Committee to commission a paper on governance and ownership. The paper, co-authored by Graham Scott (former Secretary to the Treasury) and Simon Smelt, supports a private, not-for-profit trust model of governance on the grounds that this minimises risks for the Crown while increasing the commercial freedom of the universities. We provide a critique of Scott and Smelt's arguments. Some of the constitutional consequences of privatisation are noted, and the division between 'representation' and 'technocracy' arising from the not-for-profit trust model of governance is examined.

Chapter 6 the tense relationship between the universities and the New Zealand Qualifications Authority. Formed under the Education Amendment Act of 1990, the NZQA has been heavily criticised by a range of tertiary education groups over the years. The green paper on qualifications policy issued by the government in mid-1997 makes some significant concessions to critics of the NZQA reforms. We argue, however, that the proposals in the qualifications green paper are consistent with the wider process of marketisation in the education sector. The chapter furnishes an overview of new developments and priorities in the qualifications arena and sketches possibilities for the future. We find fault with the technocratic assumptions underpinning unit standards and the development of a National Qualifications Framework and express our support for a more holistic, contextualised and dynamic approach to learning and assessment in tertiary education.

Chapter 7 provides a critical analysis of New Zealand's tertiary education review green paper, released in September 1997, and the Dearing Report on higher education in the United Kingdom. Brief reference is also made to the interim report of the West Committee in Australia. Key differences between the green paper and the Dearing Report are identified under four headings: the concept of education, resourcing, globalisation, and the role of the humanities. We argue that the green paper represents a further step toward a fully consumer-driven system of tertiary education in New Zealand. The Dearing Report is built upon the more expansive educational ideal of 'The Learning Society'. While not devoid of potential problems, the Dearing Committee's ideal recognises both the need for change in a globalised world and the importance of preserving intellectual and cultural traditions through the arts and humanities. We suggest that should New Zealand follow the path set out in the leaked Ministry of Education document (Ministry of Education, 1997d), the result will be a tertiary education system bearing many similarities to the uncompromising vision portrayed by an appendix to the interim West Committee report. Produced by Global Alliance Limited (1997), the appendix heralds a highly marketised, heavily commercialised, customised educational future.

Elements of this vision are given more extended critical treatment in Chapter 8, where some of the implications of further neoliberal reform for staff and students in tertiary education are explored. Situating these changes in discourses on 'crises' in higher education, we consider possible futures for higher education in New Zealand the 21st century. Special attention is paid to three themes: the emergence of the 'perpetual chooser', potential changes in conditions of work, and the reconfiguration of academic priorities in the age of the market. We comment on the impediments to resistance in an anti-intellectual environment and assess the prospects for the ideal of a scholarly mode of life in neoliberal New Zealand.

Chapter 9 addresses the development of 'virtual' learning environments in the tertiary education sector. We identify some of the forms learning might take in such environments and consider the extent to which, and ways in which, information technology issues have been addressed in recent tertiary education policy documents in New Zealand.

By comparison with other reviews of tertiary education – notably the Dearing Report in the United Kingdom – the New Zealand documents have little of substance to say about such issues. It is possible to speculate, nonetheless, about what *might* happen should current trends in the reform of tertiary education continue. Building on some prophetic comments from Lyotard on the changing role of the state in postmodern societies, the chapter discusses the decline in traditional forms of institutional authority and the emergence of new forms of control over educational subjects. We also assess the possible impact of the new technologies on scholarly publishing, and ask whether traditional modes of academic expression and legitimation will still *matter* in a virtualised and marketised educational world. The last part of the chapter comments critically on the possible emergence of 'electronic tracking' as an extension of reforms already instituted under the NZQA.

While the current New Zealand government appears to seriously entertain only one direction for tertiary education in New Zealand, we believe there are multiple possible futures for universities in this country. Even within the confines of government policy, each individual institution can determine its own distinctive response and vision. There *are* alternatives to the mantra-like call for the market as both the best allocative instrument for distributing public money and the superior form of political economy. In the face of the current political dogma in New Zealand, the thoughts of the recently appointed German Chancellor are worth recalling: his ideal was captured in the slogan 'Market economy but not market society'. This is but one alternative starting point among many. Given the wider forces at work on the tertiary sector – particularly those associated with the opening up of global commerce and the development of the new information technologies – this approach, broadly supported by just one of the major reviews of higher education in recent years (Dearing, 1997), seems more realistic than many other possibilities. Accepting such a principle would provide the university with a dual mission in the new millennium: to contribute to the formation of an innovative, stable and efficient economy while at the same time preserving 'society' – and all that 'society' represents – from the worst ravages and excesses of a market mentality.

Endnote

[1] As this book goes to press, Prime Minister Shipley has just announced a reshuffle of Cabinet, with potentially significant implications for all working in tertiary education institutions. The Education portfolio has been split, with a new separate division for tertiary education. Wyatt Creech has become Minister of Health, and Nick Smith has been appointed Minister of Education. Max Bradford will become the inaugural Minister of Tertiary Education, supported by Maurice Williamson as Associate Minister. In our view this signals another clear move to the right in the reconstruction of the tertiary education sector.

chapter one

Facing the Future:
The Tertiary Education
White Paper

In November 1998, the long-awaited white paper on tertiary education (Ministry of Education, 1998) was released by the New Zealand Government. The white paper cemented in place several crucial changes signalled in the leaked document of 1997 (Ministry of Education, 1997d) and confirmed suspicions about the way the tertiary education review green paper (Ministry of Education, 1997a) would be interpreted by policy developers (see Chapter 7). The white paper can be seen as a synthesis of neoliberal ideas developed and applied over more than a decade of social policy reform in New Zealand, and has already attracted a range of responses from the tertiary sector. The Association of University Staff of New Zealand (1998: 1) has called it 'inequitable, irresponsible, unworkable, and incoherent'. Of the major political parties other than National, only ACT has supported the overall direction signalled in the document. Both Labour and the Alliance have been heavily critical, viewing the white paper as a serious threat to a credible public tertiary education system. The policy proposals have been enthusiastically embraced by the New Zealand Association of Private Education Providers, and there has also been (qualified) support from the New Zealand Business Roundtable. This chapter summarises some of the key features of the white paper, offers brief critical comments on proposed changes and identifies a number of important omissions in the document.

Overview

In both substance and form the white paper is not dissimilar to the tertiary education review green paper, released more than a year earlier. The level of detail in the discussion is comparatively modest: the document comprises fifty-six pages of text, with a further fifteen pages set aside for appendices. There are four major sections ('The Future Tertiary Environment', 'The Process of the Review', 'The Tertiary Review Package', 'Implications for Maori') and a conclusion. The tertiary review 'package' covers five key areas: subsidies and costs; quality assurance, protected terms and financial viability; research; information; and governance and accountability. Significant legislative changes are signalled, and transitional arrangements during the period 1999–2001 are set out in one of the appendices.

Wyatt Creech opens the white paper with the following declaration:

> A high-performing tertiary sector is a key to a forward-looking, cohesive, creative, and innovative society in the 21st century. Post-compulsory education and training is going to become more and more necessary to secure career paths and quality of life and to achieve an equitable, cohesive, and culturally dynamic society in which all members can fully participate. Employers will demand higher and more diverse skills and knowledge to support the creativity and enterprise upon which their success depends. Over the course of their lives, many people will face the need to retrain, upskill, and change direction – perhaps several times.
>
> (Creech, 1998: 2)

The Minister acknowledges that rapid growth in the 1990s placed pressure on the tertiary education sector, and speaks of substantial challenges facing the tertiary education sector and the certainty of further change proceeding at the same pace. Seeking to 'advance New Zealand's needs well into the future', the white paper is, in Creech's view, a forward-looking document concerned with meeting diverse and changing demands and with upholding 'quality education that meets international standards'. Institutions, Creech asserts, will 'need to adapt to meet the challenges and opportunities created by expanding frontiers of knowledge, the changing needs of students, and new learning technologies'. Creech claims that '[a] great deal of consultation has gone into the development of these proposals' and expresses the government's hope that 'a broad political consensus can be developed around tertiary reform'. The white paper, he says, 'establishes ground rules for the successful future development of the tertiary education sector. It is up to us all to take advantage of the opportunities that the reforms create' (Creech, 1998: 2).

The first chapter of the white paper provides an overview of the proposed changes and the rationale behind them. It begins with the now-familiar refrain about the importance of tertiary education for competitiveness, economic growth, employment, productivity, and social cohesion (Ministry of Education, 1998: 3). It is noted that in 1997, over 214,000 students participated in public tertiary education courses, while 34,000 were enrolled in private training establishments. With seven universities, twenty-five polytechnics, four colleges of education, three wānanga, eleven government training establishments and seven hundred private training establishments, the number of tertiary education institutions and organisations in New Zealand is, as the white paper points out, very high for such a small country (p. 4). The small size of some of these institutions has cast doubt on their 'long-term educational and financial viability', to which a number have responded with alliances and mergers of various kinds in an attempt to strengthen their positions (p. 4). The Ministry speaks of the need to improve accountability measures and systems of governance. The importance of maintaining the quality of tertiary education is stressed. This does not require the same quality assurance mechanism for all institutions: different approaches will be appropriate for different institutions. The Ministry expresses a commitment to protecting certain terms (including 'university' and 'degree') in order to prevent them 'being devalued by misuse or abuse' (p. 8). Research, it is argued, should be 'of high quality and relevant to the purpose for which it is carried out'. It is claimed that the current legislative framework governing the tertiary sector is too prescriptive: 'the sector would benefit from having clearer and more concise legislation that enables it to adapt to meet the inevitable changes that are necessary over time' (p. 13).

The major policy changes in the white paper are set out in the third chapter, entitled 'The Tertiary Review Package'. In brief, these changes can be summarised as follows:

Tuition and Funding:

1. A new Universal Tertiary Tuition Allowance (UTTA) will be available to subsidise costs for all domestic students enrolled in approved courses.
2. Students enrolled in courses taught in New Zealand by overseas organisations will also be able to claim the subsidy, provided the courses meet quality assurance criteria.
3. From the year 2000 private training establishments will receive the same subsidies as public institutions.
4. Base grants (currently $1,000 per EFTS, up to a maximum of $250,000 per public tertiary institution) will be phased out after 1999.

Quality Assurance:

5. To receive consideration for government funding, 'tertiary providers and qualifications developers will need to be quality assured through a recognised quality validation process' (p. 21).
6. In acknowledging the range of purposes served by different tertiary education institutions and organisations, a variety of approaches to quality validation will be allowed and encouraged.
7. A new overarching regulatory body, the Quality Assurance Authority, will be established to monitor quality validation processes. Recognised quality validation processes will those judged 'sufficiently robust' by the Authority.
8. The NZQA will be 'repositioned' and renamed 'Quality Validation Services'. Its prime function will be to validate the quality of qualifications. Its other activities (including the development of unit standards) will be progressively transferred to other bodies.

Protected Terms:

9. The use of the following terms will continue to be regulated: 'university', 'polytechnic', 'college of education', 'wānanga' (for tertiary education institutions), 'degree' (including 'bachelor', 'master' and 'doctorate'). The use of the terms 'national' and 'New Zealand' in describing qualifications will also be restricted.

Financial Viability:

10. To be considered for government funding, 'tertiary providers will need to demonstrate that they are solvent and are likely to remain so' (p. 27).
11. All institutions and organisations receiving government assistance will need to provide information on their policies for safeguarding 'students' [interests] and educational interests' (p. 27).

Research:

12. From 2000, a new dual system for funding research will be introduced. A proportion (initially 80 per cent) of the government funding for research will be allocated through tuition subsidies based on student numbers; the rest (initially 20 per cent) will be allocated via a contestable pool. These proportions will, subject to a review to be carried out in 2001, have been reversed by 2002 (making 80 per cent of research funding contestable).

Tertiary Education Information:

13. An electronic database of information relating to student enrolment and a national register of 'quality-assured' tertiary institutions, qualifications and courses will be established.

Governance:

14. Councils for Tertiary Education Institutions (including universities) will be reduced in size to 7–12 members.
15. TEIs will be required to negotiate with the Minister of Education in confirming membership of their Councils.
16. The Chair and majority of members of each Council must not be

directly involved in the institution in any student or staff capacity. Only one student and one member of the institution's staff will be required on Councils.

17. The membership of Councils 'will need to reflect the skills, knowledge and experience essential for effective governance of a tertiary institution. These include skills in business management, finance, and strategic planning, and knowledge of the education and research sectors' (pp. 38–39).

Monitoring and Accountability:

18. In accordance with the government's intention of moving progressively away from 'central control of inputs' (p. 40) to an approach blending stronger accountability with greater institutional autonomy, TEIs will have to 'prepare, and report against, an annual Statement of Intent outlining strategic direction and performance targets' (p. 39).

19. Restrictions on the use of assets will vary depending on the degree of 'risk' (to the Crown) posed by an institution.

Capital Assets:

20. 'Asset rich' institutions will receive less funding through the UTTA than TEIs with fewer capital assets.

The fourth chapter of the white paper details the government's proposals for improving Māori participation in tertiary education. The Ministry of Education and Te Puni Kōkiri have developed an 'Education Strategy for Māori', the aim being to:

• establish a set of criteria and principles to evaluate policies to maximise the return to Māori [...]
• enhance the influence of Māori over education policy by improving the accountability of providers and of the whole education system
• improve the quality, capability, and diversity of schools and other education institutions
• improve communications and provide information to the Māori community; and

- strengthen the links between Māori education policy and wider government social reform policies to ensure increasing success in education outcomes for Māori.

(pp. 44–46)

The white paper suggests that the new resourcing system of 'funding following the student' (vouchers) will, together with the policies on information and quality, improve prospects for Māori students. It is claimed that the new system of governance 'could hold particular relevance to wānanga, enabling them to develop further the distinctive characteristics of Māori tertiary education' (p. 48). It is noted, however, that the question of how wānanga differ from other tertiary institutions is a complicated one. No firm commitment to resourcing the future growth of new wānanga, beyond the UTTA available to all TEIs meeting quality assurance criteria, is made. Questions about capitalisation and finances for wānanga are yet to be resolved, but are currently being considered by the government.

The document closes with a concluding statement (pp. 55–56) similar in tone to the introductory remarks. There is talk of the importance of a quality tertiary education system – one based on innovation, ideas and research – for 'our success as a nation', for international competitiveness, for 'our growth as individuals' and 'the strength of our communities' (p. 55). The government, it is said, will continue to play 'a major role' in tertiary education. Because all approved tertiary education programmes rely on 'a taxpayer subsidy', minimal barriers to innovation and growth need to be balanced with robust accountability mechanisms. The nature of the 'student–provider relationship' is important in safeguarding taxpayers' investment in tertiary education. The proposals set out in the white paper are designed to enable tertiary education institutions and organisations to adapt quickly to changing student demands while providing high quality courses and programmes.

Many of the changes in the white paper had been expected; indeed, some had been signalled in budget statements made earlier in 1998. What was surprising for some commentators was just how far the government had been prepared to go in both extending its own powers and making concessions to the private sector. We address this issue as a key element of our critique in the next section, and analyse some of the philosophical assumptions behind the proposals in later chapters.

Critique

The process of social policy reform provides a fascinating study in the dynamics of discourse, the art of political rhetoric and the exercising of political power. The white paper attests to this in many respects but perhaps most vividly in relation to the question of privatisation. In the section entitled 'The Process of the Review', the following comment on the 380 written submissions to the tertiary education review green paper is made:

> Submissions generally focused on the issues raised in the Green Paper, such as the importance of maintaining educational quality and improving accountability for the use of taxpayer funds. Some, however, focused on a mistaken belief that the Government intended to privatise tertiary education institutions (p. 14).

The white paper does little to reassure those who hold this 'mistaken' belief about privatisation. We see the proposals in the document as further steps in a process of incremental privatisation that has been under way for several years. The positive reaction to the white paper from a range of private 'providers' is hardly surprising: the public tertiary education system will, in effect, be subsidising private training establishments. As Jane Kelsey says, 'why should taxpayers' money be channelled into private education when public education is severely stretched?' (1998: A19). On the face of it, such an appropriation of public money for aiding private purposes – where those purposes might include running for-profit 'educational' enterprises from an off-shore location – seems bizarre. Such an approach makes sense, however, if the changes proposed in the white paper are viewed as transitional arrangements in a larger privatisation agenda. If the intention is to systematically reduce government involvement in (and financial commitment to) tertiary education in New Zealand, incentives for the private sector assist in allowing a new competitive, customised environment to become established. This does not, however, need to be seen as *planned* strategy (or 'grand conspiracy') for the point to hold; rather, it is a matter of viewing changes in tertiary education in the light of trends, practices and ideological positions already firmly established in recent New Zealand history. Once the fundamental assumptions of market liberalism have been accepted, as they have by successive New Zealand governments from 1984, almost *all* major policy changes tend to follow a certain direction: the emphasis will *always* be on enhancing 'choice', increasing competition, and (ostensibly) reducing government involvement in individual lives. Encouraging growth in private educational enterprises is simply one element in a larger neoliberal reform programme.

The proliferation of references to serving the 'needs' of various groups – principally but not exclusively students – reaches new heights in the white paper. Talk of meeting the 'needs' of 'consumers' has become a regular feature of recent policy statements on tertiary education. In the case of the white paper, however, this is sufficiently incessant to give the appearance of driving every major policy proposal. Statements about meeting ongoing, diverse and changing student 'needs' can be found in Wyatt Creech's Foreword (Creech, 1998: 2), the first chapter (Ministry of Education, 1998, twice on p. 3, and on pp. 12 and 13), and the third chapter (p. 38). There are also references to the 'needs' of the labour market (p. 24), different tertiary institutions (pp. 29 and 37), the 21st century (p. 31), 'stakeholders' (p. 38), and Maori (p. 52). The importance of using taxpayers' money effectively to meet (unspecified) 'present and future needs' is also noted (p. 34). Such references to 'needs', as we argue later in the book, are better understood as appeals to 'wants' and demands. The use of the term 'needs' is almost never supported by an account of what is *necessary*, as opposed to merely *preferred*, for the individual or groups being referred to. Moreover, little consideration is given to the ways in which 'needs' are *constructed*, shaped and modified; there is seldom any in-depth commentary on *why* and *how* 'needs' might change. The *consequences* of changing preferences are never examined in detail. We believe the increase in the number of references to the term in the white paper is more than coincidental: it corresponds with the shift further towards a fully consumer-driven system of tertiary education. In such a system, so-called 'needs' – the demands of students, employers and the government – are all that count in determining the distribution and use of resources. *All* decisions in tertiary institutions and organisations driven by these imperatives are ultimately based on the criterion of 'giving the customer what he or she wants'.

There are some significant omissions and silences in the white paper, the most striking of which is the almost complete absence of any discussion about the new information technologies and the bearing they may have on tertiary education in New Zealand (in the immediate and long-term future). As far as concrete policy proposals go, there is a brief reference to electronic databases of information to assist with enrolment, but little else. The Minister of Education mentions the new learning technologies in his Foreword when referring to the 'challenges and opportunities' facing the tertiary sector, yet there is virtually no elaboration on this in the body of the document. The need to 'adapt to and exploit advances in information technology' is noted as a 'key pressure' on the sector in the first chapter (p. 3), but is not clear why this might be so, or how the pressure might be felt, or where it might be emerging from, or how tertiary institutions might respond to it. The tertiary education review green paper has been criticised for its lack of attention to information technology issues (see Chapters 7 and 9 of this volume), making the omissions in the white paper all the more surprising. In the period between the release of the two documents, the government has made a renewed commitment to the further development of learning technologies in educational institutions, but this is not reflected in the policy proposals set out in the white paper.

The recommendations in the white paper signal a decisive shift from collegial, democratic and representative systems of governance to a business model, with a significant reduction in the number of academic staff serving on tertiary education institution councils. This is consistent with the reforms in governance inaugurated a decade ago under the Labour government, but takes the process several steps further. The reduction in the total number of members on Councils (from 12–20 to 7–12) is premised on the assumption that smaller governing bodies will be 'more efficient and clearly focused while still enabling the workload ... to be adequately spread among members' (Ministry of Education, 1998: 39). No evidence is cited in support of this view. The arguments in favour of changing the composition of Councils are based on equally dubious and ambiguous claims. Academics, we are told, will continue to have 'an essential role' given their knowledge of the 'core educational and research functions' of tertiary education institutions (p. 39), yet with so few represented on Councils their views could easily become swamped by other concerns. The balance is heavily weighted in favour of 'skills, knowledge and experience' drawn from the commercial world. Council members will be required to make decisions based entirely on their judgements of 'the short- and long-term best interests of the institution' (p. 38), but it is not all clear how 'best interests' will be defined. Ensuring the financial viability of the institution is certainly a part of this, but apart from vague references to 'accountability' other demands remain ambiguous. The call for greater accountability in the tertiary sector, repeated several times throughout the document, is based in part on unsubstantiated statements about Council members putting their own interests ahead of the overall good of their institutions under representational systems of governance (pp. 4–5). The notion that accountability mechanisms need to be improved is allegedly 'widespread' (p. 5), but no evidence is provided to support this claim. Nothing is said about *who* might be critical of current systems of governance and accountability and what interests *they* might be serving.

The introduction of contestable research funding was anticipated (see, for example, Roberts, 1999a, 1999b), but the precise form this would take was open to considerable speculation. As the proposals stand, no indication of a reduced overall budget for research funding is given, but neither is this eliminated as a possibility. Several features of the proposed system are problematic from our point of view. First, the shift from an EFTS-based distribution of monies for research to a contestable system forces academics to negotiate new layers of bureaucracy in seeking support for their work. More time will be spent completing application forms and less time will be spent actually *doing* research. Second, and of perhaps greater concern, academics lose (even more) control over the nature of their research activities and the focus of their scholarly inquiries. An EFTS-based system grants institutions considerable autonomy in determining research priorities (within a limited budget); with the progressive removal of funds into a contestable pool control shifts squarely into the hands of government officials. This might be less objectionable if researchers could be confident the total pool of funds would increase (or at least stay at current levels, after adjustments for inflation), and provided *all* domains of research activity would be eligible for funding. It is clear from the white paper, however, that some areas of research will be more likely to attract funds than others. The contestable fund will target 'advanced, high-quality research portfolios with a strong strategic focus' (p. 32). Applications will be assessed on the following criteria:

- *Demonstrated quality and capacity of researchers.* Researchers bidding for this funding will need to submit recent track records of research activity in the area for which funding is sought. Judgements will be based on such factors as recognised publications and the local, national and international significance of past research (where relevant).
- *Quality of the proposed research portfolio.* This quality will be judged on the basis of the design and purpose of the proposed portfolio, its feasibility, the research methods, the skills and technologies to be developed and used, and the relationship to other programmes and investments.
- *Strategic focus.* Researchers will need to demonstrate how their portfolios will develop the innovation and human resource capabilities of New Zealand.
- *Cost-effectiveness.* All elements of proposed research portfolios will need to be appropriately costed.

(pp. 32–33)

Few researchers would object to the idea that research should be of 'high quality' if it is to receive funding. Many, however, would want to debate questions about how 'quality' is to be determined. In universities, the 'acid test' of quality has long been international peer review. The white paper places this convention under threat, transferring control over criteria for quality to government officials. This is ostensibly because accountability arrangements for the use of EFTS-based funds 'have not been strong' (p. 28). As with other claims about accountability in the document, this remains merely an *assertion*, with no argument or evidence mustered to support it. Several groups of researchers will be disadvantaged under the new system. Those just beginning their academic careers will find it difficult to compete against experienced researchers with lengthy funding and publications records. Those with interests and expertise falling outside the 'strategic' criteria specified in the white paper will find little or no support. Finally, those whose research depends more on *time* than money will find themselves short of the former precisely because they will not gain the latter.

The implications of the new system are far-reaching. A small group of experienced researchers in selected strategic areas (particularly those with quantifiable and readily discernible economic benefits) will do well under the new system, and might expect to gain both funding and the necessary time, space and resources to do their work. Others will become 'outcasts' in the new order. They may continue to hold academic posts if their courses meet 'student needs' (current enrolment preferences), but they will be required to undertake more teaching and administration, with little or no time for research. This is made explicit in the stipulation, foreshadowed by the tertiary education review green paper, that teachers of undergraduate degree courses do not need to be active in research (that is, 'research' as it has traditionally been defined in universities). For the early years of undergraduate study at least, 'research can reflect a personal involvement by the teacher characterised by the continual refreshing of the mind through the updating, investigation and scholarship in the given discipline' (p. 29). For the moment, a largely arbitrary line is drawn between undergraduate and (post)graduate teaching; in the future, relaxation of the concept of research might apply at higher levels as well. This could produce what might in the past have been called 'teaching' (as opposed to 'research') institutions, many of which might still want to claim the name 'university' while simultaneously reducing the perceived obligation on the part of the government to provide support with research funding. Some domains of inquiry are likely considered 'irrelevant' in a system driven by student demands and economic imperatives, and entire fields of study could disappear from New Zealand tertiary education curricula. (These problems are addressed in greater detail in Chapter 8.)

In earlier writings (e.g. Roberts, 1997a) attention has been drawn to the tenuous position of the NZQA given its heavily bureaucratic structure and growing unpopularity among members of the university, polytechnic and secondary school communities. In the white paper we see a 'thinning' of the NZQA, with many of its former functions to be taken over by the new Quality Assurance Authority of New Zealand. While the new body spreads the load of quality-control responsibilities, it also adds another layer to the bureaucracy. Whether this will have the effect of 'streamlining' the qualifications reform process or making it more cumbersome remains to be seen. In an unusually forthright letter to *New Zealand Education Review*, David Hood (1999: 6), former chief executive of the NZQA, offers some strong criticisms of the proposed changes. He sees the NZQA as being 'demoted' under the new system. The government, he believes, has caved in to vocal protests about unit standards from those who purport to speak for the universities and polytechnics. In his view, the National Qualifications Framework and the associated Skill New Zealand strategy have been 'highly successful'. Indeed, he goes so far as to suggest that the NZQA has perhaps been *too* successful and is now being 'punished' for challenging 'the conventional and traditional'. Critics, he says, have tended to attack unit standards from a theoretical or technical point of view, when in practice they work well. Much of what is in the white paper will, Hood maintains, force New Zealand into taking a 'giant leap backwards'. Hood favours a flexible ('shopping basket') approach to the acquisition of tertiary qualifications, whereas the white paper wants to 'return to qualifications as the end point of a fixed length, seemingly because it fits more readily to a particular funding model'.

Hood's letter is all the more remarkable given his previous position as a senior official and his firm support for a market model of education. To us, Hood's similarities with those he criticises in the government are far greater than his differences with them. His letter is replete with the language of neoliberalism; he describes students as 'consumers' and the 'primary customers' of tertiary education. In discussing why the NZQA was established, he speaks (approvingly) of opening the education 'market' to private training establishments, the shift in emphasis 'from inputs to outcomes' and the 'flexible provision' of educational programmes. Hood seems to us to have placed undue emphasis on one element of the restructuring process proposed by the white paper while downplaying other elements highly compatible with the vision he had for the NZQA. A reduction in the regulatory authority of the NZQA has long been a possibility and was predicted nearly two years ago (Roberts, 1997b). While the new structure may appear to Hood as a reaction to noisy detractors in two tertiary interest groups, it is unlikely to provide much comfort for such critics. As we try to show in Chapter 6, the target of university criticisms – from individual academics, the New Zealand Vice-Chancellors' Committee and the Association of University Staff – of the NZQA reform process was never simply unit standards; rather, the concern at a deeper level was with the technocratic and managerialist assumptions underpinning unit standards, among other features of the NZQA reform process. It is the very conceptions and practices of education flowing from the sort of language Hood employs in his letter to which many university critics object. The white paper may allow universities to side-step unit standards, a concession signalled in the 1997 green paper on qualifications policy (Ministry of Education, 1997b), but the broader ideological and political parameters within which quality assurance processes will have to operate remain the same.

We turn finally to the question of academic freedom under the new system. Here we want to join John Codd (1998) in arguing that this is perhaps the most worrying feature of white paper. Under the indicative legislation detailed in the third appendix to the document, the Minister of Education is granted unprecedented new powers in the governance of tertiary education institutions. The Minister must appoint the first Council of a new tertiary education institution (section 165A). Every Council will be 'accountable to the Minister for the efficient and effective governance of the institution, including the discharge of its statutory functions, and for the educational and financial performance of the institution' (181A). Proposed amendments to Council charters can only be made with ministerial approval (184/2). It is a requirement that charters specify the 'goals and purposes of the institution' together with '[t]he number of members of the Council ... and the manner in which they are appointed, hold office, and may resign or be removed' (184/1). New powers of intervention go far beyond those extended to Ministers in the past. Sections 222B to 222L of the indicative legislation have been set up to allow the Minister of Education 'to intervene in the operation of a tertiary education institution, where, *in the opinion of the Minister*, the effective operation of the tertiary education institution is at risk, in a manner that is appropriate to address the nature and severity of the risk' (222A, emphasis added). Under the new legislation, the Minister will have the power to appoint an observer to the Council of a tertiary education institution (222D), and direct a Council to take 'independent' advice (222E) or prepare an action plan (222G). The Minister will be able to appoint members to a Council (222F/1), subsequently terminate those appointments (222F/4), and even dissolve the entire Council. The Minister will have the right to appoint a Commissioner who will act in the place of a dissolved Council (222J). The reinstatement or replacement of a dissolved Council will also be at the discretion of the Minister (222L).

These extraordinary new powers constitute a direct and serious threat to both academic freedom and institutional autonomy. The authors of the white paper draw a distinction between the two ideals, conceding that the new arrangements 'may impinge on institutional autonomy' but claiming that 'neither the governance nor the accountability arrangements will encroach on the principle of academic freedom' (p. 41). We disagree. In our view, the two principles are – or have been historically – linked. Exercising the 'critic and conscience' role ascribed to universities demands a high degree of autonomy over substantive and procedural matters in the day-to-day running of an institution. This does not mean, of course, that institutions should be free from the scrutiny of those who provide some or all of their funds. But if a university is to discharge its responsibility of upholding rigorous standards of critical inquiry – which may include the investigation, teaching and discussion of controversial or unpopular ideas – tight limits need to be placed on the circumstances and the ways in which the funding body might intervene in the affairs of the institution. The new powers granted to the Minister under the indicative legislation place few limits on what might be considered necessary grounds for interference. There is little to prevent a Minister of Education, should he or she be so inclined, from appointing political allies or removing those known to hold contrary views to his or her own. There is an increased possibility of a government withdrawing support for programmes of study considered 'too radical' or undesirable for some other (politically motivated) reason, given the new powers the Minister has over charters, judgements about the performance of the Council, and the appointment or termination of Council members. The new powers of intervention allow the other elements of the white paper reform package to fall more neatly into place. Ensuring emphasis is placed on research and teaching in areas of 'strategic' (economic) importance will be easier if the governing bodies of tertiary institutions are subject to all the avenues for possible interference noted above. The balance between the different functions of a tertiary education institution – research, teaching, administration, community activities, etc. – can be controlled with greater ease, given the composition of Councils and the Minister's powers of 'correction' under the new system.

We would argue, as Codd does, that what is needed is neither a lack of accountability from institutions to the government (or students, or anyone else involved in tertiary education), nor a situation in which the government has excessive powers over matters of governance, but rather a buffering mechanism between the institution and the government. The University Grants Committee used to perform this role as a body 'independent of the government, while being accountable to it' (Codd, 1998: 11), but there are other means of ensuring the proper balance between accountability and autonomy is retained. Codd suggests a financial auditing unit attached to the New Zealand Vice Chancellors' Committee as one possibility; another might be an organisation comprising representatives from students' associations, academic staff organisations, university management, and various community groups. The motives for dispensing with the University Grants Committee a decade ago were, at least in part, financial in nature; the current government, we suspect, would object to the idea of a buffering body on ideological grounds as well. The proposed new powers granted to the Minister under the indicative legislation show just how far the government is prepared to go to avoid such a possibility. Codd neatly captures what is at stake in the debates over governance and accountability:

> It is self-evident that some (perhaps most) governments do not favour the provision of funds to support ideas, views, teachings or even research, that is contrary to their ideologies or policies. In a society that upholds liberal democratic values, however, the independence of its universities is essential to their purposes as 'critic and conscience of society'. That independence must be protected in legislation against the actions of a future government that may seek to control what is taught in universities and suppress the social criticism that arises within them. We need to be reminded often that the price of freedom is eternal vigilance (p. 11).

Concluding Comments

The battle lines over the future of New Zealand universities were drawn more than a decade ago with the publication of the Watts Report (Universities Review Committee, 1987) and the Treasury (1987) brief to the incoming government. The Watts Report, commissioned by the

New Zealand Vice-Chancellors' Committee, expressed broad support for the standard of university education in New Zealand and argued for a substantial increase in state funding to encourage greater numbers of students into full-time study. No changes to existing systems of governance were suggested. The Treasury brief, by contrast, advanced a case for a reduction in state expenditure, an increase in 'user' charges and an emphasis on 'consumer' choice. As Boston (1988: 1) notes, both reports recommended special assistance for students from poorer backgrounds and advocated major reforms in university administration, staffing and remuneration. In the years following the release of these two reports, the Treasury vision has prevailed and the Watts Report has been largely forgotten or ignored. The policy proposals set out in the white paper follow along the same path established by the 1987 Treasury brief and will, over time, radically alter the face of tertiary education in New Zealand.

We see some positive features in the white paper. For example, the notion of providing full and accurate information for students attempting to choose between institutions is difficult to argue against, although we would hasten to add that this is a necessary rather than sufficient condition for good decision-making. The choices we make and the *way* we make them may be heavily influenced by a host of experiences and encounters, including those we have in other educational settings (e.g. schools). Conversations with other students and/or staff members, family circumstances and expectations and the 'marketing' of educational programmes (e.g. via television advertisements) are also significant factors in shaping choices. The expressed goal of improving Māori participation rates in tertiary education is also admirable, as is the recognition that many Māori students may prefer to study in a wānanga learning environment. Yet the white paper makes no firm commitment to Māori in terms of providing the necessary resources for the further development of wānanga. Indeed, while many of the issues relating to the establishment of wānanga are still 'being considered' by the government (p. 50), it seems clear that the variable subsidy regime will be insufficient to meet capital requirements for new institutions.

Overall, the white paper provides disheartening reading for those committed to a comprehensive, properly resourced public tertiary education system. The document lacks any sense of history; it conveys no commitment to, or critical engagement with, intellectual ideals developed over hundreds of years in universities and other institutions of higher learning such as the traditional whare wānanga in Aotearoa. There is little thought given to the contribution the arts and the humanities might make to New Zealand society. The cultural dimensions of higher education are, with the exception of brief comments on the distinctive role of wānanga, ignored. The idea that tertiary education might serve ends other than those generated by self-interest is never taken seriously; the notion that tertiary study ought to be *its own end*, and that this alone might justify continued public investment in universities and other institutions, is even more foreign to the discourse of the white paper. When the justifications for policy changes occasionally shift from the language of serving the so-called 'needs' of individuals, the appeal is typically to some other goal consistent with neoliberal political philosophy (e.g. national economic competitiveness).

The early reference to 'social cohesion' needs to be contextualised as part of the same neoliberal discourse. This term, which is not defined or explained in the white paper, has found currency in marketised societies around the world. References to the term can be found as far back as the Hawke Report (Department of Education, 1988a), but in recent times it has become a 'buzz word' for government officials and has appeared in a number of recent New Zealand policy documents (e.g. the Foresight Project materials). We see the goal of 'social cohesion' as the latest attempt by governments in neoliberal societies to secure the 'social bond' (Lyotard, 1993: 13) to bind citizens to the prevailing economic and philosophical doctrine of neoliberalism. The adhesive in this case is competitive individualism, and the citizens who cohere have been reconstructed as 'consumers'. Promoting 'social cohesion' demands the denial of difference, the containing of criticism within pre-defined parameters, and the suppression of alternatives to market liberalism. After more than a decade of breaking communities down, right-wing politicians are now – through appeals to social cohesion or the closely related term 'social capital' – attempting to bring them back together again. (Former Prime Minister Jim Bolger was one of the most prominent proponents of such a synthesis near the end of his parliamentary career.) This involves a reconfiguration of the notion of community: the replacement of an ethic of collective care with the apparently paradoxical idea of people being bound together by their commitment to serving their own individual (competitive and economic) interests.

The fate of the white paper over the next few years will, to some extent, be determined by the results of the next general election. The two major opposition parties, Labour and the Alliance, differ somewhat in the detail of their approaches to tertiary education policy, but both are committed to maintaining a credible public system. Steve Maharey, Labour Associate Education (Tertiary) Spokesperson, has this to say about the white paper: 'It is now 'crunch time' as the white paper proposals would destroy New Zealand universities to such an extent that academics world-wide would no longer recognise them as peer institutions' (Association of University Staff of New Zealand, 1998: 4). Labour sees the new system of research funding introduced in the white paper as 'punitive' and opposes tertiary capital charging. Alliance Education Spokesperson Liz Gordon has argued that the competitive behaviour encouraged under the new student funding system would lower standards and further weaken the international standing of New Zealand universities. The 'sinking lid' policy applied to universities could no longer be sustained (Association of University Staff of New Zealand, 1998: 3). The path from policy to practice also rests in the hands of voters, for whom tertiary education has become an increasingly important issue in recent years. There has been extensive publicity in the popular media over the past year about growing levels of student debt. The injustice of one generously supported generation making the next pay heavily for taking up the same opportunities in tertiary education has not been lost on young people, their parents, and many members of the wider voting community. The reduction in government support for tertiary education has been initiated by politicians who, for the most part, enjoyed the benefits of universal health care, higher welfare payments and comparatively low educational fees. In a world demanding perpetual (re)training, the momentous changes signalled in the white paper will have a bearing on many New Zealand lives. Policy proposals of such significance warrant close critical scrutiny and ongoing debate.

chapter two

Universities, Futurology and Globalisation

... if we create market universities run purely on market principles
they may be of their age, but they will not be able to transcend it.
(Federico Mayor, UNESCO Director-General,
Times Higher Education Supplement, 3 October 1997, p. 12)

Bill Readings (1996) argues that three ideas of the university dominate
the modern era: the Kantian idea of reason, the Humboltian idea of
culture and the technological idea of excellence. With the advent of
globalisation and the consequent decline of the nation state as the
principle of economic and cultural organisation, both the Kantian and
Humboltian conceptions have become problematic. Universities now
function as one bureaucratic subsystem among others. In the age of
global capitalism, Readings suggests, universities have been reduced to
a technical ideal of performance in the discourse of 'excellence'. The
crisis of the idea of the modern university has also been addressed by
theorists such as Jürgen Habermas (1987), Jean-François Lyotard
(1984), Jacques Derrida (1983) and many others (see e.g. Clark &
Royle, 1995), and is investigated in detail in Chapter 3 of this book.

The crisis of the idea of the modern university has been brought about largely by changes to the nature of capitalism and through the attempts by governments to structurally adjust their national economies to these new conditions. The new global economy is not just the universalisation of capitalism after the collapse of actually existing communism; it also involves the rise of finance capitalism, supported by the emergence of new information and communications technologies, and a series of agreements concerning the liberalisation of world trade. The neoliberal paradigm for economic restructuring has dominated the policy agendas of most Western countries during the decade of the 1980s. Some of its distinguishing features include the abolition of subsidies and tariffs, the floating of the exchange rate, the privatisation of state assets, the encouragement of foreign direct investment, tax reforms, and the downsizing and commercialisation of the public sector.

Fundamental to understanding the new global economy has been a rediscovery of the economic importance of education (Papadopoulos, 1994: 170). The OECD and the World Bank have stressed the significance of education and training for the development of 'human resources', for upskilling and increasing the competencies of workers, and for the production of research and scientific knowledge as keys to participation in the new global economy. Both Peter Drucker (1993) and Michael Porter (1990) emphasise the importance of knowledge – its economics and productivity – as the basis for national competition within the international marketplace. Lester Thurow (1996: 68) suggests that 'a technological shift to an era dominated by man-made brainpower industries' is one of five economic tectonic plates which constitute a new game with new rules: 'Today knowledge and skills now stand alone as the only source of comparative advantage. They have become the key ingredient in the late twentieth century's location of economic activity'.

Equipped with this central understanding and guided by neoliberal theories of human capital, public choice and new public management, Western governments have begun the process of restructuring universities, obliterating the distinction between 'education' and 'training' in the development of a massified system of higher education designed for the twenty-first century. In 1997 the British, Australian and New Zealand governments convened reviews of higher education to determine the shape and imperatives of the sector for the twenty-first century. The terms of reference for these inquiries were written against the kind of changes to the global economy and policy issues identified above (see Chapter 7).

This chapter investigates the notion of university futures – defined in the plural. In the first section we identify the main trends and pressures facing the university and examine the discourse of globalisation as it appears in the Dearing Report (the most substantial of the three reports on tertiary education). In the second section we analyse the emphasis on the 'knowledge society' as a policy narrative designed to provide something of a philosophical and coherent vision underlying recommended policy changes to higher education. The third section investigates the discourse of futurology itself and the ideological function it serves.

To Sound Out Idols

Traditionally universities have been concerned principally with two main functions: research or the production of knowledge, and teaching or its dissemination and acquisition. Universities are now and have been historically the central knowledge institutions of the modern state. Knowledge has been seen not only as an end in itself but also as an essential and defining element of the Western tradition, closely tied to scientific and material progress, cultural preservation, and the nature of both the market and democracy. The knowledge functions of the university, especially since the time of Kant, have also carried a critical function, together with certain privileges and responsibilities. Accordingly, the university has served as the critic and conscience of society and the critical function has been protected from political interference and the vagaries of the market through the historical development of notions of institutional autonomy and academic freedom. This has been the essence of the idea of the liberal university. In an important sense, the liberal university epitomised the idea of a *public* institution designed to serve the needs of society. It was the exemplar of a public discursive space where knowledge could be pursued in a disinterested and scholarly fashion and ideas could be exchanged freely on the basis of academic interests. Today this ideal is undergoing radical change: in short, as the knowledge functions have become even more important economically, external pressures and forces have seriously impinged upon its structural protections and traditional freedoms. Increasingly, the emphasis in reforming the university institution has fallen upon two main issues: the resourcing of research and teaching, with a demand from central government to reduce unit costs while accommodating further expansion of the system, on the one hand; and changes in the nature of governance and enhanced accountability, on the other.

In the post-war period, and especially since the 1980s, national university systems have experienced a huge growth in both participation and demand, leading to the phenomenon of 'massification'. This growth is, in part, the result of demographic changes, but also of deliberate policies designed to recognise and harness the economic and social importance of 'second chance' education and 'lifelong' education. In a competitive global economy the accent has fallen on the development of human capital. Universities have become more market-oriented and consumer-driven as a consequence of funding policies designed to encourage access at the same time as containing government expenditure. As a result, the cost of a university education in many countries has been transferred to the students themselves and governments have moved away from the premises of universal provision to favour targeting as a means of addressing questions of equity of access.

Main Pressures and Trends

New Zealand universities, like other universities in the Western world, have had to face external pressures which come with increased access, 'lifelong learning', continuing reductions in the level of state resourcing (on a per capita basis), and greater competition both nationally and internationally. Overall, since 1988, the public tertiary education system in New Zealand has been incrementally privatised: a regime of competitive neutrality has increasingly blurred the distinction between public and private ownership; the introduction of user-pays policies has created a consumer-driven system; and recourse has been made to various forms of contract including 'contracting out' and the institution of performance contracting. Incremental privatisation has involved reductions in state subsidy (and a parallel move to private subsidy), reductions in state provision, and reductions in state regulation (Association of University Staff of New Zealand, 1997) as shown below:

Reductions in State Subsidy (parallel move to private subsidy)

- cumulative reductions in government subsidy for tuition costs
- increased student charges
- increased reliance on student loans
- the avoidance or passing on of costs by the state (salaries; compliance costs, insurance and superannuation)
- institutions increasingly forced to find other sources of funding
- proposed full funding of PTEs.

Reduction in State Provision

- increased contracting out of services
- contestable funding for research
- active encouragement of private provision, including individual student entitlements
- full funding of PTEs
- the competitive neutrality for public and private institutions.

Reductions in State Regulation

- deregulation of the setting of student tuition fees (1991)
- moves to have public institutions operate as businesses
- to operate under legislation based on the Companies Act 1993
- imposing a capital charge (tax) on public institutions
- proposals to deregulate statutory terms: 'polytechnic', 'college of education' etc., and to relax criteria for university status, including the role of critic and conscience.

Source: Association of University Staff of New Zealand, 1997

In addition, universities in New Zealand and elsewhere, like other parts of society and economy, face the challenges inherent in the new communication and information technologies (C&IT) which, effecting a shift from 'knowledge' to 'information' and from teaching to learning, threaten to further commercialise and commodify the university, substituting technology-based learning systems for the traditional forms of the lecture, tutorial and seminar. The introduction of technology-based learning systems is blurring the boundaries between on-site and distance learning. It is transforming the nature of scholarship and research, and brings in its wake many problems for reconceptualising academic labour. Some policy-makers view C&IT as the means by which the problem of growth and expansion in age of steadily reducing state subsidy (and unit costs) can be overcome. The virtual university, the virtual classroom and the virtual laboratory are heralded by techno-utopians as *the* answer.

The main trends facing the university, together with the pressures they bring to bear, are:

- increased globalisation (as world economic integration)
- increased levels of national and international competition
- increased power and importance of global and multinational corporations
- increased importance of research to global multinationals
- importance of regional and international trade and investment agreements
- the growing economic and political importance of the Asian economies, including China
- declining sociopolitical priority of higher education as an entirely state-funded activity
- corporatisation and privatisation of the public sector
- interpenetration of public and private enterprises
- managerialism and new contractualism
- increased demands for efficiency and accountability
- increasing economic, social and cultural importance of knowledge
- commodification and mercantilisation of knowledge
- increasing role and importance of telecommunications and information technologies
- new political, legal and ethical problems of 'information economy' (e.g. intellectual property)
- changing nature of advanced economies to knowledge-based industries

- changing structure of labour market (e.g. casualisation, feminisation of workforce)
- demand for highly skilled technically competent workforce
- increasing multicultural and international nature of societies and universities
- increased demand from a highly diversified, 'massified', student population
- need for lifelong learning and 'second chance' education
- the vocationalisation of higher education.

The Discourse of Globalisation: The Dearing Report

These trends are, of course, very much interrelated phenomena and each one by itself represents a significant level of political-economic complexity. Considered together, the whole is both uncertain and unpredictable; certainly one can say the future has not been 'written upon' or determined. To briefly illustrate the level of complexity we will take one trend, globalisation, and schematically consider the way the UK review of tertiary education – the Dearing Report (1997) (named after its chairman, Lord Dearing) – elaborates the implications for higher education:

Main Causes

- technological changes in telecommunications, information and transport
- the (political) promotion of free trade and the reduction in trade protection

Main Elements

- the organisation of production on a global scale
- the acquisition of inputs and services from around the world which reduces costs
- the formation of cross-border alliances and ventures, enabling companies to combine assets, share their costs and penetrate new markets
- integration of world capital markets

- availability of information on international benchmarking of commercial performance
- better consumer knowledge and more spending power; hence more discriminating choices
- greater competition from outside the established industrial centres

Consequences for the Labour Market

- downward pressure on pay, particularly for unskilled labour
- upward pressure on the quality of labour input
- competition is increasingly based on quality rather than price
- people and ideas assume greater significance in economic success because they are less mobile than other investments such as capital, information and technology
- unemployment rates of unskilled workers relative to skilled workers have increased
- more, probably smaller, companies whose business is knowledge and ways of handling knowledge and information are needed

Implications for Higher Education

- high quality, relevant higher education provision will be a key factor in attracting and anchoring the operations of global corporations
- institutions will need to be at the forefront in offering opportunities for lifelong learning
- institutions will need to meet the aspirations of individuals to re-equip themselves for a succession of jobs over a working lifetime
- higher education must continue to provide a steady stream of technically skilled people to meet needs of global corporations
- higher education will become a global international service and tradeable commodity
- higher education institutions, organisationally, may need to emulate private sector enterprises in order to flourish in a fast-changing global economy
- the new economic order will place a premium on knowledge and institutions; therefore, will need to recognise the knowledge, skills and understanding which individuals can use as a basis to secure further knowledge and skills

• the development of a research base to provide new knowledge, understanding and ideas to attract high technology companies.

Source: Compiled from Dearing (1997), 'The Wider Context'.
http://www.leeds.ac.uk/niche/index.htm

Clearly the Dearing Report recognises globalisation as a strong influence upon the UK economy and the labour market, with important implications for higher education. Analysing the Dearing Report, it is possible to consider the globalisation of tertiary or higher education according to three interrelated functions: the *knowledge* function, the *labour* function and the *institutional* function. The primacy of the knowledge function and its globalisation has a number of dimensions: knowledge and its production and transmission or acquisition is still primary as it was with the idea of the modern university, but now its value is legitimated increasingly in terms of its attraction to and service of global corporations. The globalisation of the labour function is formulated in terms of both the production of technically skilled people to meet the needs of global corporations and the ideology of lifelong learning, where individuals can 're-equip themselves for a succession of jobs over a working lifetime'. The institutional function is summed up in the phrase 'higher education will become a global international service and tradable commodity'. The competitive survival of institutions is tied to the globalisation of its organisational form (emulating private sector enterprises) and the globalisation of its 'services'. Clearly with this function there are possibilities for the emergence of both a closer alliance between global corporations and universities, especially in terms of the funding of research and development, and, in some cases, the university as a global corporation. The latter is a likely development with the world integration and convergence of media, telecommunications and publishing industries (see Cunningham *et al.*, 1998).

The developments described here under the banner of globalisation, which accentuate the primacy of knowledge, are further underwritten by recent advances in so-called 'growth theory'. Neoclassical economics does not specify how knowledge accumulation occurs. As a result there is no mention of human capital and there is no direct role for education. Further, in the neoclassical model there is no income 'left over' (all output is paid to either capital or labour) to act as a reward or incentive for knowledge accumulation. Accordingly, there are no externalities to knowledge accumulation. By contrast, new growth theory has highlighted the role of education in the creation of human capital and in the production of new knowledge. On this basis it has explored the possibilities of education-related externalities. In short, while the evidence is far from conclusive at this stage, there is a consensus emerging that (i) education is important for successful research activities (e.g. by producing scientists and engineers), which are, in turn, important for productivity growth, and (ii) education creates human capital, which directly affects knowledge accumulation and therefore productivity growth (see Report 8, 'Externalities in Higher Education', Dearing, 1997).

The Knowledge Society and the Discourse of Futurology

In the attempt to reposition and structurally adjust their national economies to take advantage of the main global trends, British, Australian and New Zealand governments have begun to recognise the importance of education, and especially higher education, as an 'industry' of the future. There is an emerging understanding of the way in which higher education is now central to economic (post)modernisation and the key to competing successfully within the global economy. This understanding has emerged from the shifts that are purportedly taking place in the production and consumption of knowledge which are impacting on traditional knowledge institutions like universities.

Shifts in the Production and Legitimation of Knowledge

The role of the university is undergoing a transition in late modernity as a result of structural shifts in the production and legitimation of knowledge. The older goal of the democratisation of the university has now been superseded by new challenges arising from the dual processes of the globalisation and fragmentation of knowledge cultures. These arise from the following developments:

• the separation of knowledge (research) from the post-sovereign state that no longer exclusively supports Big Science

- the rise of new regulatory regimes that impose an 'audit society' on the previously autonomous society
- a separation of research from teaching (education)
- the decoupling of knowledge from society and the replacement of the public by target constituencies
- the functional contradiction between science and economy in the increasing specialisation of knowledge and the decline in occupational opportunities
- the de-territorialisation of knowledge as a result of new communication technologies and knowledge flows
- the crisis of scientific rationality under conditions of the 'risk society', reflexivity and the new demands for the legitimation of knowledge.

Source: Delanty (1998)

Senior managers and policy analysts have begun to develop over-arching concepts or visions of the future as a method of picturing these changes. Thus, the terms 'information society' (which has been around since the late 1960s) and 'global information economy' abound in policy documents. More recently, the terms 'knowledge' and 'learning' have been moved to centre stage by those reviewing higher education. The Dearing Report uses the central concept of the 'learning society' to interpret the likely impact of imminent global trends on the national economy and, accordingly, to reform higher education. In New Zealand, the term adopted by the Ministry of Research, Science and Technology (MoRST) is the 'knowledge society'. In both cases, the concepts are embedded in what we call the discourse of futurology. In this section we briefly examine the MoRST Foresight Project, which trades heavily on the 'knowledge society'.

The Foresight Project

The Foresight Project is a future-oriented public discussion exercise designed to encourage a consensus among various sector groups in New Zealand concerning a 'desirable future'. The exercise is based on a notion of foresight which is neither a form of prediction or planning, but rather an analysis of global trends, how they will affect us and how (given our resources) we might take advantage of them. The Foresight

Project links government investment with New Zealand's development towards becoming a knowledge society. MoRST sees the path by which this will be achieved as an active process that recognises four key imperatives:

- The focus on the future must not be constrained by what we have been doing in the past.
- Technology (in its broadest sense) is a key driver for the knowledge revolution. It will have wide-ranging implications for the structure of society and the way in which we deal with environmental issues.
- A globalised economy requires us to be internationally competitive.
- The government's strategic investment in public good science and technology must be used effectively to underpin New Zealand's development as a knowledge society.

Over a two-year period, a comprehensive review of the priorities for public good science and technology is being carried out (under the umbrella of the Foresight Project) with the following four phases: Foresight Overview (establishing a context for thinking about the future); Development of Sector Strategies (developing a widely shared and compelling understanding of what is important for New Zealand); Priority and Allocations Decisions (identification of the priorities for public good science and technology); Implementation (implementation of new priorities and investment processes from July 2000).

It is claimed that while the future is not entirely predictable, there are trends which are presently unfolding that must be taken into account in the foresight process. The Foresight Project specifies seven such trends, including: The Knowledge Revolution; Globalisation; Global Science and Technology Trends; Changing Consumer Behaviours and Preferences; Industry Convergence; Environmental Issues; and Social Organisation. In this account we will concentrate on the so-called 'knowledge revolution'. We are informed that the 'knowledge revolution' constitutes a significant global paradigm shift that is changing the structure of New Zealand's economy and society. Knowledge is the key to the future because it, rather than capital or labour, drives productivity and economic growth. Unlike either capital or labour, it cannot lose its value and may even increase in value with future applications. Knowledge, we are informed, 'includes information in any form, but also includes know-how and know-why, and involves the way we interact as individuals and as a community' (MoRST, 1998: 8).

> Knowledge economies are those which are directly based on the production, distribution and use of knowledge and information. This is reflected in the trend towards growth in high-technology investments, high-technology industries, more highly-skilled labour and associated productivity gains. Knowledge, as embodied in people (as 'human capital') and in technology, has always been central to economic development. But it is only over the last few years that its relative importance has been recognised, just as that importance is growing.

This description of the 'knowledge revolution' is sprinkled with references to Toffler, Drucker, Tapscott, Negroponte, Handy, Kelly, Henderson and Hawken.

The framework, the philosophy and the process of planning for the future in the 'knowledge age' that MoRST adopts is a form of management theory called 'scenario-building', born out of the dissatisfaction with strategic planning during the 1980s. Scenario-building theory is seen to overcome the conceptual limitations of strategic planning including, its élitism and lack of engagement with sector representatives, and its lack of vision and orientation to the future. Wallace and Packer (1998) indicate that the concept of a 'scenario' originates in film practice, as a kind of scaffolding or framework for the production of a movie. They note that it was popularised in the corporate world by Royal Dutch Shell and subsequently adopted as a tool of business management. The Foresight Project developers describe scenario-building in the following terms:

> Three key elements are required for useful scenarios. Firstly, we need to gather information – about the irrevocable events and factors influencing how we will respond to these. Next, we need to assemble scenarios, in terms of social, technological, economic, political and environmental factors. Finally, we need to rehearse the future – by visualising how each of these scenarios might

affect us. We can then elucidate strategies to capitalise on the opportunities and challenges in front of us.

The hindsight process of reflecting on the past is considered a useful way of seeing the 'paradigm shifts' that have occurred in New Zealand. The Ministry offers the following description of the past and the future as a series of Kuhnian 'paradigm shifts': from the regulation, protectionism, public ownership, welfarism, egalitarianism of the 1970s to de-regulation, open markets, privatisation, self-responsibility and the age of the self-achiever in the 1990s. The big question for the Ministry futurologists is to guess what the paradigm for 2010 will be.

The Foresight Project uses scenario-building to develop an awareness of irrevocable events while reviewing priorities for public good science and technology. On this basis possible strategic responses to these scenarios are developed. Three possible scenarios for New Zealand are identified:

Possum in the Glare: New Zealand is caught like a possum in the glare of the oncoming future. But possums are hardy creatures, and New Zealand muddles along by finding new markets for traditional agricultural products and combating falling prices with new production technologies.

Shark Roaming Alone: After a period of economic difficulty, New Zealand has adapted quickly to keep up with the changes of the early twenty-first century. Rapid uptake of new technology and the Internet combined with the success of the entrepreneurial approach have made us a highly individualised society of sharks ....

Nga Kahikatea Reaching New Heights: Around the world, there is much interest in the social change that has occurred in New Zealand over the first decade of the twenty-first century. What highlights New Zealand among other countries is a strong and widely shared sense of purpose – a national intent. A nation of kahikatea, standing together ....

Is this really scenario-building? Are these equally valid or possible options? Can data be found to distinguish these three possible scenarios? Of the three scenarios, which are to be considered desirable futures?

What are the implications for the role and status of universities as knowledge institutions in these scenarios?

We are not at all happy with either the notion of the 'knowledge revolution' underlying the Foresight Project or the management scenario philosophy. If strategic planning has its problems, so too does scenario planning. We are surprised, given the alleged importance of the 'knowledge revolution', that so little attention is paid to the role of universities as axial knowledge institutions. The focus is investment-driven science and technology policy, which makes some simplistic assumptions about the concept of knowledge and the 'knowledge revolution'. We shall confine our critique to five key points.

First, the Foresight Project does not make the standard philosophical distinction between 'knowledge' and 'information'. Based on the traditional 'true, justified belief' account of knowledge which goes back to Plato, the following logical conditions apply. For A (a knower) to know that p (where 'p' is a proposition or statement): (1) A must believe that p; (2) P must be true; and (3) A must be justified that p. In other words, there is a belief condition, a truth condition and a justification condition, all of which must be met for something to count as knowledge. For data to qualify as information, none of these conditions must be met: there is no belief condition, no truth condition, no justification condition. All that has to occur is for data to be sent from a sender to a receiver. Data as information may not be true, believed or justified. There are forms of 'disinformation', 'infomercials', increasingly 'edutainment' and so on that clearly do not count as knowledge. This is a serious error for the Foresight Project, which, while based of the concept of 'knowledge', conflates 'knowledge' with 'information', collapses the two and, thereby, also perpetrates flawed accounts of both the production and consumption processes of knowledge and of knowledge institutions.

Second, the Foresight Project embraces a discourse of futurology in a very narrow sense: the discourse is at once populist and ahistorical. The discourses of futurology and of futurisms (in the plural) have always been a defining feature of modernism and modernity and these discourses, it could be argued, seem to become most popular at the end of centuries. Are they millennium products? At any rate, the futurisms of European formalist thought originate in pre-revolutionary Russia and have strong conceptual links with a formalist poetics. We must remember that there is a strong future-orientation and element of prophecy in the counter-Enlightenment thought of both Schopenhauer and Nietzsche, both of whom strongly influenced the cultural sites of *fin-de-siécle* Vienna and the northern Italian cities, which were sites for Filippo Marinetti's futurism. Futurism was the first attempt in the twentieth century to reimagine life as it was then being transfixed by new technologies and to invent a machinic utopia that both extended and remodelled culture.

Third, the Foresight Project is grounded in the corporatist management theory of scenario building. While we may acknowledge that such a theory is inclusive of sector interests and less élitist than its predecessor, strategic planning, it still carries with it the ethos of the corporation and reflects the interests of business rather than the interests of the wider society or nation. Wallace and Packer (1998) ask of MoRST's Foresight Project's scenarios, 'who is telling the story, and therefore whose perspective is at least implicitly being privileged?' They also suggest that scenarios, normally used as a business tool for controlling the future of a company, tend to assimilate the nation to the status of a corporation. They comment that the almost exclusive focus of the scenarios is upon the relation between technology and the economy (and, in particular, economic growth and productivity). Not only are social and cultural issues consigned to economic ends in so far as they are mentioned at all, but the technological forces that are allegedly responsible for propelling us into the future are acultural and asocial; they exist some how apart from culture and society, and impact upon it.

Fourth, the Foresight Project does not consider the history of the notion of the 'knowledge society' or the 'information society' or associated concepts like the 'global information society'. These are not uncontested terms. They are value-laden and theory-laden concepts that have been part of social and cultural theory for over thirty years. What this means is that there is no innocent approach to these terms or their unproblematic use which can be hived off from the accumulation of theory, especially the sociology of post-industrialism and post-Fordism to which they belong. We would argue that there is a public obligation on the part of MoRST officials to acknowledge these theory contexts and to present them clearly as part of the overall discussion.

Fifth, and in related terms, the Foresight Project tends to focus upon the investment side of the ledger and attempts to answer the question of national priorities in science and technology. It does not move from the question of the 'knowledge society' to questions of the main 'knowledge institutions' or the way these are being transformed. There is, for example, little or no attention given to New Zealand's universities or other tertiary education institutions and there does not seem to be any linkage between science and technology policy on the one hand, and the review of tertiary education on the other. Arguably, in the United Kingdom there is a better articulation between these related policy areas.

Globalisation, Universities and Democracy

Roger Dale (1998: 3) argues that 'globalisation does represent a new and distinct shift in the relationship between state and supranational forces and that it has affected education, profoundly and in a range of ways'. He maintains that while globalisation effects have been experienced in more extreme forms in developing countries, they have been experienced directly, sectorally and organisationally in developed countries, and he is quick to point out that globalisation is not unidirectional:

> National modes of regulation, social structures of production, societal and cultural effects, all not only interpret, modify, mediate, resist, support or are indifferent to the direct or indirect effects of globalisation, but they may both transform or invert those effects and bring about changes in them. National states and societies are not helpless in the face of globalisation, nor are the outcomes of globalisation bound to bring about a greater transnational homogeneity of practice of education.
>
> (Dale, 1998: 3)

Dale recognises that while globalisation does present all countries with 'a much more common agenda of problems', even for the richest and most powerful states this does not mean that responses to those problems necessarily will be uniform. Yet, as he argues, 'the state can discharge its national responsibilities only by prioritising its extra national responsibilities' which he identifies as the major source of the indirect effects of globalisation on education.

The major question that the analysis of the discourse of globalisation and its relation to higher education policy poses is whether it simply represents a capitulation to the strength and influence of transnational corporations (TNCs). Are universities to become research and teaching centres servicing the needs of global capital, providing TNCs with human capital and providing the basis of innovation by stimulating R&D? Is this the only alternative? In policy-making terms is globalisation undermining the possibilities of national sovereignty? What are the implications of globalisation for democracy?

There can be little doubt that there has been a shift from a system of distinct national economies to a global economy in which both production and consumption has been internationalised and finance capital and information flow freely and instantly between countries. This development has been both a cause and a consequence of the so-called information revolution and the dramatic improvements in telecommunications. The international regulatory framework is increasingly defined by world policy institutions such as the WTO, the IMF, the World Bank, the OECD and G7 summits, and by regional trading blocks such as APEC, the European Union and NAFTA. A recent OECD report, *Globalisation: What Challenges and Opportunities for Government?* (OECD, 1997b), argues that 'If sovereignty is defined as the ability to exercise control without outside interference, then the nation state is clearly experiencing diminishing sovereignty'. The report outlines its support for this assertion in terms of the following:

- Monetary and fiscal policy decisions can no longer be taken on the basis of exclusively domestic considerations
- Competition for international investment – encouraged by the activities and mobility of multinational enterprises – means that most traditionally domestic policies such as education and training, taxation, social protection, economic regulation or labour legislation have become international
- Policies must increasingly be made more consistent or competitive with trends in main trading partners

- Participation in international organisations or the adoption of international agreements puts limits on policy options available to governments, or 'ties their hands'
- Many other important policy goals cannot be met by governments acting alone (e.g. environmental degradation, international crime and drugs trafficking).

The report suggests that at the same time as globalisation is forcing the transfer of major domestic policy decisions to the international arena, public management reforms in many countries have attempted to institute policies of decentralisation and devolution, transferring many decision-making functions to regional or local levels. Of course deregulation policies are entirely consistent with globalisation, and, indeed, together with other policies, including the privatisation of state assets, tax reform, trade and financial liberalisation, and the promotion of foreign direct investment comprise a significant part of the underlying set of principles for economic globalisation. Genuine devolution policies appear at odds with these developments, for they devolve power and responsibility to regions, local government, communities and institutions exactly at the point when national governments have the least power and political will to mediate in conflicts with multinationals.

The OECD report suggests that international cooperation opens up new opportunities for progress such as sharing policy strategies or working together to establish rules of the game for international information highways or a global financial system. The report argues:

> Firstly, there is a need for adjustment in the structures or machinery of government to enable governments to function effectively in an interdependent world. Secondly, governments must examine the impacts of globalisation on national and international policy-making processes, and the relationships between various policy actors therein, so as to protect and strengthen the basic democratic underpinnings sought for national and global governance.
>
> (OECD, 1997b: 6)

In terms of the first issue the report suggests adapting the role of foreign ministries to an environment such that they no longer have a monopoly over foreign relations; improving the internal management of external relations, including the need for greater internal policy coordination, mechanisms to manage participation in international fora, and developing strategic direction; exploiting opportunities for international problem-solving and the international exchange of policy strategies; and developing international skills among public officials.

In terms of the second issue the report is more equivocal, indicating that while there are opportunities for greater international cooperation and the prospect of an emerging set of world institutions that point to global governance, there are also distinct limits, problems and dangers. We summarise these aspects of the report in terms of a register of problems and prospects:

The changing balance of power and relationships

- International or multilateral agreements, particularly in the area of trade policy, are changing the international balance of power.
- Globalisation strengthens strong states at the expense of small peripheral players in the global economy.
- Regional groupings may be one way for 'small' countries to maximise their influence in global fora and to equalise the power relationships in international decision-making between heterogeneous players.
- The bargaining power of individual member states in international fora could be enhanced by collective action.

Globalisation and participatory democracy

- Increased access to information may have a 'democratising effect', politicising citizens and mobilising them into action (e.g. referenda on EU membership), helping to build democracy in traditionally closed societies.
- Globalisation allows people to organise themselves more quickly and effectively across national borders (e.g. Greenpeace, the 1993 Rio Summit and the 1994 Cairo Conference on Population Growth, the Beijing World Conference on Women) to exert international pressures on governments.
- Collaboration of domestic interest groups, linked by race, religion or conviction, with their foreign counterparts (e.g. indigenous peoples

such as New Zealand Māori, Australian Aboriginals and native Canadians) to share strategies across national borders.
* Both global media and policy processes are open to capture by powerful interests with special access to information and its dissemination, but it may make international relations and events more visible and transparent.

The democratic deficit

* Governments may take policy processes to the international level as a strategy to escape domestic opposition and to limit the number of players involved in policy.
* Claiming 'tied hands' as a result of international agreements may be a way for governments to present unpalatable policies at home.
* The tendency to resort to international decision-making (including treaties and international agreements) seems to be increasing the power of executive government at the expense of parliaments, resulting in a shift of power from elected to non-elected bodies.

The future for 'global governance'

* There is currently no 'world government', only a range of uncoordinated international institutions (e.g. UN, WTO, EU, IMF, WB, OECD) that set guidelines or make rules in selected policy areas.
* The impacts of globalisation on democratic accountability at both the national and international levels will need to be carefully monitored and new international forms of democratic accountability need to be developed.
* Countries must invest more in building effective and legitimate international organisations and institutions that are capable of delivering results while maintaining democratic values.
* Governments must prove that sovereignty can actually be enhanced rather than diminished by active participation in international decision-making.

Source: Edited and abridged from OECD (1997b)

Universities have always been 'world institutions' imbued, at least in the modern era since Kant, with a critical function. In the context of globalisation, one might argue that this critical function undergoes both a transformation and enhancement from the role of 'critic and conscience of society' to 'critic and conscience in the world community'. This does not mean that universities relinquish their previous critical functions in home societies; indeed, this domestic critical function becomes even more important in protecting domestic democratic rights, decision-making processes and institutions, enhancing processes of participatory democracy and scrutinising the 'democratic deficit'.

In the context of globalisation, universities, acting alone or in concert with each other, may, in addition, take on other critical functions related to what might be called 'an agenda for alternative globalisations':

Promotion of a global social contract

- promoting sustainable development
- promoting ecological standards
- consolidating the democratic process
- enhancing the development of international labour standards
- promoting world trade union rights
- monitoring the social dimension of global and regional trade agreements.

Promotion of global governance

- building standards of global governance
- protecting the public institutions of civil society
- developing transparency and accountability of international fora and world institutions
- developing approaches to institutions of an international civil community
- encouraging greater north/south dialogue and better world representation.

Promotion of cultural globalisation

- promoting cultural diversity and exchange
- developing genuine multicultural structures and processes
- promoting and enhancing the notion of cultural rights
- protecting indigenous property rights
- promoting political and cultural self-determination.

An agenda for alternative globalisations recognises that the neoliberal 'free market' approach represents only one paradigm among a range of possibilities. The neoliberal paradigm, which has been dominant over the last decade, advocates: the reduction of the role of the state; the privatisation of state assets; the abolition of state subsidies and tariffs, allowing 'free market forces' to prevail; and the encouragement of high levels of foreign direct investment with the consequence of providing a high degree of 'freedoms' to multinational corporations at the expense of civil society and public good institutions at the national level. Within the neoliberal paradigm, universities are increasingly being divested of the public good functions as they are progressively privatised. Their institutional autonomy is imperilled and their form of democratic governance curtailed. Universities, in this paradigm, become service centres for multinational corporations. Accordingly, the role of critic and conscience of society is relaxed, or limited, or disappears entirely. There are other approaches – for instance those of UNCTAD (the United Nations Conference on Trade and Development) or of the ILO (International Labour Organisation) – which either seek a more balanced approach to the roles of the market and the state in contrast to neoliberal initiatives, or emphasise the social dimension to economic globalisation, based upon recognising core labour standards and developing a 'socially acceptable' model of competitiveness (see Evans, 1997). Secretary-General Rubens Ricupero of UNCTAD believes that globalisation has been 'oversold' to the public and that there has been a too-exclusive emphasis on market forces at the expense of the need for an effective state and good public institutions. Others have called for a strengthening of civil society's democratic outlook. Still others recommend an international relations paradigm based on inclusive consensus-seeking, greater world partnerships, the integration of environmental and development concerns, and the intervention of the state and the international community to control and regulate market forces in the public interest so as to ensure social equity and bring about more sustainable patterns of production and consumption. Universities have an important role to play in making these alternatives the subject of rigorous discussion and ongoing debate.

chapter three

Challenges to the Concept
of the Modern University

In the previous chapter Bill Readings' work provided the starting point
for a broad account of the crisis in the concept of the modern university.
For anyone working in an Australian, Canadian, British, American or
New Zealand university over the past decade, Readings' account of the
shift to the discourse of excellence in higher education must constitute
an easily recognisable and frightening description. The language of
managerialism, focusing on strategic planning, mission statements and
performance indicators, seems to have nothing to do with the traditional
governance of the university. The further the university moves away
from the old structures the more it loses its institutional uniqueness and
looks like just another corporation. The neoliberal policy paradigm now
dispenses with any pretence to anything other than the underlying
market logic: contestable funding, 'providers' and 'consumers', student
loans and so on, have real consequences and now form the parameters
of our daily working lives. In short, the establishment of a new language
of the university has been accomplished, and while we might distance
ourselves from the ideology of managerialism or even attempt to subvert
it in various ways, we cannot help but be effectively reshaped by it.

In this chapter we examine Readings' arguments in closer detail, concentrating in the first instance on a paper published posthumously in a special issue of the *Oxford Literary Review* in 1995. We suggest four major areas where we differ from him. In Chapter 2 we maintained that the position of the university is significantly altered under neoliberal economic globalisation. This chapter draws upon the work of Michel Foucault and Gilles Deleuze in developing this thesis further. We argue that the idea of the modern university was intimately interwoven with the development of the liberal nation-state and that its crisis is part of the decline of the modern nation-state under the impact of globalisation.

Dwelling in the Ruins of the University

In the lead article for a special issue of *Oxford Literary Review* commemorating his work, Readings (1995: 16) argues that we must recognise that the university is a *ruined* institution, and he asks us to ponder the question of what it means to dwell in the ruins without falling back on romance or nostalgia. Readings restricts himself to the notion of the culturally-oriented humanities, noting that under the impact of the market and the adoption of consumerism as a way of life, the (Humboldtian) idea of culture has dropped out of the discourse purporting to give the university a foundation or, at least, no longer appears serviceable. As the editors remark, the university no longer functions as a 'privileged site of national cultural self-definition' (Clark & Royle, 1995: 16). Readings (1995: 21) suggests that the animating idea of culture in cultural studies 'is not really an idea in the strong sense proposed by the Modern University'.

In the face of such an overriding economic imperative, Readings wonders 'how thought may be addressed within the University' (p. 22) or rather 'how to think in an institution whose development tends to make thought more and more difficult' (p. 23). His answer is partly construed as an historical response, although clearly it also contains faint traces of a German idealism with its concern to protect, if not an idea, then a *space*. He implicitly defines thought in terms of its disciplinary structures while acknowledging the dissipation of such structures and the opening up of a certain interdisciplinary space. To dwell in the ruins of the university without nostalgia, Readings suggests we ought to abandon disciplinary grounding but retain as structurally essential 'the *question of the disciplinary form that can be given to knowledges'* (p. 25). In this new context disciplinarity has become a permanent question: 'we must keep open the question of what it means to group knowledges in certain ways', to ask not only of what it consists but also what it excludes.

We are sympathetic to Readings' interpretation and wish to acknowledge the significant role he has played in prompting new work on the changing nature of the university. In the spirit of critical thinking, we want to offer four points on which we differ with Readings. First, we think Readings conflates the Kantian and the Humboldtian ideas: he talks of disciplinarity in the humanities, acknowledging the decline of the Humboldtian idea of culture as a central organising idea for the university, yet the idea he wants to defend, in some limited sense, is a variant of the (Kantian) idea of reason – the idea of thought or thinking and its institutional space. Some clarification is required here: we think there is a suppressed argument in Readings' paper that does considerable work concerning the definition of thought or thinking in humanities in terms of its disciplinary structures. For our part we would want to talk of the *multiplicity* of thought, of the difference between disciplinary and interdisciplinary thinking, of thinking without the disciplines, perhaps even of thinking despite the disciplines.

This new multiplicity of thought in the humanities is not just a kind of postmodern *bricolage*, assemblage or blind eclecticism driven by the academic market; it is also a kind of unravelling of the disciplinary purposes of the Modern University. It is not without considerable care that Foucault chose the notion of discipline as part of the title of his famous work *Discipline and Punish*. 'Discipline' – a systematically ambiguous term – as a form of moral training establishes the liberal rationality of governance required for our autonomy as subjects and, therefore, also the self-regulating autonomy of the university as a whole. Barry Hindess (1995: 44), for example, argues that 'the most influential Western models of a university should be seen, at least in part, as belonging to a liberal rationality of government' in the Foucauldian sense of individual self-regulation. Indeed, the neo-Foucauldian trope of disciplinarity has proved remarkably productive for understanding not only the university and the rise of cultural studies but also modern institutions per se[1].

Second, we disagree with Readings when it comes to giving up entirely on the idea of culture and on the university as a privileged site for national cultural self-definition. Readings is still wedded to the idea of the Modern University, an idea largely born out of German idealism and one certainly bearing all the traces of a Eurocentric conception. While Readings does entertain a certain resistance to the history of the idea – we now live amongst its ruins and we must learn to do so without nostalgia – he does not seek to displace it or dislodge it entirely. More importantly, he does not want to interrogate its cultural expression, its native tradition or the way it expresses a certain typical Euro-universalism and ethnocentrism. The time of the idea is a European time which must be questioned. In non-European cultural traditions the task of the post-colonial university, *in a different cultural time*, may be precisely to focus upon the question of national cultural self-definition and to do so as a means of coming to terms, confronting, engaging with, or resisting forces of cultural homogeneity which threaten to erode indigenous traditions in the wake of a globalisation which commodifies both word and image[2]. We cannot presume that the university will take place or perform the same functions in non-European cultures as it does or did in European cultures. Some indication of this might be gained from the prescribed purposes of national universities (for example, the National Islamic University of Malaysia) which have a statutory function of protecting and enhancing national religious and cultural traditions.

Third, by concentrating upon the disciplinary shifts in the humanities alone, Readings is not able to provide an analysis of the way in which these shifts respond to or interact with other shifts – for instance between the sciences and the humanities – or the way the whole disciplinary regime is modulated together. His allusion to the shift of philosophy and the presence of certain strands of European philosophy in departments of literature and cultural studies, which are almost totally ignored by philosophy departments, is a good example. Such a question almost certainly requires reference to disciplinary developments in science and the adoption of a 'scientific' philosophy. Let us briefly elaborate: a genealogy of American philosophy reveals the fracturing of a public intellectual tradition under such figures as Emerson and Dewey, when Jewish émigré philosophers, strongly influenced by the Vienna Circle (Reichenbach, Feigl, Carnap) migrated to the United States. In general, analytic philosophy became very narrowly professional and technical, turning in upon itself and, accordingly, was less interested in communicating with other disciplines. Under the influence of twentieth-century formalism and logicism, it ditched its 'humanity' and 'literariness' to become a highly professionalised and a purely technical discipline (see Rorty, 1982, Dyke, 1993, Barradori, 1994)[3].

Fourth, we do not think that Readings sufficiently distinguishes between two kinds of market liberalism: that construed in national economic terms and a neoliberal economic globalisation. They have both impinged upon the university in distinctive ways and in different eras. Neoliberal economic globalisation, at least, presents *new* problems – legal, ethical, epistemological – to the university. It is these issues which we want to tease out in more detail, focusing particularly on the role of science, the emergence of the research-based university and its harnessing by the liberal nation-state.

Globalisation, Knowledge and Control

The idea of the modern university was first formulated in different but related ways by Kant, Schleiermacher, Scheller, Humboldt and Newman and became the basis of national (German and English) discourses which both consigned an idea to the university and purported to justify its institutional essence in philosophical terms. Kant and Newman, as representatives of different national traditions, emphasised in common the importance of the search for truth or the role of critical reflection and its relation to the question of the governance of the institution. They also shared a similar understanding of the industrial or quasi-industrial organisation of the university as a *modern* liberal institution based upon a division of (academic) labour.

The emergence of the modern university is a phenomenon of the nineteenth century: its development as the principal knowledge-producing institution, Wittrock (1993) asserts, is concomitant with the rise of the modern liberal nation-state, in its newly formed (e.g. Germany or Italy), reformed (e.g. France), or 'new world' colonial-satellite status (e.g. Australia and New Zealand). Wittrock (1993: 303–4) argues that the development of the research function is 'co-terminous with the nineteenth-century transformation of universities from institutions for the transformation of a received body of knowledge to generally immature adolescents into research institutions, the "axial" institutions of the modern world'. He suggests that specialisation within universities (the emergence of an academic division of labour based upon the development of the disciplines) and the move from gentlemen amateurs to professional specialisation can also be seen in a Foucauldian way as precipitating a new kind of epistemic regime. Interesting in Wittrock's analysis of the transformation of the university is his historical observation that while the emergence of a new epistemic regime was co-terminous with the resurrection of the idea of self-governance proposed by the Humboldt brothers, such an idea was at odds with the process of ever-increasing disciplinary specialisation (p. 342).

It is important to recognise that the accounts offered by Newman and by the German idealist tradition differed on this crucial point. Newman did not see the advancement of knowledge as a central function of the modern university. He gave no room to research per se, suggesting that teaching was the principal function which defined the essence of the institution. In his Preface to his famous work of 1852, he wrote:

> The view taken of a University in these Discourses is the following:
> That it is the place of *teaching* universal *knowledge*. This implies that its object is, on the one hand, intellectual, not moral; and, on the other, that it is the diffusion and extension of knowledge rather than the advancement. If its object were scientific and philosophic discovery, I do not see why a University should have students; if religious training, I do not see how it can be the seat of literature and science. Such is a University in its *essence*, and independent of its relation to the church.
>
> (Newman, 1996: 3)

What was genuinely new about the *modern* university, Wittrock (1993: 345) argues, was that the task of research, of advancing knowledge, became a central part of the university's mission, and increasingly that part of the university developing self-image was what separated it from other institutions offering post-secondary education. A large part of Wittrock's (1993: 361) argument is that 'two of the three institutions of modernity, namely the nation-state and the university, can no longer take their continued existence for granted – certainly not in the form in which they have appeared for over a century'. The third institution, the modern corporation, has also undergone changes to its form. Wittrock concludes that while there is no reason to expect the demand for higher education or scientific knowledge to diminish, 'such may well occur in a fashion that makes any discussion of the "idea" of a university appear hopelessly antiquated' (Wittrock, 1993: 361)[4].

A conference held in Copenhagen in 1994 (OECD, 1996) was designed to address the conceptual difficulties economic theory faces in coming to terms with the core concepts of 'knowledge' and 'information'. One paper, by Dominique Foray and Bengt-Åke Lundvall (1996: 29), gives a very real sense of the stakes involved. Having provided interpretations of the knowledge-based economy, considered the empirical evidence and trends, and made some conceptual clarifications (going back to Polanyi's *tacit* knowledge), they conclude:

While information technology makes more kinds of knowledge codifiable, and thereby accelerates the processes of innovation, change and learning, some elements of tacit knowledge have become more important than ever for economic performance and success. The traditional dichotomy between public and private knowledge is becoming less relevant. Hybrid forms of knowledge which are neither completely private nor completely public are becoming increasingly important. More and more strategic know-how and competence is developed interactively and shared within sub-groups and networks.

They continue:

These changes may be regarded as parts of an ever further-reaching process of socio-economic change – we are moving towards a networked learning economy where the opportunity and capability to access and join knowledge- and learning-intensive networks determine the relative success of individuals and firms.

What we find fascinating about this statement (and the paper as a whole) is the absence of any reference to traditional knowledge-institutions, the acknowledgement of the tacit dimension in knowledge, and the recognition of the hybridisation of knowledge forms.

Of course, the new policy prescriptions for the university have not been welcomed by everyone. Nor have 'populist' market interpretations of globalisation as the triumph of capitalism and democracy been accepted by all. These views may be contrasted with a range of 'critical' positions from the Gramscian writings of Robert Cox to the more 'technical' approach adopted by Susan Strange or the 'developmental' perspective of Anthony Giddens and Roland Robertson. There is not space enough here to engage or to distinguish these positions further. Instead we would like to put forward, in outline, a neo-Foucauldian – or better, a Foucauldian-Deleuzian – approach to globalisation which has clear implications for the institution of the university.[5] To a large degree this approach continues to focus upon Foucault's notion of 'rationality of government' (see Burchell, *et al.* 1991; Barry, *et al.* 1996): it understands neoliberal economic globalisation as a deepening of world political order through marketisation effected by the spatialisation of both time and knowledge.

In his 'Postscript on the Societies of Control' (1992) Deleuze claims:

We are in a generalized crisis in relation to all the environments of enclosure – prison, hospital, factory, school, family. The family is an 'interior', in crisis like all other interiors – scholarly, professional, etc. The administrations in charge never cease announcing supposedly necessary reforms: to reform schools, to reform industries, hospitals, the armed forces, prisons. But everyone knows that these institutions are finished, whatever the length of their expiration periods. It's only a matter of administering their last rites and of keeping people employed until the installation of the new forces knocking at the door (pp. 1–2).

Drawing on the work of Paul Virilio as well as Foucault, Deleuze argues that new modes of free-floating control are replacing the closed systems of disciplinary societies. Deleuze speaks of enclosures as 'molds' with distinct castings; in controls, by contrast, we find a form of 'modulation'. The new processes of control are based on the model of the network, with greater flexibility and continuous change. In disciplinary societies 'one was always starting again (from school to the barracks, from the barracks to the factory)', whereas in societies of control 'one is never finished with anything' (p. 2). In place of the signature (which designates the person as an *individual*) and the number (which indicates a person's position within a *mass*), it is the *code* that is important in societies of control:

> [T]he code is a *password*, while on the other hand disciplinary societies are regulated by *watchwords* (as much from the point of view of integration as from that of resistance). The numerical language of control is made of codes that mark access to information, or reject it. We no longer find ourselves dealing with the mass/individual pair. Individuals have become *'dividuals'*, and masses, samples, data, markets, or 'banks' (p. 3).

We live, Deleuze suggests, in a capitalism of higher-order production. The factory has given way to the market, where control tends to be short-term, with rapid rates of turnover, but also continuous and without limit. The model of the school will be replaced by the ideal of perpetual training (driven by corporations), and university research will no longer seem necessary. Societies of control allow people to be *tracked* – continuously monitored, via computer networks and sophisticated electronic devices – while ostensibly granting new freedoms. In this sense they are no less oppressive than the disciplinary societies that proceeded them. Indeed, Deleuze notes, '[t]he coils of a serpent are even more complex than the burrows of a molehill' (p. 4).

In a recent interview Eric Alliez (1997: 86) provides a graphic description of Deleuze's 'societies of control', linking them, above all, to the question of knowledge and the new spatialisation of knowledge and education under a *capitalism of circulation* based upon the mode of information:

> The analysis that Deleuze gives us of the passage from 'disciplinary societies' to 'societies of control' aims to throw light on the forms taken by the accelerated substitution of a *capitalism of circulation and communication* for a capitalism of production centred on the exploitation of paid industrial labour alone (the factory being the paradigm for milieus of enclosure). The technological mutations of the age of planetary informationalisation are thus related to a mutation of capitalism (a Hypercapitalism of services) which knows no discourse of legitimation other than the purely horizontal one of the market (from enlightened

neo-liberalism to the hallucinated anarcho-capitalism of the Internet ...),
and no practice of domination other than that of a purely immanent
social control by universal marketing in continuous variation and
modulation (with the 3 M's ruling the New International order: Money,
Media and Military).

The new spatialisation of knowledge and education in the postmodern
age is based on the 'soft architecture' of the *network,* which increasingly
defines the nature of our institutions, our practices and our subjectivities.

Two signposts in the study of the university in relation to globalisation
can be distinguished: (i) a Foucauldian one pointing historically to
'disciplinary societies', to the notion of disciplinarity, to the study of
enclosed institutional spaces, and to the study of the university as part of
the 'rationality of government'; and (ii) a Deleuzian one, indicating the
road ahead of us: the understanding of the university as an institution
undergoing transformations based upon the dispersed logic of the
network. Both sets of studies are required; they are, indeed,
complementary. Yet neo-Foucauldian studies of disciplinarity (i.e. of the
emergence and transformation of disciplines) may appear as isolated
historical accounts oriented toward a modernist understanding of space:
they sometimes lack a directional politics, a politics of the present.

Let us give a brief example. In an important and insightful paper,
Alison Lee and Bill Green (1997: 21) argue for a re-assertion of the
notion of pedagogy as a means for 're-inventing the university in and for
postmodern times'. They make reference to the work of Keith Hoskin
(1993) and claim that it was the conjuncture of three emergent sets of
practices – writing, examination and grading – together with the three
pedagogical sites of the seminar, the laboratory and the classroom, that
'caused a great discontinuity in Western intellectual history' (p. 7). The
danger here, however, is that insufficient attention will be paid to
questions of political economy and their relevance to the formation of
new knowledges. Such an analysis can become too oriented to the
'economy of disciplines' rather than the 'discipline of the economy'.
Will the rehabilitation of pedagogy *vis-à-vis* research and detailed
empirical studies be adequate in helping us to confront the political
difficulties faced by the postmodern university? We think the critical
questions concerning the survival of the university (for example, its
privatisation, the cuts to staff and budgets, the closing down of

departments, the separation of teaching and research) have less to do with 're-inventing' pedagogy than with understanding the nature of neoliberal economic globalisation and its effects upon the university[6].

It is possible, we think, to understand globalisation fruitfully in terms relevant to the university through the concept of the spatialisation of knowledge, a concept promoted by both Foucault and Deleuze, and also given a specific determination by their countryman Henri Lefebvre (1991). One idea central to Lefebvre's view is that we are never confronted by a single social or cultural space; instead, a multiplicity of social spaces can be found, and growth and development does not annihilate these spaces. Indeed, Lefebvre seems to argue that in the development of world wide networks of communications and knowledge these social spaces emerge in all their complexity and diversity (1991: 86)[7]. Lefebvre argues that an understanding of the social distribution of knowledge and power requires a critique of space – its production over time and within its numerous social contexts.

In this regard, and in the context of a Deleuzian capitalism of circulation and communication, it is interesting to examine the way intellectual property rules create emerging structures of political space. Intellectual property regimes (IPRs) have been traditionally regarded as territorial but more recently they have been 'increasingly detached from the individual state through international agreements, including those which create extra-territorial rights, and are now policed by corporations and their lawyers or by international institutions' (Farrands, 1996: 179). These agreements focus more on products and core technologies than on territories, thereby rewriting cultural and social space.

Farrands (1996: 179) argues that these globalisation processes tend more toward some form of reconstitution of difference than they do toward a homogenisation; that is, IPRs remain diverse. Yet whatever form they take, 'they shift or reupholster existing power relations much more than they make any radical shift in them'. This is a point he develops in more detail:

> There is ... no single intellectual property regime in the international political system. Different rules cover different areas – patents and copyright, licensing and so on – and have their origins in different national jurisdictions and international agreements. Together, they constitute a system of governance in which a variety of stakeholders

have some interest in stable management. That is to say the control, legitimation and regulation are managed by a variety of interests only some of which are governments.

(Farrands, 1996: 183)[8]

He charts the shift in GATT talks around IPRs, and the moves by the USA after 1986 (before this date IPRs had not figured in such talks) to make intellectual property an agenda priority. Electronic data transmission, satellite broadcasting, the development of rapid copying systems, and the 'writing' of software on microchips have tended to confuse questions of copyright and raise new legal issues in defining and policing fraud. In this climate trade policy has focused on the language of 'economic security' and become increasingly protectionist.

The investigation of IPRs is one way of investigating the problematic of *extra-state governance*, its language and its practices – what Foucault (1970: xxii) called 'the *space* of knowledge'. This extra-government space has, in part, been expanded by the way neoliberals have withdrawn from aspects of the management of the national economy. In many instances their 'downsizing' and deregulation have simply shifted management to another level beyond the state, where the grid of power–knowledge is harder to detect.

Jane Kelsey (1997) has given attention to the implications of New Zealand and other countries becoming signatories to the GATS (General Agreement on Trade in Services) talks, which were part of the Uruguay GATT negotiations concluded in 1996. She argues that the consequences of exposing tertiary education to strong pressures of international competition, without suitable constraints and protections, are potentially very damaging for a small country like New Zealand. One such consequence is the risk of cultural homogenisation, where cheaper, standard, satellite-broadcast, courses and programmes could threaten to displace local content and cut across indigenous rights. Under a trade paradigm, education loses its capacity to transmit cultural values and to critically reflect issues of identity or national self-definition. In her opinion the GATS offer works to reinforce trends towards commercialisation, internationalisation and privatisation. In this worst case scenario, perhaps, we can no longer talk exclusively of 'the rationality of government' but also of 'the rationality of corporation'.

Endnotes

[1] See, for instance, Caputo & Yount (1993), Hunter, (1994, 1995), Messer-Davidow *et al.*, (1993), Roberts & Good (1993), Sosnoski (1995), Elam (1994), Nelson & Gaonkar (1996), Lee & Green (1997).

[2] The question of the postcolonial university and cultural self-definition is addressed, in part, by so-called 'Subaltern Studies' (Guha, 1982; Guha & Spivak, 1988) but also by Edward Said (1994a, 1994b), especially in terms of imperialism in literature and representations of the intellectual, and also by Ashis Nandy (1988) in his study of the impact of British science in India.

[3] In this respect we find fascinating the comment Foucault makes on Anglo-American philosophy in 'La Philosophie analytique de la politique' (orig. 1978, 1994) cited in Davidson (1997: 3):

> For Anglo-Saxon analytic philosophy it is a question of making a critical analysis of thought on the basis of the way in which one says things. I think one could imagine, in the same way, a philosophy that would have as its task to analyze what happens every day in relations of power, a philosophy that would try to show what they are about, what are the forms, the stakes, the objectives of these relations of power. A philosophy, accordingly, that would bear rather on relations of power than on language games, a philosophy that would bear on all these relations that traverse the social body rather than the effects of language that traverse and underlie thought. One could imagine, one should imagine something like an analytico-political philosophy.

[4] For a contrasting and more optimistic view, see Clark Kerr (1994: xiv) who embraces a 'convergence' thesis:

> I see a convergence going on, with national systems of higher education facing many of the same problems and working towards solutions that are more like each other than the historical points of origin of each system. As knowledge becomes more universal and as needed skills around the world become more similar, and as people are more liberated in their aspirations, systems of higher education tend to become more alike. Under the impacts of spreading industrialization and democratization, we have been moving away

from more culturally bound systems of higher education, nation by nation, to a more uniform world of learning.

Kerr (1994) contrasts the 'internationalisation of learning' against the intensification of interest by nation-states in institutions of higher education and the 'nationalisation of their purposes'. He neglects entirely the effects of economic or cultural globalisation on higher education.

5   For a broader discussion of Deleuze's work, see Peters (1996a).

6   We are also somewhat perplexed by the claims made by Hoskin, and Lee and Green, concerning the status of 'education'. For instance: 'Education, appropriately theorised is, we argue, central to an understanding of the genesis, maintenance and renewal of disciplinary knowledges' (Lee & Green, 1997: 3); or Hoskin's claim that 'Education is a subdiscipline ... best disregarded in serious academic company' though it might have been otherwise had the discipline claimed Durkheim or Dewey as its founding fathers; and now 'education, far from being subordinate, is superordinate' within the project of the university (cited in Lee & Green, 1997: 4). Such statements seem to us to convey a problematic 'field-centric' view of education.

7   See also in this connection Gianni Vattimo's (1992: 4) *The Transparent Society*, where he argues that the mass media play a decisive role in the emergence of postmodern society. Mass media do not make postmodern society more 'transparent'; rather they make it more complex, even 'chaotic', yet it is precisely in this relative 'chaos' that our hopes for emancipation lie. In arguing this line Vattimo wants to attack the ideal of a 'transparent' public sphere that underlies the work of Adorno & Horkheimer, and Habermas, who believe that under the same logic of production, mass media and the 'culture industries' have become commodified, such that original use-values are reduced to a common set of exchange values. The result is that communication has become systematically distorted.

8   We think this point is worthy of further elaboration in the sense that the boundaries here become blurred between states and firms, among states and between firms. In this new international arena the notion of 'rationality of government' requires rejigging. The extent to which the corporation now takes over some state functions in the exercise of modern political rationality, mobilising individuals for the goal of productivity, remains to be seen.

chapter four

Re-reading Lyotard:
Knowledge, Commodification
and Higher Education

It is difficult to avoid the term 'postmodernism' in the contemporary academic world. Postmodern ideas have surfaced in a remarkably diverse range of scholarly fields, including sociology, philosophy, anthropology, geography, women's studies, literary criticism, art, architecture, cultural studies and education. Of the various authors frequently cited in articles and books addressing postmodern themes, Jean-François Lyotard is arguably one of the most important for educationists. This claim cannot be made lightly, given the company Lyotard often keeps in postmodern bibliographies: Foucault, Derrida, Barthes, Bataille, Baudrillard and Rorty, among others, also feature regularly. Our assertion about Lyotard's educational significance rests, in large part, on a reading of his classic text *The Postmodern Condition* (1984), first published in 1979. Following the release of an English translation of the text in 1984, *The Postmodern Condition* has been widely cited, and now no major work on postmodernism is 'complete' without reference to it.

This chapter returns to Lyotard's concise account of the changing nature of knowledge in late capitalist societies and reconsiders some of his statements about performativity, commodification and the future of the university. An appraisal of the New Zealand policy scene suggests Lyotard was stunningly accurate in his predictions about many features of the changing higher education landscape. While some commentators, following Lyotard, have announced the 'death of the professor' in computerised societies, others believe academics have a vitally important role to play in postmodern universities. The chapter analyses the views of A.T. Nuyen – a theorist who takes the latter position – in the light of the New Zealand context, and assesses prospects for pedagogical resistance.

The Postmodern Condition

When *The Postmodern Condition* (Lyotard, 1984) was published almost two decades ago it became, as has been noted elsewhere (Peters, 1995: xxiii), 'an instant *cause célèbre*'. Indeed, it can be likened – in one sense, at least – to Kant's famous discourse on ethics and reason, *Groundwork of the Metaphysics of Morals*: both texts have exerted an influence seemingly quite out of proportion to their size (cf. Paton, 1948: 7). Kant's *Groundwork* has, of course, stood the test of time as a philosophical work of enduring value; the fate of *The Postmodern Condition* over the next two centuries remains to be seen. It is undeniable, however, that in the space of less than seventy pages Lyotard captured much of what has subsequently come to be regarded as important in postmodern work. We shall concentrate here on a number of key statements near the beginning and the end of the book. Collectively these passages provide a summary of Lyotard's ideas on the commodification of knowledge, the logic of performativity, and the impact of computerisation on teaching and learning.

Following a brief introduction, where the often-quoted comment about the postmodern condition being defined by 'incredulity toward metanarratives' is made (1984: xxiv), Lyotard offers a working hypothesis: 'that the status of knowledge is altered as societies enter what is known as the postindustrial age and cultures enter what is known as the postmodern age' (p. 3). Observing that this trend has been under way since at the least the end of the 1950s, Lyotard goes on to predict that knowledge – which has become the major force of production in recent decades – will increasingly be translated into quantities of information with a corresponding reorientation in the process of research.

Lyotard notes that 'the miniaturization and commercialization of machines is already changing the way in which learning is acquired, classified, made available, and exploited' (p. 4). Knowledge in computerised societies is becoming 'exteriorised' from knowers. The old notion that knowledge and pedagogy are inextricably linked has been replaced by a new view of knowledge as a *commodity*:

> Knowledge is and will be produced in order to be sold, it is and will be consumed in order to be valorized in a new production: in both cases, the goal is exchange. Knowledge ceases to be an end in itself, it loses its 'use-value' (pp. 4–5).

Lyotard continues:

> Knowledge in the form of an informational commodity indispensible to productive power is already, and will continue to be, a major – perhaps *the* major – stake in the worldwide competition for power. It is conceivable that the nation-states will one day fight for control of information, just as they battled in the past for control over territory, and afterwards for control of access to and exploitation of raw materials and cheap labor (p. 5).

Indeed, with the rise of multinational corporations, the very idea of autonomous nation-states begins to break down. The new technologies will hasten and reinforce this development. The state, Lyotard postulates, will come to be perceived as 'a factor of opacity and 'noise'' (p. 5) in the commercialisation of knowledge. The idea that 'learning falls within the purview of the State, as the mind or brain of society' will give way to the view that 'society exists and progresses only is the messages circulating within it are rich in information and easy to decode' (p. 5). Lyotard envisages a shift in the whole system of organised learning:

> It is not hard to visualize learning circulating along the same lines as money, instead of for its 'educational' value or political (administrative, diplomatic, military) importance; the pertinent distinction would no longer be between knowledge and ignorance, but rather, as is the case with money, between 'payment knowledge' and 'investment knowledge'

– in other words, between units of knowledge exchanged in a daily maintenance framework (the reconstitution of the work force, 'survival') versus funds of knowledge dedicated to optimizing the performance of a project (p. 6).

Lyotard argues that knowledge and power are 'two sides of the same question' (p. 9). In the West, narrative knowledge has been subjugated by scientific knowledge. The latter is 'governed by the demand for legitimation' and, as a long history of imperialism from the dawn of Western civilisation demonstrates, cannot accept anything that fails to conform to the rules (the requirement for proof or argumentation) of its own language game (p. 27). Narratives, by contrast, are legitimated by the simple fact that they 'do what they do' (p. 23).

In the computer age, 'the question of knowledge is now more than ever a question of government' (p. 9). The function of the state will change: machines will come to play an important role in regulatory and reproductive processes, and the power to make decisions will increasingly be determined by questions of access to information (p. 14). Eventually, 'professors' (academics) will no longer be needed: much of their present work will be taken over by computerised data network systems (p. 53). Computerisation 'could become the 'dream' instrument for controlling and regulating the market system, extended to include knowledge itself and governed exclusively by the performativity principle'. This would involve the use of terror. Alternatively, computerisation could 'aid groups discussing metaprescriptives by supplying them with the information they usually lack for making knowledgeable decisions'. Lyotard believes we should take the second of these two paths and provide free public access to databanks. This would respect both 'the desire for justice and the desire for the unknown' (p. 67).

Neoliberalism and Educational Reform in New Zealand

The broad features of the economic and social revolution in New Zealand were noted in the Introduction, and will be discussed in more detail in the next chapter. Here we limit our focus to some of the features of educational reform which mirror, in remarkably close detail, the move toward the commodification of knowledge and learning signalled in *The Postmodern Condition.*

As we noted in the Introduction, the marketisation of education, a trend consistent with Lyotard's analysis, has in New Zealand been built on a neoliberal political philosophy, at the heart of which is a view of human beings as self-interested, rational, autonomous individuals (Marshall, 1995). The public sphere has been transformed. In place of the old ideals of welfare, community and a sense of obligation toward others, the new rules are those of the market. State involvement in individual lives is, for the most part, seen as highly undesirable. A generous system of universal benefits, it is believed, is inefficient, inequitable and likely to promote 'welfare dependency'. The state, for the most fervent supporters of neoliberal reform, has a legitimate role to play in ensuring the conditions for 'free' market activity are in place, but, save perhaps for also providing a police and/or defence force, there is little else for government to do. Others generally supportive of the move toward privatisation of public services see a continuing role for government in overseeing and regulating institutional activities. Either way, the legitimacy of the market as the ideal platform on which to base social life remains unquestioned.

The educational changes implied by this form of thinking have been clear for some years now (see, for example, Treasury, 1987; New Zealand Business Roundtable, 1987; Crocombe *et al.*, 1991) and have been introduced in successive stages. The trend to date has been to privatise educational processes, programmes and responsibilities while at the same time strengthening control and power at the centre. Teachers, boards of trustees and tertiary administrators have been held accountable for decisions relating to the day-to-day running of educational establishments, yet the parameters for undertaking these duties have been defined elsewhere. The market has been the seen as the ideal model on which to base educational arrangements. Competition between students, staff and institutions has been encouraged. Students have been redefined as 'consumers' and tertiary education institutions have become 'providers'. Bureaucrats now talk of 'inputs', 'outputs' and 'throughputs' in the education system. Any notion of educational processes serving as a form of collective public good has all but disappeared; instead, participation in tertiary education is now regarded as a form of private investment. As such, the expectation is that students will pay a growing proportion of the costs associated with their chosen programmes of study (Peters, 1997a). The philosophy of 'user pays', routinely cited as a justification for charges in a whole range of public service areas, has become the order of the day in education. Education, in short, has become a commodity: something to be produced, packaged, sold, traded, outsourced, franchised and consumed.

The rhetoric of 'choice' has permeated many official statements on education in recent years (Codd, 1993a, 1993b; Olssen, 1997). Students are regarded as roving, perpetually choosing, rationally autonomous consumers, always seeking out the best value for their educational dollar. Educational institutions, on the other hand, are forced to compete – if they do not their viability is threatened – with other 'providers', the imperative being to 'sell' themselves and their programmes effectively in order to keep enrolments and revenues at healthy levels. There has been a significant change in the teacher–student relation. This is now no longer seen as a pedagogical relationship but a contractual one (Codd, 1995). Students, in paying ever higher fees for the privilege of attending an educational institution, expect good value for their (private, self-interested) investment. When the services they 'purchase' do not measure up to expectations, 'providers' can – as a recent case at Victoria University in Wellington demonstrated – be threatened with legal action for breach of an implied contract. On this contractual model, students pay fees in exchange for the delivery of an educational service and/or product. The product in this case is the sum of knowledge, drawn from specialist expertise which must be purchased given its scarcity, and encapsulated in the course programme. The service is the delivery ('teaching' is the old-fashioned word for this) of course content – including not just lectures, tutorials and the like, but also the provision of reading materials, the setting of assessment tasks, systems for student consultation and feedback, and so on. In making purchasing decisions of this kind (i.e. in enrolling in a particular course of study), students are presumed to be making rational, self-interested choices about the 'market value' of specific programmes. Tertiary institutions must, we are constantly reminded, be 'accountable' for what they do, and when they fail to 'deliver the goods' they should pay a (legal and/or financial) price for this. Faith in the authority, commitment and professionalism of institutions and the staff within them can no longer be taken for granted. In the current environment, a long tradition of university education is simply one more factor for students to take into account in attempting to maximise utility through the tertiary purchasing decisions.

The logic of performativity is writ large over the entire reform process. There has been a constant drive – initiated from the centre and bolstered by influential business organisations (such as the New Zealand Business Roundtable and the Employers' Federation) – to make education more 'efficient', more closely tied to the 'needs' of industry and employers, and more 'businesslike' in its processes and practices. Gaining greater value from the educational dollar has been a key goal, but the battle has also been an ideological one (Butterworth and Tarling, 1994). The appeal to 'efficiency' signals a concentration not on human relations and the quality of care or teaching but on technocratic processes. Excellence has become a product of efficient management, not (just or even necessarily) the commitment of dedicated professionals. Organisational systems exhibiting the same characteristics as those found in (financially) successful businesses have been held up as models for social organisations to aspire to. It has often been asserted that clear lines of authority and responsibility need to be drawn in organisations and institutions. These have typically been constructed on managerialist principles rather than in terms of professional experience or expertise. The best people to head organisations of *any* kind, some have argued, are those who might serve as chief executives in corporations. Traditional forms of university governance are no longer seen as appropriate; the best model for optimum performance, it is believed, is a 'board of directors' system with fewer people involved in key decisions and a smaller proportional representation from university staff.

There is, business leaders and Treasury bureaucrats claim, considerable 'wastage' in the education system. Devoting taxpayer dollars to courses that lead nowhere (in the business sense), attract few students, and pursue esoteric or trendy lines of theoretical inquiry is seen by some as pointless and to be resisted (see, for example, Kerr, 1997). The solution, some assert, is to promote intense competition and maximise the choices available to consumers (students, their parents and employers) while progressively withdrawing state support (cf. Myers, 1993). This 'consumer-driven' system avoids the problem of 'provider capture' – a situation where institutions have excessive control over the content, processes and valorisation of educational programmes – and allows all committed, entrepreneurial players in the tertiary marketplace to flourish. Regular 'performance reviews' of all kinds – for individuals, departments, programmes, and entire institutions – have been seen as necessary to ensure these efficiency objectives are being met. Various 'performance indicators', most inspired by a blend of technocratic and managerialist thought, have been developed to (ostensibly) give clear evidence of success or failure in the discharging of contractual obligations.

As an extension of the same logic, a complex system for ensuring efficient trading in information about educational qualifications has been developed. This has been underpinned by a strong push to break down divisions between 'academic' and 'vocational' learning (compare Hood, 1995; Barker, 1995). The development of a National Qualifications Framework (NQF) under the auspices of the New Zealand Qualifications Authority (NZQA) has been a crucial and often underestimated step in the standardisation of trading within the educational marketplace. In building a system for exchanging information about qualifications and assessment through unit standards – the 'building blocks' of the NQF to use the NZQA's own words – a decisive shift away from the knowledge-based, institutionally-generated standards of old has been made. The transformation has proceeded hand-in-hand with changes elsewhere in the education system. *The New Zealand Curriculum Framework* (Ministry of Education, 1993), for example, is lacking in substantive discussion of knowledge and understanding but replete with talk of skills and information (Marshall, 1995). The context for this shift in focus is the language of 'enterprise culture' and 'international competitiveness', neatly encapsulated in Maris O'Rourke's opening comments in the *Framework* (O'Rourke, 1993) but elaborated and extended in numerous other policy statements issued in the early to mid-1990s.

It is important to acknowledge some of the positive features of the move toward a 'seamless', standards-based system. The NZQA reforms have allowed greater flexibility in the accumulation of qualifications – an advantage for many adults seeking to return to tertiary education while maintaining other commitments (e.g. to their families) – and have recognised, at least in principle, the value of prior learning. Students excluded from a programme of study in one institution are more likely in the current tertiary environment to find opportunities for gaining certificates, diplomas or degrees elsewhere than they may have in the past. As we note in Chapter 6, the NZQA has, following extensive criticism from the universities and other tertiary sector groups, recently given ground on some crucial issues. Yet the NZQA has become a substantial bureaucratic body in an otherwise 'hollowed out' (Peters, 1997b) educational world, and the development, approval, assessment and auditing of unit standards – now numbering into the thousands – has become a cumbersome and time-consuming task. A system based on unit standards allows educational 'products' – the qualifications students acquire in 'purchasing' degrees and other programmes from competing 'providers' – to be packaged, moved, compared and traded with ease. In this sense the NZQA reforms are highly compatible with a marketisation agenda, fostering just the sort of standardisation and portability necessary for efficient 'trading' in the educational marketplace.

Neither the white paper on tertiary education (Ministry of Education, 1998) nor the tertiary education review green paper (Ministry of Education, 1997a) have much to say about information technologies, but the green paper on teacher education (Ministry of Education, 1997c) places this issue squarely on the agenda (we pay more extended attention to this issue in Chapter 9). The government appears to have only recently been roused from a sort of pre-cyberspatial slumber, with the enormous potential in the new technologies for saving money and meeting neoliberal policy objectives coming into clear focus at last. The possibilities for a convergence of 'virtual' technologies with neoliberal tertiary reform have yet to be adequately theorised in this country, but the money-saving potential in 'thin', 'for-profit' universities on the Internet (Luke, 1996, 1997a) is surely not going to escape the attention of an administration obsessed with fiscal matters (above all other considerations) for long. The notorious leaked version of the tertiary education review green paper (Ministry of Education, 1997d) is, it might be postulated, driven by similar motives and ideological assumptions as the University of Phoenix's Online Campus. Indeed, there are some striking similarities:

> Responding to the life-long learning market of nontraditional students
> and aiming to control costs, the University of Phoenix has forsaken all
> Mode 1 [culturally concentrated] knowledge system obligations; it has
> a narrow practical curriculum, nondisciplinary structure, no library
> resources, no research commitments, a flat, small central administration,
> and only part-time semi-professional faculty. Moreover, it runs on a for-
> profit basis; market performance, not peer review, valorizes its products.
>
> (Luke, 1997a: 21)

In short, there is much in the history of educational reform in New
Zealand over the past fourteen years that bears an uncanny resemblance
to the scenario described by Lyotard two decades ago. Several phases
in the commodification of knowledge can be identified: the development
of standardised units for trading qualifications (and parts of
qualifications); the concentration on skills and information in curriculum
policy; and, most importantly, the redefinition of the concept of
'education' itself. Universities, along with all other tertiary institutions,
are now expected to measure up to the new imperatives of performativity,
and ongoing state support for programmes at odds with this logic
cannot be guaranteed. Faith in the metanarratives of days gone by – and
in particular support for a variant of democratic socialism inaugurated
by the first Labour government's extensive welfare programme more
than half a century ago – has been systematically undermined, only to
be replaced, it must be added, by a new grand narrative: market
liberalism.

Some changes to tertiary education in New Zealand were (and are)
necessary. It was not difficult, fifteen years ago, to identify a number of
potentially worrying trends at work. There was sometimes excessive
overlap between different programmes of study, uneven attention to
(sometimes outright disregard for) teaching quality, a proliferation in
the number of courses, an unhealthy conservatism in peer review
processes, heavy bureaucratic barriers to change, and inadequate
transparency and consistency in promotion and appointment procedures.
It would be unwise to deny that certain inefficiencies existed in the old
system. Ironically, however, the neoliberal reforms have *exacerbated*
rather than solved many of these weaknesses. The emphasis on

performativity has contributed to a sharp increase in administrative work, with endless forms to be filled in and numerous new organisational tasks to be completed for most academics. Student evaluations of teaching effectiveness have become a routine feature of academic life, but these, in their more technocratic ('tick the boxes') and reductionist forms, have been heavily criticised. Advancement up the academic ladder has become a slower, less consistent, more difficult process. There are now more courses and more organisations offering programmes of higher education than ever before in New Zealand. If unnecessary duplication of course content across institutions was observable in the past, this is now a problem of far greater proportions. This point finds perhaps its most dramatic illustration in teacher education programmes, with a plethora of degrees, certificates and diplomas currently available at universities, polytechnics, teachers colleges and private training establishments.

In one sense, the full impact of computerisation has yet to be felt in the tertiary sector: academics have not yet been replaced (at least not in large numbers) by machines. Given what we know to be possible (in terms of processing power and technical sophistication), there is at present only rather limited use of the sort of data exchange systems envisaged by Lyotard. The emergence of the Internet is, to be sure, a development prefigured in Lyotard's analysis, but politicians and bureaucrats are, as we note in Chapter 9, only just beginning to see its potential in deepening – perhaps completing – the neoliberal agenda. Once the possibilities for a consumer-driven system of 'virtual' tertiary education, with minimal state funding but continuing governmental and/or corporate control over participants, become apparent, the future for academics – in New Zealand and elsewhere – could look very bleak indeed. Alternatively, the Internet could become highly significant in *resisting* neoliberal reforms. 'Wired' academics might collectively constitute a formidable force against standardisation and the external regulation of minds and bodies. But will academics still *exist* as a professional class in the next century? The next section addresses this issue in relation to Lyotard's provocative claim about the impending demise of the professoriate.

The Role of Academics in Computerised Societies

While *The Postmodern Condition* raises many issues of educational significance, Lyotard's proposition that computerisation could signal the 'death of the professor' is obviously of special interest to academics. The threat to what some see as a livelihood, others a vocation (for most it is probably both), is bound to stimulate debate. Lyotard's own words should be conveyed here:

> [T]he process of delegitimation and the predominance of the performance criterion are sounding the knell of the age of the Professor: a professor is no more competent than memory bank networks in transmitting established knowledge, nor more competent than interdisciplinary teams in imagining new moves or new games.
>
> (1984: 53)

Some believe Lyotard is astray in this prediction. Nuyen (1995), drawing on the work of Rorty (1990, 1991), attempts to turn Lyotard's argument on its head. He maintains that the predominance of grand narratives diminishes the role of the professor, whereas their demise enhances the need for people (including professors) who can promote *understanding* over mere information retrieval. This is because ...

> ... [a] grand narrative is meant to provide the grounding for, and thereby legitimate, other discourses. It does not allow for the questioning of its role and its nature, for to do so is to engage in another narrative. Thus, a grand narrative requires imposition and demands obedience, leaving no room for teaching and learning (p. 49).

Nuyen points out that computers and other machines cannot ask *why* something should be this way or that; nor can they inspire imagination in students. In the postmodern university, Nuyen argues, we need a new kind of professor, one who can ...

> ... think up new viewpoints, who can construct alternative intellectual worlds, who can transfigure tradition with 'original and utopian' fantasies, like those of 'Plato's and St. Paul's', who are 'world-disclosing' thinkers rather than 'problem-solving' thinkers (p. 55).

Nuyen prefaces his conclusions with a series of claims about narratives, understanding and information. He argues that Lyotard's predictions about the death of the professor are built on two premises: (i) that the role of the professor is to educate students in the understanding of narratives, and (ii) that narratives have zero performativity in proving scientific claims. Against Lyotard, Nuyen maintains that the fascination many people have in narratives – in stories about 'great thinkers', for example – is, when combined with increases in leisure time, likely to create further demand for people (professors) who can teach others about these narratives. The demand for learning about narratives is unlikely to be affected by the performativity criterion because it is not led by the market (p. 47). Moreover, if Lyotard is right about delegitimation, performativity and the collapse of grand narratives, professors (rather than computer programmers or technocrats) will be needed to spread the word about this. Nuyen suggests that Lyotard's target is a particular *kind* of professor: it is the Hegelian academic,

> ... [the] guardian of Truth, the one who knows about the Absolute and who can *profess* about the system that leads to it, that is, one who can tell us with absolute authority that such-and-such is legitimate knowledge and so-and-so is not (p. 49).

The appropriate role for the professor, Nuyen believes, is not to train students in routine skills, but to set examples – to inspire, excite and encourage others to new heights of creativity and imagination.

While many aspects of Nuyen's argument have considerable appeal to us, we want to begin by problematising some of the assumptions in his analysis. First, it seems to us that his claim about the fascination with narratives does not deal adequately with the question of how dispositions and choices come to be formed. The desire to study narratives could, given the right combination of social and ideological circumstances, disappear or be reshaped along lines conducive to the interests of, say, corporate giants. The history of capitalism has demonstrated that if there are dollars to be made from selling the 'products' of culture, considerable effort will be expended in fashioning tastes and attitudes to best serve the profit-making imperative. The interests people have in great stories (and stories of greatness) are not merely intrinsic to those individuals and are certainly not 'natural' for all human beings. Rather, our conceptions of what might be worth studying or investigating are conditioned by the complex web of experiences and relations – in the realms of politics, culture, the family, education, etc. – we encounter and develop in our daily activities. A longing for narratives only creates jobs for academics if that desire is nurtured in a manner compatible with further stimulation by those who have already undertaken a particular approach to understanding narratives.

Second, there is nothing to stop technocrats and computer specialists from spreading a wide variety of messages, including some relevant to discourses on delegitimation, the collapse of grand narratives, and so on. Lyotard happens to have advanced a position on these matters, as have other professors. But messages about the postmodern condition might be conveyed by any number of different individuals and groups, and indeed by institutional structures, practices and processes, or by machines. The manner through which the message is conveyed in such cases may differ from that employed by a philosopher, but these alternative modes of transmitting ideas may – if Lyotard is correct – be more in keeping with our (postmodern) times. If at this moment in our history relentless consumption provides the dominant motive behind human activity, ideas generated in an 'easy to consume' form are likely to be more palatable. Regrettably, perhaps, the utterances of 20th century philosophers and others in academic positions have only infrequently been given serious consideration by many beyond the confines of the university. There are, of course, some important exceptions here – ranging from Jean Paul Sartre to Allan Bloom – but by comparison with television personalities, popular music heroes and newspaper commentators, academics have exerted relatively little influence in shaping (and challenging) public opinion. There are few readily discernable signs that the professoriate will be granted greater respect, or listened to more attentively, as we move into the new millennium. The need for professors as people who will explain the postmodern condition is thus, in the eyes of many, highly questionable.

Some would even question the need for any form of explanation: postmodern narratives, as Lyotard himself argues, legitimate themselves by doing what they do. But if knowledge of postmodernism, or anything else, is required, the logic of the system – of the postmodern condition we find ourselves in as we try to address these problems – would suggest it will be sought not with criteria of truth or academic authority in mind, but rather with a view to maximising efficiency. Information (and it will be 'information' rather than knowledge) should, in other words, be gathered as quickly, effortlessly and at the lowest cost possible. Some of us *want* to say professors will be needed to 'do the explaining' because *we* value traditions of scholarship, academic rigour, and face-to-face teaching; but this view is not shared by all. A clean, 'neatly packaged' answer to difficult questions is, for many, preferable to the complicated systems of argument and counter-argument typical of theoretical discourses in the university.

Like Nuyen, we believe making students aware of alternative ways of understanding (and living in) the world is of the utmost importance. This, for us, is one of the key features of a good university education (see further, Roberts, 1996b; 1997c). An appropriately self-critical and open-minded attitude is essential, however, if academics are to perform this role with distinction. Part of the problem lies in the politics of selecting 'alternatives'. In this respect, the arguments of J.M. Fritzman (1995) are helpful. Writing in the same volume as Nuyen, Fritzman draws our attention to a key difference between Rorty and Lyotard:

> Rorty believes that all disputes either are litigations or can be transformed into such. In contrast to Rorty, Lyotard argues that there are disputes that cannot be regulated. Such disputes are differends rather than litigations. Further, not all differends can be transformed into litigations. To attempt to adjudicate a differend as though it were a litigation necessarily wrongs at least one of the parties (p. 66).

Lyotard's notion of the differend is succinctly summarised in the opening comments of his book of the same name. A differend, as distinct from a litigation, is 'a case of conflict, between (at least) two parties, that cannot be equitably resolved for lack of a rule of judgement applicable in both arguments' (Lyotard, 1988: xi). Conflicts – differends – are inevitable, but applying a single rule of judgement to settle a differend always damages at least one of the parties. This, for Lyotard, means politics should be concerned not with pursuit of the good but rather with minimising damage through preferring the lesser evil. A politics of the lesser evil attempts to 'leave open as wide a set of political options as possible' (Fritzman, 1995: 68).

Fritzman finds Rorty's pluralism wanting. In response to Rorty's call for universities to 'take in representatives of every conceivable movement – deconstructionists, Marxists, Habermasians, Catholics, Straussians' (cited Fritzman, 1995: 70), Fritzman reminds us that many movements not currently 'conceivable' – that is, those positions not recognised as either legitimate or minority views – tend to be excluded. Carol Nicholson's (1989: 204) argument that 'no serious voice' should be left out of the 'great conversation that shapes our curriculum and civilization' is, in Fritzman's view, similarly suspect: 'persons left out of conversations are always said to be insufficiently *serious* by those who would exclude them' (1995: 70). Lyotard, by contrast, 'would recognize that besides attempting to persuade professors and administrators to recognize positions, frequently there are other options to be employed in obtaining a hearing for unpopular opinions and gaining legitimation'. 'It is,' Fritzman says, 'the role of the imagination to create and discover these options.' The options might include:

> ... creating interdisciplinary academic journals; founding alternative educational institutes; writing letters of protest to trustees, legislators, state and national accreditation boards, and newspapers; occupying the administration building; seizing the library; and pseudonymously submitting papers to reputable journals (p. 71).

Fritzman summarises some of the pedagogical implications of Lyotard's position thus:

> [E]ducation should encourage students to develop new ideas and to challenge critically what passes as common knowledge and accepted wisdom. In addition, education should teach students to be sensitive to the inevitable presence of differends (p. 69).

This might involve: demonstrating incommensurability in beliefs concerning the meanings of 'citizen' and 'subversive' through examples from current events; allowing students to encounter new forms of literature, music, painting and philosophy; and teaching about historical and cultural differences. Students should be encouraged to believe that all concepts – including 'critical thinking', 'teaching' and 'learning' – can be questioned and redefined (pp. 69–70).

While Fritzman's suggestions for pedagogical activity have their limitations, the strength of his approach lies in the promotion of a respect for and willingness to investigate and live with uncertainty (as well as differends). This idea figures prominently in the work of a number of post-structuralist thinkers. Lyotard himself, in *The Differend*, argues that the philosopher is not certain of what he or she wants or knows and values reflective 'ignorance' as a form of resistance against the 'accountable or countable use of time' (1988: xvi). This is an extension of his famous remarks in the Introduction to *The Postmodern Condition*. Stressing that he is a philosopher and not an expert, Lyotard adds: '[t]he latter knows what he knows and what he does not know[;] the former does not' (1984: xxv). Derrida advances a not dissimilar view: 'A philosopher is always someone for whom philosophy is not a given, someone who in essence must question him or herself about the essence and destination of philosophy' (1994: 3). Nietzsche, the thinker to whom all post-structuralist are indebted, has this to say: 'What a philosopher is, is hard to learn, because it cannot be taught: one has to "know" it from experience – or one ought to be sufficiently proud *not* to know it' (1990: 144). These comments all refer to a particular kind of thinker, who may or may not be a professor: this is the figure of the philosopher. Perhaps, though, there is a point of significance here for the debate over the future of the university and of academics in particular. In our view, assisting the development of an attitude of constructive, investigative, curious uncertainty is one of the most important roles academics might play in postmodern universities. Acquiring an appreciation for uncertainty demands that the world be rendered problematic, that nothing be beyond questioning, that 'what we have now' be contrasted with that which was or might be.

It does not follow that if some views may be excluded from the range of alternatives, none ought to be considered. The reasons behind an act of exclusion may vary widely and could include our ignorance, lack of knowledge, prejudices, history and experiences, or simply lack of time. To put nothing on the table does as little good as telling students there is only one way to view the world: this simply allows the dominant discourses of the day to prevail. The New Zealand context provides an especially interesting case study. It is precisely because students in New Zealand *have*, in effect, been told there is only one real (or true or viable or sensible) path to follow, that alternatives are needed. Market liberalism has become *the* metanarrative of our times. For the powerful promoters of this creed, there are no alternatives (see, for example, Myers, 1996a). All problems – whether economic, cultural, political, or personal in nature – are addressed through neoliberal lenses.

A classic example of a differend has emerged. On matters of tertiary education, the gulf between those who play this language game – subscribe to the grand narrative of market liberalism – and those who wish to defend almost any other position on the purpose and character of a university is enormous. There is no rule that might be found to adjudicate between the parties involved in this dispute without one side being wronged, but to date the battle has been overwhelmingly one-sided. The litigating activities of politicians, bureaucrats and business élites have ensured that differends are hardly ever acknowledged, and questions about 'lesser evils' are seldom seriously considered. Igniting even a small spark of uncertainty about the direction of the reform process by encouraging students to question – to analyse, to criticise, to wonder, to become aware of alternatives – would be a significant achievement in the contemporary New Zealand climate. There is a need for academics to tell other stories about New Zealand – our histories and contrasting contemporary experiences – but the creation and continuation of opportunities for maintaining this role cannot be taken for granted. The struggle to be heard against the dominant voices of the times will, as always, be agonisingly difficult, time-consuming and ongoing.

chapter five

Ownership and Governance: The Privatisation of New Zealand Universities

It was not a bad idea, whoever first conceived and proposed a public means for treating the sum of knowledge (and properly the heads who devote themselves to it), in a quasi-industrial manner, with a division of labour where, for so many fields as there may be of knowledge, so many public teachers would be allotted, professors being trustees, forming together a kind of common scientific entity, called a university (or high school) and having autonomy (for only scholars can pass judgement on scholars as such); and, thanks to its faculties (various small societies where university teachers are ranged, in keeping with the variety of the main branches of knowledge), the university would be authorised to admit, on the one hand, student-apprentices from the lower schools aspiring to its level, and to grant, on the other hand – after prior examination, and on its own authority – to teachers who are 'free' (not drawn from the members themselves) and called 'Doctors', a universally recognised rank (conferring upon them a degree) – in short, *creating* them.

(Kant, 1992: 4)

It has been easy for the public to believe that the main object of the
changes since 1984 has been to save money. The 'reforms' have often
been advanced under that guise. It is, however, a mistaken view. The
object is ideological. The millenarian vision of ideologues involves an
unremitting attack on the structures of democratic pluralism. Their
central project is the negation of community values and the redefinition
of the citizen as merely consumer. The aim involves the destruction of
that sense of communal responsibility which infused the creation of the
modern democratic state, but which Hayek traduced as an inconvenient
hangover from tribal consciousness. When public activity is privatised,
the very idea of society is undermined. These are the issues that New
Zealanders have to consider.

(Butterworth and Tarling, 1994: 250–251)

Questions about 'ownership' and 'governance' have been thrown
into prominence during the last decade as a result of a set of policies
designed to 'restructure' or adjust national economies to the dramatic
changes in the world economy that have occurred in the last twenty
years: the growing competition among nations for world markets; the
emergence of world trading blocs and new 'free trade' agreements; an
increasing globalisation of economic and cultural activities; the
decline of the post-war Keynesian welfare state settlement in Western
countries; the collapse of actually existing communism and the
'opening up' of the Eastern bloc, and the accelerated world-wide
adoption and development of the new information and communications technologies.

Martin Carnoy (1995: 653) comments that 'structural adjustment is
normally associated with the correction of imbalances in foreign accounts
and domestic consumption ... and with the deregulation and privatisation
of the economy'. He suggests that such policies are identified with a
fiscal austerity programme designed to shrink the public sector, and in
some countries, with growing poverty and the unequal distribution of
income. Yet as Carnoy observes, the practice of structural adjustment
followed by the high-income OECD countries and the newly
industrialising countries (NICs) of Asia does not conform to this picture.
He suggests that the focus in these countries has been on:

... increased exports, reduced domestic demand, various constraints on government spending and some privatisation; with a few notable exceptions, it has not entailed policies that greatly increase inequality or poverty. Rather, many of the richer economies have focused on 'self-adjusting' mechanisms to rationalise production and the public infrastructure that serves productive and social functions. Their educational systems have not suffered and, in general, their education professionals have made income gains. In the best of cases, education has improved and teachers have participated in making that improvement happen.

(Carnoy, 1995: 654)

Drawing upon this difference in practice, Carnoy surmises that there are several categories of structural adjustment and that in the case of the richer nations the term stands for *a set of policies* which originated in the United States during the 1970s as the dominant view of how economies in crisis, typically those of developing countries characterised by high indebtedness, should reorganise to achieve growth. Such policies called for cuts in public expenditure on services, including education, precisely at the point when a shift to a global information economy required massive public investment in an information infrastructure, with an attendant emphasis on mass education, which was necessary to take advantage of changes in the nature of the world economy.

Carnoy attributes the emergence of the dominant view to two factors: the richer nations of the OECD already enjoyed favourable conditions which allowed them to self-adjust and to respond positively to rapidly changing technology, and the paradigm shift from Keynesianism to neoliberal monetarism led to 'a dramatic increase in real interest rates to reduce inflationary tendencies ... and to sharp cuts in foreign loans' (p. 655). The neoliberal monetarist paradigm also became the dominant view at the international level, shaping the outlook of world institutions such as the International Monetary Fund (IMF) and the World Bank, which imposed Structural Adjustment Policies (SAPs) on developing countries as a response to their continuing and exacerbating debt problems.

The so-called 'New Zealand experiment' (Kelsey, 1995) is something of an anomaly in terms of Carnoy's analysis. While it started the process of structural adjustment relatively late in comparison to the United States and the United Kingdom (i.e. in the mid-1980s rather than the late 1970s), it did so under conditions of crisis management, which enabled the Labour government to gain a kind of legitimacy and momentum for neoliberal policies that ran against the historical mission of a left-wing party traditionally affiliated to the labour movement. It is also the case that New Zealand during the period 1984–96 sustained a programme of 'reform' across different and successive governments which, contrary to the main thrust of Carnoy's analysis, resulted in both increased poverty and social inequalities (see Peters, 1993; 1996b).

Based on a relatively pure neoliberal model of structural adjustment, applied by the fourth Labour government (1984–90) and by the National government (1990–96) up until recently, the 'New Zealand experiment' has been touted by the World Bank and the OECD as an example for the rest of the world. Jane Kelsey (1995: 1) outlines the four distinctive features of the 'New Zealand experiment' in the following terms:

- This radical exercise in structural adjustment was not implemented by a 'third world' government as a condition of securing credit from the international financial institutions, but was unilaterally undertaken by a democratically elected government within an advanced capitalist economy.
- Successive governments applied pure economic theory to a complex, real-life community, with generally cavalier disregard for the social or electoral consequences.
- The programme was implemented in 1984 by a Labour government, whose party had traditionally embraced a social democratic philosophy, and was continued after 1990 by a purportedly free enterprise, but traditionally interventionist, conservative National government.
- The 'fundamentals' of the programme – market liberalisation and free trade, limited government, a narrow monetarist policy, a deregulated labour market and fiscal restraint – were assumed to be 'given', based on common sense and consensus, and beyond challenge. These fundamentals were systematically embedded against change.

Against this policy background, issues of ownership, governance, monitoring and accountability acquire new significance. This chapter reviews current debates on governance and ownership of New Zealand universities, commenting in some detail on the not-for-profit trust model advanced by Scott and Smelt (1995), and on recent attempts to develop a model of ownership monitoring for TEIs (tertiary education institutions). The chapter begins by contextualising the discussion in terms of both structural adjustment policies and New Zealand's model of public management before focusing on two opposing models of devolution. We then proceed to review the governance of higher education in New Zealand against the background of the shift from so-called 'state control' to 'state supervision', focusing on public sector reform, the constitutional consequences of privatisation, and the issue of 'representation versus technocracy' arising out of the consideration of the not-for-profit model of governance.

New Zealand's Model of Public Management

As we noted in the Introduction and the previous chapter, the New Zealand education system – like education systems in many other Western countries – was fundamentally 'restructured' during the late 1980s. Broadly speaking, the restructuring of education involved a shift from direct 'state control' to 'government by the market' (Self, 1993) which has been variously described as 'devolution', 'decentralisation' or 'privatisation', and theorised under the notion of 'governance'.

The policy context and the parameters for the debate over the notion of governance in education, as with the restructuring of the rest of the public sector, were set by the New Zealand Treasury based upon neoliberal principles. Christopher Hood (1990: 210), commenting on the Treasury's (1987) treatise, *Government Management*, described it as 'remarkable', implying that it was vastly more coherent and intellectually sophisticated than its equivalents elsewhere: 'Neither Canberra nor Whitehall has produced anything remotely comparable in quality or quantity to the New Zealand Treasury's "NPM manifesto"'. He cites the cardinal principles of what he terms 'New Public Management', set out by the Treasury, as goal clarity, transparency, contestability, avoidance of capture, congruent incentive structures, enhancement of accountability and cost-effective use of information. These features have been substituted for a public service which used to operate on the principle of anonymity, secrecy and political neutrality.

What is often not made clear is the way these changes spring fundamentally from two basic assumptions: the revival of faith in the assumption of *homo economicus* underlying classical liberal economic theory and the assumption underlying the catallactic approach, that the exchange paradigm can be extended to politics – the major innovation of public choice theory. The first asserts that all human behaviour is to be understood in terms of self-interest – that we are 'rational utility maximisers'; the second rests on the principle of spontaneous order most thoroughly developed in Hayek's work – that order in society is a function of spontaneous formation which is best exemplified in the economic theory of market exchange. 'Catallactics' is the term given to the study of institutions of exchange. The major innovation of public choice theory, according to James Buchanan (1986: 20) is the extension of the catallactic approach beyond simple exchange (two persons/two commodities) to complex exchange and, finally, to all processes of voluntary agreement, so that economists can look on politics and on political processes in terms of the exchange paradigm. These two assumptions – one based on an economic rationalism construed in extreme individualistic terms and the other, by extension, applying the exchange paradigm to politics – constitutes the most elementary form of the economic theory of politics governing the means by which the state has been reshaped.

The key features of the New Zealand model of public management have been identified by Boston *et al.* (1996: 4–5) as comprising three separate aspects: the broad objectives, the administrative principles and the specific policies. In specific policy terms, the New Zealand model in the mid-1990s embraces the following:

• A preference for retaining key governmental powers and responsibilities at the central government level with only limited devolution to sub-national government despite considerable rhetoric about devolution in the 1980s.

- A strong emphasis on the use of incentives to enhance performance at both the institutional and the individual level (e.g. short-term employment contracts, performance-based remuneration systems, promotion systems, etc.).
- An extensive use of explicit, generally written 'contracts' of various kinds, which specify the nature of performance required and the respective obligations of agents and principals (e.g. performance agreements between ministers and department CEs, purchase agreements between ministers and departments, and contracts between funders and purchasers and between purchasers and providers). In addition to the emphasis on ex ante performance specification, more exacting monitoring and reporting systems have been introduced.
- The development of an integrated and relatively sophisticated strategic planning and performance management system throughout the public sector. Key elements include the specification by ministers of strategic result areas and key result areas and the integration of these into CEs' performance agreements and departmental purchase agreements.
- The removal, wherever possible, of dual or multiple accountability relationships within the public sector, and the avoidance of joint central and local democratic control of public services.
- The institutional separation of commercial and non-commercial functions; the separation of advisory, delivery and regulatory functions; and the related separation of the roles of funder, purchaser and provider.
- The maximum decentralisation of production and management decision-making, especially with respect to the selection and purchase of inputs and the management of human resources.
- The implementation of a financial management system based on accrual accounting and including capital charging, a distinction between the Crown's ownership and purchaser interests, a distinction between outcomes and outputs, an accrual-based appropriations system, and legislation requiring economic policies that are deemed to be 'fiscally responsible'.

- Strong encouragement for and extensive use of competitive tendering and contracting out, but few mandatory requirements for market testing or competitive tendering.

Two Models of 'Devolution'

The debate on devolution and accountability in New Zealand can be seen within the context of two predominant models. The first has been advocated by the Royal Commission on Social Policy (1988), the Task Group on Devolution (1988), and the green paper, *He Tirohanga Rangapu* (1988). The second, which promotes an economic perspective of devolution, viewing it essentially as a form of delegation, has been strongly advocated by the Treasury and underlies changes to educational administration, the Gibbs Taskforce Report and the reform of local government in New Zealand. The Royal Commission on Social Policy sees devolution, in contradiction to the Treasury view, as one way of increasing public participation with the overall objective of enhancing social wellbeing. For the Commission, devolution is a form of decentralisation which takes 'a more relaxed approach to the development of local answers to local problems' and recognises that 'there is a need for a shift from the institutional approach towards a style of delivery involving the community with greater responsibility for social programmes being given to structures other than Government' (1988: 318).

Mason Durie (1988: 43) identifies the framework within which discussion of devolution ought to take place:

> There must be clear objectives, relating to the overall objective of enhanced social wellbeing. Three principles, participation, partnership and subsidiary, are particularly relevant, and four criteria are particularly recommended in the application of those principles: equity, efficiency, transitional fairness and transparency.

The Commission recognises five prerequisites for effective participation in decision-making and these are worth noting here:

- The structures of government should be designed so as to maximise and encourage participation.

• Public participation should be part of the regular decision-making processes of government.
• Participation in decision-making is time-consuming and has implications for the speed with which decisions can be made.
• Participation can take many forms.
• Participation should not be compulsory, but rather a free choice as to exercising a right to have a voice.

The principle of partnership will be familiar now to most New Zealanders as a central concept underlying a constitutional recognition the Treaty of Waitangi. By 'subsidiary', the Commission means that decisions and actions be taken at the lowest appropriate level of social organisation. The Task Group on Devolution (1988) sees devolution as a form of power-sharing and explicitly recognises a link of accountability (in terms of legitimacy and responsiveness) to clients as well as the traditional bond of accountability (value for money and compliance) to Parliament.

The Task Group (1988), reporting to the Steering Group of Permanent Heads and taking its mandate from the report, Pauo-te-Ata-tu (recommendation 13c), which 'seeks a holistic approach to supporting community initiatives', uses the framework of 'administrative responsiveness' developed by OECD to consider questions of power-sharing and accountability within a client-centred view of the statutory social services. The Task Group (1988: 6) outlines the key characteristics of 'administrative responsiveness' in the following terms:

• comprehensibility of policies and programmes to clients
• access of clients to services that meets their needs
• relevance of policies and programmes to clients
• ability of clients to participate in the design, delivery and evaluation of programmes.

The principles of comprehensibility, access, relevance and participation of a client-centred system are seen as underlying the future development of social services in New Zealand. They highlight '[t]he need for government departments to acknowledge two sets of accountability relationships in power sharing arrangements (i.e. one set inwards, to Parliament and the other set outwards, to clients)' (Task Group, 1988: 6).

On the other hand, Bushnell and Scott (1988) view devolution simply as a process of delegation: from government to the local level and from principal to agent. The economic perspective on devolution as delegation is defined in terms of a contractual relationship which itself is structured in such a way so as to counter tendencies to opportunism on the part of the agent and to ensure that the agent remains faithful to the interests of the principal. The essence of this approach is that first, objectives should be clearly identified and conflicts avoided; second, performance must be monitored, which 'requires adequate flows of high-quality information to assess the performance of agents'; and third, 'incentives and sanctions should be in place to encourage managers to act to meet agreed objectives rather than to follow their own goals' (Bushnell & Scott, 1988: 23).

It immediately becomes clear that the two models of devolution and accountability are at odds with one another. The former, which might be termed the 'strong' democratic model, places a high value on active participation in the process of government and views such participation as an empowering process for communities and individuals. Accordingly, it recognises a dual accountability: to Parliament (or the minister) and to clients. The latter, which by contrast might be termed the 'thin' democratic model, emphasises a passive element of participation generally in the form, if at all, of a management-led consultative process. An important corollary of this model is to recognise that 'each agent must have only one principal with respect to each set of activities' (Bushnell & Scott, 1988: 22). In other words, dual accountability is rejected as ineffective and leading to conflicts of interest which would make it difficult to assess the performance of the agent.

The Hawke Reforms

It is in terms of these two approaches to devolution and accountability that administrative 'reforms' in higher education in New Zealand should be assessed. *Learning for Life*, (Department of Education, 1989a; 1989b) the policy translation of the Hawke Report, (Department of Education, 1988a) strongly advocates a model of devolution and accountability which is based closely on that developed under Brian Picot as chairman of the Taskforce to Review Education Administration in New Zealand (The Picot Report). The introduction to the *Report on Post Compulsory Education and Training in New Zealand* (the Hawke Report) states:

> The Picot Report advocates essentially devolution and accountability, opportunities for local initiatives within national guidelines. It argues that the essential features of a new structure are:
>
> - a simple administrative structure
> - decisions made as close as possible to where they are executed
> - national objectives, clear responsibilities and goals
> - coordination in a structure in which decision-makers have control over available resources and are accountable for outcomes
> - the system should be open to scrutiny
> - the system should promote responsiveness to client demands.
>
> These are equally appropriate for PCET. All the debate is about how to achieve the right mixture of devolution and accountability, and the right balance of local initiative and national uniformity.
>
> (Department of Education, 1988a: 4–5)

Later in the body of the text (section 3.9) the crucial accountability mechanisms are identified as consisting of:

1. A set of contractual relationships between:

   (i) the government on the one hand and the chief executives of the Ministry of Education and other educational agencies (such as the Educational Review Office, NZQA) on the other
   (ii) PCET providers (councils and boards) and their chief executives

2. Charters setting out intended outcomes and performance measures
3. Audits of performance in accordance with charters.

It is also clear that universities, polytechnics and colleges of education are expected to develop forms of asset value accounting in order to promote greater public financial accountability.

The charter forms the basis of agreement between the council of an institution and the government. It outlines education, financial and social goals in consultation with the community it serves, which becomes a basis for negotiation with the Ministry 'within funding parameters and provide the basis for performance review' (p. 4). Accountability requires a statement of goals (a charter): 'a statement which translates these goals to measurable objectives' (a corporate plan); 'the capacity to manage efficiently (which requires ownership and/or control of assets)'; and a variety of reporting mechanisms. The main accountability mechanisms are: clarity of objectives; freedom to manage; incentives and sanctions; adequate information flows; effective assessment with a basis for judgements and comparisons. Institutions are required to provide an annual report, including audited accounts and information about educational, financial and equity performance allowing comparisons with previous years. In addition, there is external monitoring by the Education Review Office (ERO) and the NZQA and, lastly, self, peer and internal reviews. Traditional forms of professional accountability receive minimal recognition and are overshadowed by external forms of monitoring. The major stakeholder identified is the government. The government is seen as having an interest in accountability to reflect its role both as 'provider of assets' and as 'principal founder for outputs on behalf of students'. Students and communities are recognised as having an interest in accountability for the quality and quantity of outputs. Additionally, 'some communities have a particular interest in the equity provisions provided' (p. 6). It is abundantly clear that the model of accountability developed here is managerialist in orientation, heavily emphasising an economic perspective which centres around questions concerning the control of assets/resources and a potentially technocratic measurement of relative performance, both individually and institutionally.

It is evident that accountability in the Picot model conforms to the economic perspective advocated by Bushnell and Scott (1988: 20) which views devolution as a form of delegation. They define devolution within the context of principal/agency theory:

In our view accountability is inseparable from devolution or delegation. A principal (government, board or council) would be willing to delegate duties or devolve processes if confident that the agent would act in line with the intentions of the principal. Of particular importance is the ability to hold the agent to account for the performance of the duties. Devolution, therefore, should be favoured to the extent that this furthers the objectives of the principal.

The overriding consideration here is one to do with 'the efficiency of relationships between agents and their principals'. In this approach to accountability once objectives and goals are agreed upon, performance is measured, and any tendency to opportunism by the agent is countered through the use of incentives and sanctions. The State Sector Act, 1988, performs the function of formalising and structuring the contractual relationship between agent and principal, allowing a 'more explicit accountability of performance'.

From 'State Control' to 'State Supervision'

Western countries have experienced a change in the relationship between higher education institutions and government and, in particular, a shift in models of governance from 'state control' to 'state supervision' (Neave & Van Vught, 1991; Goedegebuure *et al.*, 1992). Van Vught (1992: 18) has identified the two primary traditions as follows.

The state control model treats higher education as a homogeneous enterprise, with government attempting to regulate all aspects of the dynamics of the higher education system: access, curriculum degree requirements, the examination system, appointment and remuneration of academic staff, etc. The state control model does not recognise the loosely coupled, multidimensional character of higher education. In contrast, in the state supervising/facilitory model the influence exercised by the state is weak, with many of the basic decisions on such matters as curriculum degrees, staff recruitment, and finance left to the institutions themselves. The state sets the broad parameters in which higher education operates, but fundamental decisions about missions and goals are the province of the system and its individual institutions.

Van Vught argues that the state supervision model is better able to recognise certain characteristics of higher education, such as the plethora of organisational goals espoused by diverse constituencies, the relatively flat governance structures, the norm of collegial participation, and the diffusion of decision-making power. By limiting itself to global forms of steering and putting its confidence in the self-regulatory capacities of professionals, the state supervision model can stimulate the innovativeness of the system as a whole (Van Vught, 1989). The trend towards a state supervision model has been accompanied by deregulation in a number of areas and, correspondingly, a greater emphasis upon coordination through the market mechanism.

The move towards state supervision, while granting greater institutional autonomy on the one hand, has entailed the strengthening of managerial authority on the other, with an emphasis on greater management efficiency and the institutionalisation of accountability and quality systems. The trend toward steering at a distance has favoured changes to funding as the most powerful policy instrument to bring about change. While funding has remained stable or fallen in real terms, student intakes have increased dramatically, forcing institutions to diversify their funding bases and to develop entrepreneurial functions. In many countries, the effects of a massified system of higher education have exhausted the limits of public expenditure and, accordingly, many governments have moved away from earmarked funding to the allocation of block grants, to formulae funding based on actual student places provided or to 'conditional contracting'. Several countries have introduced user-pays schemes, supplemented with student loans and various forms of graduate tax.

The move away from state control has encouraged a variety of new planning systems emphasising forms of 'remote control', including, for example, the establishment of institutional profiles in Australia within a system characterised by a 'new mutuality' (Mahoney, 1994) or the development of new planning cycles in the Netherlands based upon a conception of 'communicative planning'. These new systems of 'remote control' planning aim to preserve flexibility, often through the employment of new forms of institutional evaluation based upon set criteria, indicators or targets tied closely to issues of accountability and quality.

The issue of governance per se is one that is beginning to receive some attention in the literature. The so-called 'new governance' has been referred to as 'governing without government'. Rhodes (1996) suggests that current use does not treat 'governance' as a synonym for 'government'; rather it signifies a change of meaning, referring to a new process of governing or changed condition under which society is governed. He suggests that the term has at least six separate uses: as the minimal state; corporate governance; the new public management; 'good governance'; a socio-cybernetic system; and self-organising networks (p. 653). Rhodes examines each of these usages in turn and argues that the British government can choose between 'governing structures'. He specifically suggests that 'networks' can be added to 'markets' and 'hierarchies' as structures for authoritatively allocating resources and exercising control and coordination[1]. Rhodes (1996: 660) provides the following stipulative definition of *self-organising, interorganisational networks* which incorporates elements from its other uses:

1. Interdependence between organisations. Governance is broader than government, covering non-state actors. Changing the boundaries of the state meant the boundaries between public, private and voluntary sectors became shifting and opaque.
2. Continuing interactions between networks members, caused by the need to exchange resources and negotiate shared purposes.
3. Game-like interactions, rooted in trust and regulated by rules of the game negotiated and agreed by network participants.
4. A significant degree of autonomy from the state. Networks are not accountable to the state; they are self-organising. Although the state does not occupy a privileged, sovereign position, it can indirectly and imperfectly steer networks.

On the basis of such a definition, Rhodes explores its potential contribution to understanding the hollowing out of the state, the contradictions of the new public management and the rise of interorganisational management. Rhodes suggests that 'the new governance' points to four weaknesses in NPM: that NPM as a form of managerialism adopts an *intra*-organisational focus, thus paying no attention to *inter*-organisational links or to negotiating shared purposes where there is no hierarchy of control; that NPM resurrects management-by-objectives, a form of goal-directed activity more suited for understanding rats than human decision-making or managing network relationships; that NMP focuses on results, where in an inter-organisational network if 'no one actor is responsible for an outcome ... there may be no agreement on either the desired outcome or how to measure it; and the centre has no means of enforcing its preferences' (p. 663). Finally, 'there is a contradiction between competition and steering at the heart of NPM' (p. 664). He concludes that a 'key challenge for government is to enable these networks and to seek out new forms of co-operation' (p. 666).

Roger Dale (1997: 280) has argued that in the restructuring of the education–state relationship, the state's control of education, if anything, has been strengthened. He traces the shift from state control to governance and examines governance in terms of the three activities of funding, regulation, and provision/delivery to argue 'state control of funding, the curriculum and the teaching profession has clearly been strengthened ... but it can also be argued that the state's grip is also tightened by decentralised, multiple nodes of accountability'. While Dale's comments are aimed at the compulsory schooling sector, his observations, at least as far as funding and accountability go, apply directly to higher education in New Zealand.

By contrast, the not-for-profit trust model of governance is a market form of governance aimed at replacing the role of the state altogether.

The Governance of Tertiary Institutions in New Zealand

Following the *Learning for Life* reforms enacted in the Education Amendment Act 1990 and the development of an equivalent full time student (EFTS) funding system and student loan scheme, a Taskforce was established to investigate the feasibility of a capital charge scheme for tertiary institutions, with responsibility also for examining the issue of governance. In May 1995 the Minister of Education established discussion groups on capital charging and tertiary governance. In 1992 the State Services Commission had submitted a paper entitled 'Governance of Tertiary Institutions' to the Taskforce on Capital Charging of Tertiary Institutions recommending that 'the owners of institutions – who may be the Government or the institutions, or the

Government and the institutions – and the Government as the primary funder of tertiary education should have the right to appoint up to half the members of councils, and that the other half be elected by students and alumni'. It is significant the New Zealand Business Roundtable (1994: 46) in their submission to the Minister of Education concerning the funding and regulation of tertiary education had recommended that the government undertake a thorough review of the governance of state providers as a matter of urgency with the aim of determining the residual ownership interest in tertiary institutions. The Roundtable (1994: 38) claimed that the residual owner (that is, the person or institution receiving any surplus after all other claims have been met) of state institutions is unclear and that monitoring by the owner is largely absent, leading to excessive costs, poor returns on investment and the dominance of the residual owner's interests by management and staff.

In late 1995 the Victoria University Council decided to be pro-active in establishing a Working Party on Governance rather than wait and face the prospect of draft legislation which would replace the representative model of existing councils with a 'political' model. The VUW Council issued a discussion paper in December 1995 and invited responses. At roughly the same time the New Zealand Vice-Chancellors' Committee in 1995 'became concerned that there were proposals for change in the relationship of universities to Government being developed at the officials level' and decided to be pro-active in reviewing proposals on governance and commissioned Graham Scott, former Secretary to the Treasury, to write a paper (with Simon Smelt) on the ownership and governance of New Zealand universities.

In essence, Scott and Smelt (1995) argue that the Crown is liable to be more active than previously in its ownership relations with universities and that the emphasis will fall primarily on containing the Crown's financial risk. On this basis they raise the question of whether such a risk is to be met by enhanced ownership monitoring or by other means. Does the Crown need to own universities at all? In answer to this question, Scott and Smelt argue that if the ownership status of universities was shifted to that of a private not-for-profit trust, such an arrangement may reduce the risk and performance concerns of the Crown while at the same time increasing the commercial freedom of universities. A trust model of governance, in particular, would give the trustees control over assets and allow them to raise debt against assets or future income. The trust model of governance, they suggest, works bests when not composed of representatives of key interest groups. In particular, they see no role for academic or general staff in governance under a trust arrangement. Instead, the trustees would be selected/ elected on the basis of their management expertise.

The remainder of this chapter specifically addresses the proposal by Scott and Smelt (1995) and argues the case against privatisation. The change of ownership status of universities[2] advocated by Scott and Smelt (1995) is interpreted as a significant step toward privatisation. The case against privatisation, in essence, is construed as an argument for a representative and democratic model of governance.

The development of universities in New Zealand receives some attention (i.e. two pages) in the Scott and Smelt paper. The major claim is that '... the framework for universities has been largely set by the Crown's financial interests ...' and that the 'shape of universities in the future ... will depend in significant part on how the formal relationship with government is specified in terms of ownership and control' (p. 6). Scott and Smelt, in addition, clearly favour greater *diversity* within the system (allegedly brought about by a trust model of governance), claiming that '... the 1990 legislation imposed uniformity on a diverse field and gave the Crown little ability to manage its ownership interest beyond input controls' (p. 5). This claim is particularly ironic given the Treasury's (1984; 1987) influence in establishing the policy parameters within which the reform of tertiary education took place: the removal of central government controls and mechanisms; the advocacy of a self-steering market model; the reduction of subsidies; the introduction of student loans; targeted assistance; the separation of research and education functions; the collapse of the distinction between education and training; the formula funding model; the introduction of systems of incentives and managerial accountability; and so on[3]. There is no argument to establish the value of diversity, the lack of it within the current system or the inference that diversity would be better fostered under the model of a charitable trust.

Scott and Smelt (1995) approach the question of the ownership of universities on the basis of the experience and principles of public sector reform in New Zealand, in which they played major policy advisory roles[4].They attempt to establish a presumption in favour of privatisation of ownership (through the charitable trust model) on the basis of public sector reforms by concentrating on the narrow question of '... containing the financial risk to the Crown and improving performance ...' (p. 3), although in reality they devote little space to exploring the question of improving performance. At one point, they write:

> New Zealand governments have taken the view in respect of the privatized State-owned enterprises at least that public ownership and control *is ceteris parabus* less efficient than alternative structures of ownership and control.
>
> (Scott & Smelt, 1995: 13)

In so far as Scott and Smelt attempt to establish a presumption in favour of the privatisation of universities on the basis of the principles underlying public sector reform in New Zealand, it is appropriate to raise some broader questions concerning the wider policy context[5].

Public Sector Reform and Constitutional Consequences of Privatisation

In the most general sense, as Le Grand and Robinson (1984: 3) comment, '... any privatisation proposal involves the rolling back of the activities of the state'. Privatisation involves three main kinds of activity which parallel the three main types of state intervention: a reduction in state subsidy, a reduction in state provision, and a reduction in state regulation. In New Zealand, examples of the first category include the continuing reductions in EFTS subsidies leading to higher tuition fees, the shift from student grants to loans, the introduction of user charges in health, and the reduction of subsidies to Housing Corporation tenants. In the second category examples include the expansion of privately owned medical care, contracting of hospital cleaning and catering, and the sale of state houses. The third category of privatisation may include policies designed to abolish restrictions on competition between private and public companies or enterprises, e.g. in transport, education and health. Privatisation can take many forms; schemes differ not only in the type of state intervention whose reduction or elimination they require but also in what is proposed instead: the replacement of the state by the market, by another form of state activity, or by non-profit-making organisations such as charities or voluntary organisations which are neither private firms nor state enterprises (Le Grand and Robinson, 1984: 6)[6].

A number of commentators (e.g. Harris, 1989) have pointed out that privatisation not only takes the form of the sale of state-owned assets and enterprises; other parallel forms include contracting out, deregulation, user fees, voucher systems and load-shedding. Others (e.g. Heing *et al.*, 1988) have concluded on the basis of comparing recent experience in Britain, France and the US that privatisation is more of a political strategy than an economic and fiscal technique. While the case for privatisation is based upon well known theories, the drive for privatisation *policies* is more complex and often involves political factors such as reducing public sector borrowing or reducing government financial risk[7]. Pitelis & Clarke (1993: 6) note that the case for privatisation policies is often strong on *a priori* theorising and weak in empirical confirmation.

New Zealand carried out its privatisation programme by virtue of the fact that it experienced few constitutional constraints, with the exception, perhaps, of the Treaty of Waitangi. There was no constitutional protection for certain types of property as in Mexico, Brazil or France and few, if any, constitutional requirements as to the manner and form of privatisation. Bollard (1994: 104) considers that among the preconditions that allowed the reforms to take place in New Zealand were '... a committed and powerful Treasury dominating the policy debate ...' and '... a thin legislative system in New Zealand, permitting radical changes to be enacted'[8]. Elsewhere (Bollard & Mayes, 1993: 309) he argues that '... it is too early to draw conclusions, and the extent of privatisation has meant that it is the state-owned enterprises with the best prospects of private sector performance that have been privatised, thus confusing the comparison'.

Janet McLean (1996) describes the instrumental changes to New Zealand government since 1986 and assesses their constitutional consequences. McLean questions the justifications offered for these instrumental changes, suggesting that the justifications for privatisation and corporatisation which issue from public choice theory are overtly political: 'By putting management and sometimes even ownership beyond elected representatives, we avoid capture and rent-seeking' (p. 216). The implication is that the market is free of self-interested strategies and there are fewer agency problems. She is concerned that the question of *how* public goods are to be delivered '... seems to have overtaken questions of what should be delivered and who should perform these delivery functions' (p. 214). The result, in terms of expressive purposes, has been that:

> ... government is removed from citizens; citizens are not themselves the state but merely select government services .... Citizens are no longer owners of the SOEs; accountability has more to do with reporting than it does with politics. Government is no longer talked about as 'of and by the people'. The legitimacy of government no longer resides (even *theoretically* it seems) in the notion of consent to be governed. The government is the 'other' with whom citizens must on occasion co-operate, conflict and cajole.
>
> (McLean, 1996: 218)

McLean proceeds to investigate the consequences for elected central government, for courts and for communities, detailing, among other things, the difficulties of maintaining open government – the uneasy relationship between the ombudsmen and SOEs – and documenting the way in which there exists no legal means to ensure that SOEs consider the interests of communities in making a commercial decision.

The Not-for-Profit Trust Model of Governance

Scott and Smelt (1995) present two possible options for containing the Crown's financial risk in its ownership interests of universities and improving performance (although they give little consideration to the latter): the first option is the enhancement of present monitoring regime for Crown-owned universities so as to enhance ownership monitoring; the second option, clearly favoured by Scott and Smelt (p. 19), is the change in ownership and organisational form from the current public statutory corporation status to a 'private not-for-profit status' or trust. They indicate that the government has ruled out the maintenance of the status quo as an option (although this may be still an option under a new Minister or a new government) and they confirm that the first option has already been proposed by officials.

Scott and Smelt suggest that forming universities as not-for-profit trusts may be a means of '... developing an ownership regime which increases the degrees of freedom for universities in a way which will enhance performance and reduce or contain risk for the Crown' (p. 25). They then consider the not-for-profit option in relation to the for-profit alternative, emphasising that taxation benefits, the complexities of monetary quantification of outcomes, the difficulties of linking the traditional broad roles of universities to profit objectives, the ease of seeking private endowments or public funding, and the complex organisational objectives of universities (and particularly the 'conscience and critic' function) tend to favour not-for-profit over for-profit ownership status. It is important to note that Scott and Smelt do not dismiss the for-profit ownership model out of hand: they note the existence of for-profit universities which are 'reportedly making strong progress' and suggest that there are examples of for-profit organisations which nevertheless take on a 'conscience and critic' role such as the media.

The not-for-profit trust option requires 'maximum degrees of freedom' by universities to pursue their objectives effectively, given that some universities may wish to specialise, target niches or 'focus on mass markets' (p. 18). Here Scott and Smelt confuse two notions of freedom (or at least a conceptual slippage occurs): freedom to pursue the institution's best interests in the marketplace and the traditional notion of academic freedom.

Scott and Smelt (1995: 19) proceed to outline the features of a trust in terms of:

- the trust deed which sets the objectives and while binding upon trustees allows them substantial discretion of means to pursue objectives
- the trustees, while they may hold legal title to the property of the university, are not the beneficiaries and therefore are not the ultimate owners
- the beneficiaries are the ultimate owners, although the Crown can take the role of trustee in some circumstances
- a trust could operate with or without Crown guarantees or with limited or conditional guarantees.

The main advantages are seen to be that a university could operate freely in terms of its trust deed and in control of its own assets, without

Crown ownership monitoring and with the ability to raise debt against either assets or future income. The question of reducing the Crown's financial risk – the sole rationale for questioning current governance arrangements – is construed positively in terms of the trust model. Scott and Smelt argue that the nature and strength of the incentives on the governing body could be such as to reduce risk and encourage efficiencies, especially given the fact that trustees under New Zealand trust law would carry considerable personal liability. However, they acknowledge that a trust arrangement will not entirely remove the Crown's financial risk and are somewhat cautious in claiming with any confidence that the trust model will reduce risk. They seem to think that a trust model provides a form of organisational flexibility for universities such that '... it could relatively easily be dis-assembled and reconfigured, perhaps into a number of institutions' (p. 20), various specialist areas 'may pursue profit on a joint-venture basis' (p. 19) or, presumably, be disaggregated and be sold off.

It is clear that Scott and Smelt's exploration of the trust model of governance is not based upon empirical evidence; rather it is argued on *a priori* grounds. It is not argued with great confidence that the model will, in fact, either reduce the Crown's financial risk or necessarily improve performance, or, indeed, even enhance the present monitoring regime. The main advantage mentioned in respect of the trust model is that it permits the governing authority, i.e. the trustees, to pursue objectives with greater commercial freedom.

There are weaknesses on several points concerning the trust model. First, it does not adequately spell out the financial risks to the Crown, to the trustees, or the beneficiaries (the nominal owners) and, therefore, to the university. It is conceivable that a group of trustees may in fact expose the Crown to a greater financial risk than is currently the case, especially given that greater commercial freedom also entails greater financial risk. Second, it does not define who might constitute the beneficiaries and, therefore, the true owners. Third, it does not entertain the notion that there may be other kinds of risks that directly impinge upon questions of governance and on the Crown's responsibilities. We can classify these other kinds of risks as: (i) risks to academic freedom (to the four freedoms noted below); (ii) risks to the public nature of universities (creeping asset privatisation); (iii) political risks to the *democratic* nature of university institutions through interest group dominance of the trust; and (iv) fiduciary risks.

Representation versus Technocracy

The State Services Commission (1992) submitted a paper entitled 'Governance in Tertiary Institutions' to the Taskforce on Capital Charging of Tertiary Institutions. The paper focuses on governance in relation to the Crown's ownership and purchasing interests and examines comparative research. The major conclusions of the paper, based upon international research findings, were that there is no optimal governance structure; that the owners of institutions are best served by single-tier councils whose composition is characterised by diversity rather than representativeness; and that the presence of members representing local or national interest groups, students or internal agents is counter-productive. The paper recommends 'that internal agents not be represented on councils, with the exception of the Chief Executive, who should not have full voting rights' (p. 2).

The SSC paper (1992) has been influential and controversial in both setting out the research literature on governance and in arguing the case against representative councils. Its arguments have been reiterated both by the VUW Working Party on Governance (1995) and Scott and Smelt (1995).

The SSC paper (1992: 19) asserts that 'The literature in general concludes that diversity and not representativeness should characterise the composition of boards'. The paper argues that 'diversity' '... means a board should be composed of both sexes, have members of minority races and creeds, and people from different ages, occupations and backgrounds', whereas the concept of representativeness involves, in addition, the '... presence of specific group interests on boards, such as faculty, students, employers, and community interest groups'.

The research referred to in the SSC paper does not establish the claim that diversity and not representativeness should characterise the composition of boards or councils; no argument or evidence is produced to support this proposition. It is alleged: 'The strongest argument against interest group representation is that trustees should not be representatives of anything except the public welfare' (p. 19, para 75). This is the crucial argument that can be contested on a number of grounds. First, it is taken for granted that existing members of a council are, in fact, 'trustees'. Second, it is not shown that 'interest group representation' cannot represent the public welfare. Third, it is simply assumed that the selection of trustees, based upon a principle of diversity, is neutral in its interests. Fourth, it does not take into account the existing composition of councils which allows for four ministerial appointees and other elected or co-opted members.

The paper quotes 'evidence' that the inclusion of 'internal agents' encourages 'board-agent' collusion and rent-seeking behaviour in non-profit organisations, while at the same time acknowledging that for-profit firms frequently include internal agents as part of their membership. This evidence is rather thin and not based upon New Zealand experience. The paper also quotes 'evidence' that 'faculty participation in governance leads to the loss of productivity' (p. 21, para. 79).

The 'strong argument' advanced by the SSC paper is reiterated by the VUW Working Part on Governance (1995: 21, para. 5.4):

A strong argument can be made that the governing body should focus on its role as stewards or trustees for the University, and not be made up in a representative fashion by stakeholders. The membership of the governing body should instead be expertise based: academic, financial, management, legal, fund raising, community relations, etc.

In this case, the argument is simply asserted without adducing grounds or providing empirical support. The implication of the VUW Working Party paper is that while different stakeholders have different interests and roles to play in university governance, these roles should not involve direct representation but rather a form of consultation based on 'two-way communication'. There is no attempt to distinguish the difference in interests between internal and external agents or to distinguish the superior claim of internal agents (or, indeed, the differences in interests among internal agents) given, minimally, their *professional interests* in what Justice Felix Frankfurter has called the four essential freedoms of the university, viz.: 'to determine for itself on academic grounds who may teach, what may be taught, how it should be taught, and who may be admitted to study' (cited in Bok, 1982: 157).

Scott and Smelt (1995: 9) base their analysis at different points upon various sets of distinctions laid out in the SSC paper. For example, they echo the distinction between academic freedom, autonomy and accountability introduced by the SSC paper (1995: 13, paras. 45-49); they (Scott and Smelt, 1995: 23) also echo the distinction between managerial, professional and consumer accountability introduced by the SSC paper (1992: 14–15, paras. 51–53). Perhaps most importantly, Scott and Smelt (1995: 23) repeat the same SSC (1992: 19–22, paras. 74–80) claim when it comes to the question of faculty representation:

> Some overseas research suggests that faculties function best when not represented on the governing body and that governing bodies may function best when not composed of key interest groups – so that they can seek to govern in the best interests of the institution rather than divide the spoils or otherwise seek political trade-offs for the chief executive to implement.

Both the SSC (1992) and Scott and Smelt (1995) refer to the same three pieces of 'international research' to warrant their claims[9]. Of the three, one adopts a property rights perspective on university governance, another adopts a principal–agent theoretical approach, and the third is clearly ideological and based more on anecdotal evidence rather than hard data or argumentation. All three pieces of 'international research' emanate from the American context and respond to the American situation. A public choice perspective held by both SSC (1992) and Scott and Smelt (1995) has determined their selection of the 'international research' evidence in this case to the exclusion of other research and evidence. It might also be argued that some forms of public choice theory, and in particular the variants which have motivated both the SSC (1992) and Scott and Smelt (1995), are profoundly and pervasively anti-democratic. This is certainly the view of one international commentator on the politics of public choice well acquainted with the New Zealand case:

> ... democracy cannot be adequately based upon the private wants of individuals but depends upon a distinctive ethos of citizenship which lies beyond the realm of most public choice thought.
>
> (Self, 1993: 197)

The arguments advanced by the SSC paper and reiterated (without acknowledgment) by the VUW Working Party and the Scott and Smelt advocate the shift from a fully *representative* model of governance of universities to a *technocratic* model based upon management expertise. The full force of these arguments is directed primarily against traditional faculty representation – so-called 'internal agents' – on grounds of economic efficiency and commercial freedom. The Scott and Smelt proposal represents a significant move towards further privatisation of New Zealand universities. The not-for-profit trust model of governance, legally speaking, involves a change of ownership status which compromises the position of academic staff as major stakeholders and thereby threatens the traditional democratic model of governance, the university as a democratic institution, and its core values of academic freedom and collegiality. The trust model of governance advocated by Scott and Smelt contains historic risks to the traditional institutional autonomy of the university and to its role as critic and conscience of society. The trust model offers no guarantees that it would contain or reduce the financial risk to the Crown; indeed, the trust model could in fact increase the Crown's financial risk under certain circumstances.

Subsequent Developments

The Scott and Smelt paper certainly provoked debate and led to the consideration of the not-for-trust model alongside other possible organisational models and ownership structures[10]. A number of tertiary institutions had been active in reviewing possible ownership/organisational models prior to the release of the paper, and have continued to work on these issues[11]. The officials too have been busy: the Tertiary Capital Charge Steering Group (TCCSG, 1996) presented a discussion paper to the Tertiary Reference Group in May 1997. Entitled 'Governance of Tertiary Education Institutions', the paper argues that current governance arrangements have confused and diffuse accountabilities which may lead to poor focus and performance, and no effective early warning of potential financial difficulties which would allow the Crown as owner to address and rectify matters at an early stage.

The TCCSG proposes a 'benchmark' model which is considered to be an appropriate basis for development of improved governance for

TEIs (tertiary education institutions). This model has the following characteristics: expertise-based councils appointed by, and accountable to, the Crown as in substance owner; smaller councils (e.g. 8–10 members); and an enhanced ownership monitoring regime matched with appropriate ownership instruments.

The TCCSG (consisting of officials from the Ministry of Education, State Services Commission, Treasury and Professor Tony van Zijl), with responsibility for developing ownership policy (related to governance, capital charge, ownership monitoring, and the relaxation of input controls), held a consultation session in June 1997 on strategic planning and ownership monitoring to outline the 'benchmark' model. At that session officials presented the case that self-management requires appropriate planning and ownership monitoring tools. The officials claimed that 1990s reforms devolved management, but that devolution was not matched with the appropriate tools. Current ownership monitoring is input-based, whereas the purchase relationship is output-based. Officials suggested that TEIs should prepare detailed financial and business plans and report regularly. The monitoring of financial performance would be carried out by a small group of officials in Wellington. Officials were at pains to persuade participants that the introduction of an ownership monitoring regime was not a return to 'hands-on' management.

After the first MMP elections in October 1996 National and New Zealand First promised, under their Coalition Agreement, to undertake a 'comprehensive review of all aspects of the tertiary sector'. The Agreement, issued on 5 December 1996, also promised to work 'towards a universal system of living allowances for tertiary students as part of a comprehensive system of youth income support that gives comparability between unemployed job seekers and students'. Both policies were part of New Zealand First's election campaign. In September 1997, the Coalition government issued the green paper, *A Future Tertiary Education Policy for New Zealand: Tertiary Education Review* (Ministry of Education, 1997a). This has, despite the collapse of the National–New Zealand First coalition, been followed in more recent times by the white paper, *Tertiary Education in New Zealand: Policy Directions for the 21st Century* (Ministry of Education, 1998). We discuss these policy documents in detail in Chapters 1 and 7. The green and white papers address several major areas for reform, including the resourcing of tuition, the resourcing of research, quality and other regulatory arrangements, and the governance and accountability of tertiary education institutions. Neither the green paper nor the white paper deals adequately with the growing problem of student debt or the escalating compliance costs faced by institutions. Both largely ignore questions concerning the impact of the new communications and information technologies (C&IT), although they assume that such technologies will promote the internationalisation of tertiary education[12]. In effect, the future directions for reform of New Zealand tertiary education institutions (and especially universities) outlined in these policy documents indicate two converging trends: one toward an incremental privatisation of the tertiary system as a whole; the other, the promotion of a neoliberal paradigm of globalisation. Trends towards the incremental privatisation of the system can be clearly seen in terms of reductions in state subsidy (e.g. increased user charges, introduction of student entitlements); reductions in state provision (e.g. proposed full funding of private training establishments, increased contracting out of services, contestable funding for research); and reductions in state regulation (e.g. deregulation in the setting of student tuition fees in 1991, the introduction of capital charging, and the move to establish tertiary institutions as businesses under legislation based on Companies Act 1993). What is of great significance in this regard are proposals to deregulate statutory terms and the possibility of relaxing the criteria for university status, including the role of critic and conscience of society, which is part of existing legislation. Should these policy directions come to fruition, then New Zealand universities will cease to exist as distinctive institutions in the tertiary education system.

Endnotes

[1]   A version of this chapter was presented at the ERA and AARE (Singapore and Australia) conference 'Educational Research: Building New Partnerships', Singapore Polytechnic, 25–26 November 1996.

[2]   See Peters (1996c; 1996d).

[3]   The SSC (1992: 28, para. 110) indicates that 'a recent legal opinion has submitted that Crown ownership of tertiary institutions is doubtful, and that tertiary institutions are not "instruments of government"'.

4   For a very different and detailed account of the relations between government and the universities during this decade of reform, see Butterworth & Tarling (1994). See in particular their account (Chapter 7) of the legal action taken by the Universities of Auckland and Canterbury in contesting the role of the university in New Zealand society and in democratic societies in general. See also Peters (1994a).

5   See, for example, NZ Treasury (1984, 1987), Bushnell & Scott (1988), Scott *et al.* (1990).

6   As the literature on public sector reform and the twin strategies of corporatisation and privatisation is now so voluminous, this chapter will confine itself to a consideration of a limited number of issues. See, for example, Duncan & Bollard (1992), Boston *et al.* (1991), Bollard & Mayes (1993), Kelsey (1993), Bollard (1994), Kelsey (1995).

7   Daintith (1994: 45) provides the following legal categorisation of privatisation techniques: (a) change of ownership from public or predominantly public to private or predominantly private; (b) change of activities or assets (*ex hypothesi*, in the direction of reduction); (c) change of legal status; (d) liquidation; (e) change of economic status (as from direct producer to indirect provider by way of contracting out ...); and (f) change of competitive environment (as by withdrawal of monopoly rights).

8   Pitelis & Clarke (1993: 2) mention the neoclassical property rights school, Hayek's view of 'dispersed knowledge', and Alchian & Demsertz's 'residual claimant' theory.

9   John Williamson, editor of *The Political Economy of Reform* (1994: 550–1), in commenting upon the New Zealand case, notes that the trade-off between efficiency and equity that occurred with the reforms (a point strongly argued by the Royal Commission on Social Policy) '... now seems to be beyond doubt ...' and he suggests that 'the price New Zealand paid was high and might well have been prohibitive in other countries'.

10   The three pieces of research in question are McCormick & Meiners (1988), Toma (1990) and Kohn and Mortimer (1983).

11   Francis (1996), for instance, considers six possible organisational models, including a statutory corporation; a not-for-profit trust; a State-Owned Enterprise model; a private for-profit model; a Crown-Research Institute model; and a private university model. She considers these models in relation to the key strategic challenges facing Lincoln University.

12   For a discussion of the importance of C&IT to New Zealand tertiary education, see Peters and Roberts (1998b).

chapter six

Qualifications Policies and the Marketisation of Higher Education

The New Zealand Qualifications Authority (NZQA) was established in 1990. Under the Education Amendment Act of 1990, the authority was charged with 'developing a framework for national qualifications in secondary schools and post-school education and training' (NZQA, 1991: 6). The Act stipulated that all qualifications should have 'a purpose and a relationship to each other that students and the public can understand'; there should also be 'a flexible system for the gaining of qualifications, with recognition of competency already achieved' (p. 7). These objectives, the NZQA proposed, could best be met through the conversion of existing and future qualifications into 'units of learning' (later to become known as 'unit standards'), each with clearly specified 'outcomes'. These units of learning were regarded by the NZQA as the 'building blocks' of the framework (p. 36). Educational institutions were to become 'providers', while students in the new system would be designated 'consumers' or 'users'. The Authority aimed to set up a national catalogue of units, the advantages of which were described as follows:

A catalogue of units will benefit students, industry and providers. Students will have increased choice. Industry and providers will be able to avoid duplication of effort in course development. Providers will be able to achieve economies of provision (p. 50).

The NZQA drew a distinction between 'norm-referenced achievement' and 'standards-based achievement', the former assessing performance through comparison with other students, the latter measuring student outcomes against (pre-specified) standards of achievement or competence (see p. 54). The Authority opted for standards-based achievement, and undertook a comprehensive process of reforming the entire nexus of certificates, diplomas, degrees and other qualifications in the New Zealand education system. A series of publications set out the path to be followed (examples include NZQA, 1992a, 1992b, 1993a, 1993b, 1993c; Education and Training Support Agency, 1993). All qualifications, if they were to be officially recognised, would fall under the NZQA framework. Units of learning would be transferable, so that qualifications gained at one time and place could be 'stacked' (as building blocks) in moving to higher levels on the framework at later stages. Eight levels, each indexed against pre-defined outcomes statements, were proposed for the new National Qualifications Framework (NQF).

The framework has attracted extensive comment (both congratulatory and critical) from the educational community in New Zealand. The relationship between the NZQA and the universities has always been a tense one, but in more recent years secondary school and polytechnic teachers have also raised serious concerns. This chapter aims to make a modest contribution to these ongoing debates by proposing a mildly 'subversive' reading of the green paper on qualifications policy issued by the government in mid-1997 (Ministry of Education, 1997b). The first part of the chapter comments on the political context within which the green paper was introduced, while the second identifies a number of important acknowledgements (of past failings) and concessions (to groups who have been critical of the qualifications reforms) in the document. This is followed in the third section by a more extended analysis of new and revitalised priorities signalled in the proposed changes to qualifications policies. The fourth and fifth sections provide a critique of the green paper, concentrating on issues of particular relevance to universities. In part four we consider why the government might have wanted to have given ground on some key areas. In the fifth section we advance a number of philosophical objections to the technocratic assumptions underpinning the NZQA reforms.

Responding to Pressure from all Sides

When the idea of a National Qualifications Framework was first introduced it appeared to have the backing of every major educational group except the universities. As the years passed, however, both the Framework itself and the NZQA as a policy organisation became subject to increasing criticism from secondary teachers, polytechnics, business organisations and individuals. The survival of the NZQA in its current form can no longer be regarded as a certainty. Unit standards – described by the NZQA as the 'building blocks' of the NQF – had become widely unpopular, and moves to subvert competency-based assessment in (some) secondary schools and other institutions were planned. The resistance seemed to reach a peak in 1996. With an election looming, the government could ill afford negative publicity of any kind, let alone in the key social policy area of education. The teacher unions and kindergarten educators were pushing hard for better wages and conditions, and university students were continuing to express their disquiet about escalating degree costs. Further controversy over qualifications policies was clearly something an administration facing an uncertain future under MMP would not want. References to NZQA, the NQF and (especially) unit standards thus faded (somewhat) in the latter half of 1996, as the National Party concentrated its efforts on minimising 'fallout' from teacher concerns and an ever-vocal tertiary student population.

With a National–New Zealand First Coalition government in place, the wheels of reform started to roll again. A re-examination of the qualifications system was one of several reviews planned for 1997. This revisiting of the qualifications reforms coincided with the recent arrival of a new Chief Executive of the NZQA, Douglas Blackmur, and followed hot on the heels of revitalised debates over excellence, the role of school examinations, and the relationship between university degrees and other qualifications. Education is always very much in the public eye as a 'hot issue', and in recent years questions about assessment and qualifications have been among those most keenly contested in debates between MPs and other government officials, bureaucrats, and representatives from educational institutions at all levels in the system.

Assessments of the qualifications reform process have been mixed in their focus and tone. The universities have been critical from the beginning. The New Zealand Vice-Chancellors' Committee (1994) raised concerns about the technocratic nature of unit standards, and argued that they were an unsuitable assessment mechanism in many university courses. The Association of University Staff of New Zealand (AUSNZ, 1995; Chapman, 1995) expressed dismay at the undemocratic processes employed in developing and implementing the new qualifications system, and believed the status of New Zealand degrees would be placed under threat if some elements of the policy reforms (e.g. the redefining of 'research' to embrace almost any form of intellectual inquiry, creative work, professional practice or consultancy) were carried through. These collective responses have been supported by numerous critical commentaries from individual academics in Education and other fields (e.g. Codd, 1995, 1996, 1997; Hall, 1995a, 1995b; Elley, 1995, 1996; Fitzsimons, 1995, 1996; Fitzsimons and Peters, 1994; Haynes and Fitzsimons, 1997; Roberts, 1996a, 1997a; and Tuck, 1994, 1995). As an effective antidote to the all-pervasive discourse of approval in the NZQA's own publications (e.g. NZQA, 1992a), a balanced collection of essays on standards-based assessment appeared in Peddie and Tuck's volume, *Setting the Standards: Issues in Assessment for National Qualifications* (1995).

Many in the private sector have expressed support for the general thrust of the qualifications reform process. Private training establishments saw an opportunity in the NQF for the development of new programmes which would receive greater official recognition (and funding benefits flowing from this) than might have been the case in the past. Similarly, many teachers and administrators in polytechnics had fallen in behind the reforms in the initial stages and were supportive of the breaking down of old distinctions between 'academic' and 'vocational' learning. The collapsing of this distinction has been doggedly pursued by the NZQA, and has been defended with conviction by Allan Barker (1995) in the Peddie and Tuck volume. By 1996, however, the tide had begun to turn. The sea of discontent continued into 1997, as several items in the *New Zealand Education Review* in that year indicated. Jim Doyle (1997), the Executive Director of the Association of Polytechnics in New Zealand, suggested that the 'overwhelming impression' is that the implementation of the legislation relating to the establishment of the NZQA (in the 1990 Education Amendment Act) had been a 'costly failure' (p. 7). The implementation process had, he says, 'polarised the education sector like no other issue before it' (p. 8). Other items in 1997 drew attention to protest action from school teachers, some of whom were openly 'discarding' NZQA advice (see Matheson, 1997: 5). In another 1997 article, Janet Rivers reported on a review of the Authority by Rob Laking (a Senior Lecturer in Public Policy at Victoria University of Wellington), Nick Kyrke-Smith (Senior Advisor with the State Services Commission) and Angela Foulkes (Secretary of the Council of Trade Unions). She noted that NZQA's 'ability to provide sound policy advice' had been hampered by '[i]nternal conflicts, conflict with the education ministry and a closed attitude to criticism' (Rivers, 1997: 1).

In June of 1997, after months of speculation about the direction qualifications policies might be taking, the government, through the Ministry of Education, released a green paper entitled *A Future Qualifications Policy for New Zealand* (Ministry of Education, 1997b)[1]. The green paper received a quieter reception than might have been expected given the controversial nature of the reforms. This could be explained in part by the structure, scope and style of the document. To the Ministry's credit, contentious issues surrounding the NQF and unit standards were set out in a balanced and fair manner, with many concessions to critics being made[2]. The discussion of the substance of critics' claims was light, but this is not unusual for a policy paper of this kind. The prose was lucid and to-the-point, and a reasonable period of time (by New Zealand Government standards) for comments and submissions was provided. A certain sincerity of purpose seemed to pervade much of the document (on the surface at least), as indicated by statements such as this from Wyatt Creech's 'Foreword':

> While the Green Paper gives an overview of the government's current thinking on future qualifications policy, the government goes into the

process with an open mind. It will carefully consider all submissions
before a decision is reached.

(Creech, 1997a: 5)

The green paper notes that before the government finalised its
policies on qualifications and other educational issues, there would be
wide consultation to ensure that the proposals for dealing with the issues
represented the best solutions (p. 5).

Such talk can, of course, be regarded in a rather cynical light given
the history of 'consultation' in reforms within education and other social
policy areas over the past decade. The Association of University Staff
has long complained, with good reason in our view, about the lack of
negotiation over reforms within the tertiary sector, and several key
government agencies (e.g. the Education Review Office) have been
strongly criticised for what some regard as 'heavy handed', 'out of
touch' judgements about schools. Nonetheless, it is instructive to take
the tone of openness and honesty, and the invitation for extensive
consultation and debate, seriously (but not at face value). The green
paper, in our view, represented an important turning point in the process
of qualifications reform, particularly as far as the universities were
concerned. Some moves to please groups who had protested against the
changes were made, and several new policy directions were clearly
signalled in the document. Teachers, academics and students appeared
to have an impact in bringing about a reversal of some trends in the
implementation of the NQF. They have continued to play an important
role as critics of qualifications procedures during the latter half of 1997
and first half of 1998.

Some Concessions

Our reading of the green paper on qualifications policy suggests that by
mid-1997 the Ministry had given ground in a number of pivotal areas.
The proposals in the green paper are premised on a series of
acknowledgements hitherto either withheld or offered in only a
fragmented and slightly 'grudging' way. These acknowledgements fall
into at least two categories: those made (more-or-less) explicitly, and
others that might be drawn by inference from a critical reading of the
document as a whole.

In the first category, the Ministry concedes that the reforms have been too expensive. Constant references are made to 'compliance costs' (see, for example, Ministry of Education, 1997b: 2, 14, 20, 25–26, 29–30) . These have, it seems, been too high in the past and need to be kept at lower levels in the future. There is also an implicit acknowledgement that elements of the reform process – notably, the implementation of a unit standards approach to assessment in secondary schools – have been, at least at times, rather too cumbersome and time-consuming (see pp. 10, 13, 23). Finally, the Ministry acknowledges that the reforms have been unpopular (or at least subject to considerable debate) in some circles. References to criticisms from various groups (not always named) are scattered throughout the green paper, and a definite effort to respond, albeit briefly, to allegations about weaknesses in the new system has been made (compare, pp. 4, 12, 13, 19–20, 23–25, 28).

At a less overt level, a desire to 'keep the major players happy' seems to underpin the green paper. The push for graded examinations from (some) secondary schools has been very strong indeed. In the green paper a clear avenue for keeping this option alive is opened up (see pp. 23–25). This reinforced earlier statements by the new Chief Executive of the NZQA about the possibility of maintaining measures of excellence as well as competence in the qualifications system (see Burge, 1997). A tacit admission that the professionalism of teachers, academics and others in educational institutions (what the Ministry would call 'provider' groups) warrants (greater) respect can also be detected in the document. This is indicated by, among other things, the expressed notion that teachers ought to play a greater role than the reforms to date may have assumed in deciding not only the best way to teach – something the NZQA claims to never have interfered with – but also the most suitable means of assessment for students in particular courses (p. 18). This represents a significant shift, and is closely related to another admission in the green paper, namely that 'unit standards' may not be the most appropriate assessment device for all subjects, or in all educational settings, or for all qualifications (pp. 18–20). Additionally, there is a much more explicit acknowledgement (e.g. on p. 20) that in matters of educational quality there is a need to focus on the course of learning as a *whole*, and not just on its constituent parts (and especially not just on discrete units *within* those parts).

There is also, importantly, a concession that certain groups already have the 'international credibility' necessary to make judgements about the quality of qualifications in their institutions. Specifically, the New Zealand Vice-Chancellors' Committee is seen as already having established its credentials to make authoritative judgements about the value of degrees and the quality of the work conducted for them (p. 29). Equally, the green paper makes it clear that other groups do *not* presently have the credentials for making quality assessments of this kind: 'Some groups (including industry training organisations, private training establishments and Māori providers) do not yet have umbrella bodies with the infrastructure, standing and competence required to approve qualifications' (p. 29).

Old Themes, New Emphases and Implied Priorities

Alongside these acknowledgements, mention must be made of implied priorities, the reinforcement of older themes, and new emphases in the green paper. Several features are worthy of note here. First, the document repeatedly focuses on *students* and *employers* as key groups with a stake in qualifications matters (compare, for example, Ministry of Education, 1997b: 8, 14, 17, 18). These groups, it is constantly noted, need to be able to choose which qualifications best suit their 'needs'. Students and employers become important assessors of quality, even if others ('NQF Approval Agencies' and, in an overseeing role, the NZQA) are also involved in this process. The question of how such choices might meaningfully be made barely warrants a mention. The authors of the green paper do admit at one point that 'people are not equally informed' (p. 30) in making decisions about educational quality, but this is more a passing comment than a substantial discussion.

This emphasis is, we think, highly significant and reinforces the move toward a fully marketised model of education – a move, we argue later, that underwrites the entire green paper. While the marketisation of education is a complex process involving a multifaceted attack on the notion of education as a public good, the relevant feature of the process in this context is the idea that educational choices (choosing which institution to enrol in, which qualification to pursue, what will be of most value or is of the highest quality, etc.) are becoming increasingly 'consumer-driven'. Students 'consume' courses and employers make consumer-style choices about which employees to take on[2]. The sub-text in this process is a critique of 'provider capture'. This notion, inscribed in New Zealand bureaucratic consciousness by the Treasury, refers to a situation in which educational institutions, teachers and academics allegedly 'take over' decisions about curricula, qualifications and pedagogy. The result of this 'capture', it is argued, is a weak relationship between educational qualifications and the 'needs' of industry and employers, and a lack of choice for students wanting to tailor programmes to their own interests, aspirations and ends. The solution, from the Treasury point of view, is to foster competition between educational 'providers' and to shift the conceptual discourse and practices of education into the private realm. The educational domain becomes similar to any other 'market', with buyers and sellers, winners and losers. Education, on this model, is a *private* good, where the only recognised benefits are those that accrue to individuals purchasing 'provider' services. The marketisation of education, including the qualifications arena, is now something the government feels no need to obscure. If the seeds of this process were planted some time ago (see, for example, Crocombe, Enright and Porter, 1991), the full flowering of marketisation is now coming into being. The qualifications green paper, like many other policy documents published in recent years, is replete with references to the importance of moving with the new economic times, of being competitive on the international stage, and of satisfying the wants (almost always erroneously called 'needs') of the corporate sector (always somewhat disguised under the heading of 'employers and industry'). At the start of the green paper, the Minister of Education observes that we live in a 'rapidly changing world', and asserts:

Skills and knowledge are becoming more and more important in people's lives. Those with expertise and innovative ideas have more opportunities and better prospects, both within New Zealand and internationally. Increasingly, firms are looking to higher levels of knowledge and skills among their employees in order to gain an advantage over their competitors. Nationally, the capability of our people drives New Zealand's overall competitiveness and our economic and social success.

(Creech, 1997a: 3)

Creech continues:

> Investment in developing skills and knowledge – whether by individuals,
> firms or the government – is therefore critical. Students and employers
> need a way of measuring the skills and knowledge that their investment
> has achieved (p. 3).

The link between the educational 'market' and the labour market is now an openly-expressed priority ('Qualifications need to match employers' and labour market requirements as closely as possible': 4), and the case for keeping qualifications and assessments processes up to date is advanced on the basis of 'recognising that we operate in a global economy and marketplace' (p. 4).

The discourse of 'flexibility' also has a strong presence in the green paper. Talk about the importance of being flexible in allowing for changes in the marketplace and the world of work and in accounting for shifts in 'consumer' preferences and possible new policy directions in the future is writ large over the document. On the other hand, the need for stability and consistency in qualifications policies is also stressed (see, for example, Ministry of Education, 1997b: 9). This is only an apparent contradiction, for the 'flexibility' referred to above is *dependent upon* rather than antithetical to a certain form of consistency in matters pertaining to qualifications – a point we discuss in more detail below. In brief, what the Ministry sees as necessary is a consistent means for *exchanging information* about qualifications: this can be met, the green paper suggests, via a system in which a common 'currency' (their word) is established. A common qualifications currency allows students and employers (and effectively *forces* educational 'providers') to adapt to changing employment relations and conditions in the world of work – at both a national and international level. The Ministry sets out its intentions as follows:

> It is ... proposed that all NQF qualifications should have clearly stated
> *outcomes* (statements about what students know or can do), and be
> capable of being related to one another through *level* and *credit values*.
> This information would give students and employers a 'common

currency' – quality, outcomes, level and credit – with which to compare qualifications across the full range, and would give providers a consistent basis for recognising learning that had already taken place (p. 6).

This means that 'any qualification, regardless of how it was designed, taught or assessed, could be registered if it met these criteria. The NQF would therefore be able to accommodate all types of qualifications, from school examinations to degrees, whether or not they use unit standards' (p. 6).

A final feature of note is the continuing dominance of 'skills' in talk of educational content and processes. This is nothing new, and has attracted criticism in the past (see, for example, Marshall, 1995). The *New Zealand Curriculum Framework* – the document upon which all other curriculum developments in specific subject areas have been founded in recent years – marked the beginning of a much more aggressive emphasis on skills in the New Zealand education system. All major learning areas, government officials seem to now believe, can be collapsed into so many skills. Thus, alongside 'physical skills', 'numeracy skills' and the like readers of the *Curriculum Framework* find 'social and co-operative skills' and a new emphasis on 'self-management and competitive skills' (see Ministry of Education, 1993).

The word 'knowledge' also appears at regular points in the green paper, almost always coupled with a reference to skills (see, for example, Ministry of Education, 1997c: 3, 5, 8). Yet there is actually very little *about* knowledge in the document. Even if the broadest definition of 'knowledge' is granted (one which might, for instance, refer to a way of understanding the world), the reasons for repeatedly speaking of both skills *and* knowledge remain unclear. All references to knowledge could probably have been eliminated from the green paper without altering the substance of the document in any way. There is no engagement with the argument, advanced by some of the NZQA's critics (see Roberts, 1997b), that some qualifications are predominantly 'knowledge-based' while others are 'skills-based'. 'Change' is an important theme in the green paper, but there is no discussion of the changing nature of knowledge in post-industrial or postmodern societies (cf. Lyotard, 1984).

The coupling of 'knowledge' with 'skills' in the document seems to be more a rhetorical device than a substantive concern with the relationship between the two concepts. Talk of skills alone is now (following widespread disquiet over it) too blatantly restrictive, too closely tied to the 'vocational' side of the 'vocational/academic' binary (which the NZQA has persistently tried to break down). It is perhaps too overtly managerialist, too readily linked with industry training (and the 'Skill New Zealand' policy in particular: Education and Training Support Agency, 1993), and too far removed from the traditions in many fields of study (particularly within the humanities disciplines) where 'knowledge' is the central organising concept. The green paper covers a very broad canvas: its subject matter is the entire qualifications and assessment policy domain. To not refer to knowledge would give the appearance of being *too* 'market-driven'; yet, while the term 'knowledge' is used – and often – it remains largely devoid of any content.

A Critical Reading of the Document

This part of the chapter addresses two questions: (i) *Why* might the Ministry be prepared to make (seemingly significant) concessions in some areas of qualifications policy? and (ii) What does the Ministry want to hold on to, and why? Further comments on some of the possible implications of the qualifications reforms are provided in our discussion of information technology issues in Chapter 9.

Why has the Ministry given ground on a number of key issues relating to the National Qualifications Framework? First, as acknowledged in the green paper, the bureaucratic weight of the NQF apparatus – particularly under a model in which all learning was to be assessed in terms of unit standards – was becoming too great. Second, for an administration supposedly committed to fiscal responsibility, the costs associated with the reforms – and the anticipated demands on funds in the future – were reaching unacceptable levels. Third, the political consequences of pushing ahead with the full NZQA programme could have been dire, particularly as the reform process might have gained full momentum just in time to (further) dampen enthusiasm for the government's educational agenda in the lead-up to the next general election in 1999. Indeed, as noted at the beginning of the chapter, the NZQA was already in deep public relations trouble prior to the *last* election. It was not that qualifications policy in itself was an 'election

breaker', or even a matter of considerable (perceived) importance for
many; but *education* was, and the growing unpopularity of the NZQA
reforms was one element, and not an insubstantial one, in the broader
mood of dissatisfaction with educational arrangements. Fourth, there
were certain divisions (obliquely hinted at in the green paper) *within* the
government over the nature of the reforms and the management of
them by NZQA officials. Finally, and perhaps most importantly, strong
pressure was being exerted not just from what the government might
call 'militant unions' (e.g. the PPTA), but from very powerful wings in
the business community.

The response of the New Zealand Business Roundtable (NZBRT)
provides a fascinating case study of tensions, within a single organisation,
between moral and academic conservatism on the one hand and
economic liberalism on the other. The opposition to key elements of the
NZQA reforms, and particularly unit standards, came both from
individuals (e.g. Michael Irwin) and groups (principally the Education
Forum) associated with the NZBRT. As might have been expected, the
NZBRT supported the closer link between qualifications and the worlds
of industry and commerce, but raised concerns about unit standards and
the undermining of academic or general education. Michael Irwin, in an
address to the Principals' Forum in 1995, saw the NQF as ushering in a
potentially rigid system which would lower educational standards and
damage the reputation of New Zealand qualifications. He favoured a
focus on core subjects in primary schools and the junior secondary
school, and the creation of three potential pathways for students at the
F5 level: academic, technical and vocational (Irwin, 1995: 5–6).

The green paper can, to a significant extent, be seen as a pragmatic
(but perhaps also reflective) response to these criticisms. It succeeds,
as a preliminary policy document, in maintaining a very clear commitment
to strengthening links with the business community: this was essential if
the support of groups such as the NZBRT and the Employers Federation
was not to be lost. At the same time, there is now scope for reintroducing
external examinations and scales of excellence, the universities have
been granted authority to (largely) manage their own affairs on matters
of educational quality, unit standards will no longer be the only means of
assessing students, and the NZQA (ostensibly at least) retreats somewhat
into the background. Private educational establishments can continue to

develop as before, and ongoing support for industry training has been confirmed.

This might be expected to please many, and, on the surface, should be viewed as an admirable exercise in reflexive policy reformulation. While acknowledging that those in government and the Ministry of Education responsible for putting the green paper in place may have been motivated by a sincere desire to work democratically with affected groups in addressing their concerns, we suggest that there is the *potential* for a more sinister scenario. Our comments here will be speculative and necessarily brief; aspects of the analysis are given fuller treatment in Chapter 9. Acknowledgement must also be made of an excellent paper addressing similar themes by Patrick Fitzsimons (1996), who examines the possible educational and epistemological implications of the managerialist practices of the NZQA in an electronic environment.

Given the battles university representatives (from both the AUSNZ and the NZVCC) have engaged in with the NZQA over the past six years, the green paper can be regarded as something of a breakthrough. Real gains appear to have been made. In a discussion of quality in qualifications, it is suggested that degrees 'are a special case'. 'It is vital,' the green paper continues, 'that New Zealand's degrees are of the highest quality if they are to continue to be highly regarded internationally, and the term "degree" is not to be eroded' (Ministry of Education, 1997b: 9). The authority of the NZVCC in making decisions about educational quality in degrees in New Zealand universities is confirmed in the document (p. 29). (This is despite the proposed policy that those granted this delegated authority – 'NQF Approval Agencies' – should not themselves be providers or developers of qualifications (p. 28). The vice-chancellors are, at law, employers of all staff in their respective institutions. In this sense they are at least indirectly involved in the development and provision of qualifications. There thus seems to be something of a contradiction between two elements of the proposed new qualifications policy.) The new space for promoting excellence as well as competence (which reinforces the universities' right to award grades), and the abandonment of a 'unit standards or not at all' approach to qualifications policy, can be seen as significant victories for the universities. Yet these developments simply take the universities back to where they started before the whole reform process began in 1990. In the meantime, the marketisation agenda has been pushed steadily forward. The green paper offers nothing to stem the flow of marketisation policies in the tertiary sector. Indeed, when viewed in relation to other policy changes, the document can be seen as an important step in *accelerating* and deepening the process. Two closely related key features of the green paper become especially pertinent here: first, the persistent and renewed emphasis on *'portability'*, and, second, the emerging talk of a *'common currency'* in the qualifications system. References to the latter have already been made earlier in this chapter. On the issue of 'portability', the green paper has this to say:

> NQF registration should help to make learning achievements more *portable* – that is, to facilitate the transfer of credit from one qualification or provider to another, so that credits towards a desired qualification may be accumulated easily. Portability is guaranteed across qualifications which have unit standards in common because they represent identical 'blocks' of learning. In qualifications which do not use unit standards, the NQF can improve portability by making clearer the goals of each component (course or paper) of the qualification, the level at which it is pitched and the amount of learning it involves.
>
> (Ministry of Education, 1997c: 9)

Marketisation demands some kind of common currency – or, rather, several forms of standardised currency for different transactions within the educational sphere – if the efficient trading or information, skills, products and services is to occur. This process of exchange must be based on a system in which prospective students are encouraged to make (what parade, falsely, as) 'free' consumer-style choices among competing 'providers'. Clearly understood, or at least routinely practised, patterns of exchange need to be developed if the system is to work. 'Vouchers' provide one type of common currency: they provide 'buying power' for educational 'consumers' (not just students, but their parents and perhaps some employers as well) to choose which goods and services to purchase in the educational marketplace. The implementation of a vouchers scheme clearly never left the government agenda, as indicated, somewhat notoriously, by comments from Lockwood Smith near the end of his tenure as Minister of Education.

But vouchers for 'purchasing' education need to be coupled with some form of currency for *'measuring'* it, and this is where talk of a common currency in the qualifications arena becomes significant. Students, as self-interested, utility-maximising 'consumers' in a marketised system of education, need not just the option of choosing – presumably from a uniform starting position – which 'providers' among those competing for their dollars best suit their 'needs' (i.e. wants, or 'consumer preferences'). They also require a form of currency that will allow them to compete amongst *themselves* as they jockey for positions of advantage within the wider marketplace. The student, through a qualifications system that explicitly frames learning ('skills and knowledge') in currency terms, becomes – in a much more overt way than was hitherto the case – an *entrepreneur*. Students of the future will be informed, via constant implicit and explicit messages from politicians, bureaucrats, the media, and perhaps their parents, that the world 'out there' is ruthlessly competitive. The notion of seeking to gain superiority of all kinds (but particularly financial superiority) over others will become instilled in young minds almost from birth, and educational experiences – whether through schools (if they continue to exist) or other means – will play an important part in reinforcing this point.

This is not to say that such a system or pattern of thinking has been uppermost in the minds of the authors of the green paper or that tendencies along these lines are part of a deliberate strategy. It *can* be said, however, that such a scenario becomes possible – indeed more feasible as the 'portability' thrust is advanced – if the policy changes signalled in the green paper are carried through to their logical conclusion. A 'thinning' of the centre – in this case, the NZQA – is consistent with the (supposed) 'withering' of the state in recent New Zealand history. The NZQA was clearly becoming something of an anomaly in the implementation of New Right social policies. Reducing bureaucratic structures at government and government agency levels has long been a Treasury goal (even though Treasury appears to have been reluctant to turn such thinking back upon itself). 'Getting the state out of people's lives' has been a catch-cry for many in government circles (e.g. Simon Upton, Jenny Shipley, Ruth Richardson, Richard Prebble) under both National and Labour administrations. Some of the apparently generous concessions in the green paper (ostensibly advanced on ethical, epistemological or educational grounds, after listening carefully to criticisms) can thus be seen as supportive of a new phase in the marketisation/privatisation process. The government *wants* to let 'providers' do their own administrative work in managing qualifications – to a far greater extent than the NZQA reforms to date have allowed – because such a stance not only saves money (a point that finds ready admission in the document), but also falls more squarely in line with other enacted or proposed policy planks in the marketisation process.

Education, Ethics and Qualifications Reform

There is a deep division between the NZQA and many university critics over the nature of education. For the NZQA, education is a commodity to be sold by provider institutions (and other organisations) and purchased by individual consumers. For many academics (but by no means all) education is seen as a complex, humanising social learning process with intrinsic as well as extrinsic benefits. The two accounts begin from quite distinct ethical and political positions. The NZQA approach is premised on a business model of the social world, in which private utility-maximising individuals compete for goods and services against others in an ostensibly open marketplace. Against this view, it can be argued that students do not 'consume' education or educational courses, but rather *participate* (with their teachers and their peers) in the learning process. Universities and other institutions are not 'providers' of education, but sites where education might reasonably be expected to take place. Many academics see the teacher–student relationship as a pedagogical one; under the market model of education promoted by the NZQA, where institutions such as universities are expected to operate on the principle of 'user pays', teachers and students exist in a contractual relationship to one another (see Codd, 1995: 8). The commodification of education is not merely linguistically bizarre (imagine, for example, a university teacher speaking of students 'consuming' a philosophy course); it is also utterly dehumanising for both teachers and students. The complexities of the act of knowing are reduced, under the NZQA system, to a series of finite competencies (unit standards), to be stacked one on top of the other as a series of building blocks and traded in an educational marketplace. Knowledge, if it can be said to remain in any meaningful way at all under a unit standards system, comes closed between fixed covers: it is necessarily limited to that which can be specified in advance in outcomes statements. The notion of education involving the open-ended pursuit of knowledge, the results of which cannot be known until the journey is undertaken, disappears.

The NQF certainly gives structure to the process through which students gain qualifications, but it wraps learning within overly restrictive boundaries: all qualifications – if they are to 'count' within the New Zealand education system – must fall within the logic of standardised competencies. In their 1994 response to the NZQA reforms (NZVCC, 1994: 6), the vice-chancellors of New Zealand point to the disintegrative impact of a unit standards methodology upon the coherence of degrees and reinforce the importance of qualities such as intellectual independence and critical thought – neither of which can be adequately understood as measurable skills (p. 14). These sentiments are extended by Codd (1994):

> The assessment of competencies is generally carried out in relation to *minimum* standards of attainment. Standards of competence set 'floors' rather than 'ceilings'. University courses aspire to standards of criticism and judgement leading to excellence rather than competency. A set of competencies can never equate with the manifold range of personal attributes which define the scholar, the scientist, the artist or the educated professional (p. 5).

The NZQA system purports to be a contextless methodology for assessing standards in myriad settings. Given that quality is assessed on the basis of *pre-determined* statements about learning, the framework can theoretically be applied in any geographical location at any institution in any historical period. We would contend, however, that learning is always context-dependent (cf. Codd, 1994: 9; Roberts, 1996a, 1996b, 1996c). The quality of learning in an educative setting can only be assessed when the particulars of that setting have been taken into account. The logic of pre-defined unit standards, however, allows for a clean separation between the assessment of standards and the development (and teaching) of curricula. Codd (1995: 3) argues that this separation of means from ends reflects the instrumental reasoning behind outcomes models of teaching and learning. He continues:

Qualifications Policies and the Marketisation of Higher Education   161

Essentially, this is a technocratic model of the educative process founded
upon a positivist epistemology that asserts a rigid dichotomy between
facts and values, implying that measurement and observation can avoid
the problems of value justification (p. 4).

Measurable people are, potentially at least, manageable people (cf.
Roberts, 1995: 416). The NQF, in attempting to place *all* qualifications
on a single scale, is without doubt one of the most elaborate measuring
mechanisms in New Zealand educational history. For several years the
NZQA, while ostensibly democratic in its consultation with the various
groups affected by the qualifications reforms, occupied a unique and
powerful position in the formation and evaluation of New Zealand
education policy. The Authority set the parameters within which questions
about quality were expected to be addressed, effectively silencing those
who approach matters relating to educational standards from opposing
points of view (cf. Fitzsimons, 1995: 177). This policy process has not,
however, been free of contradictions. The NQF purports to give overall
coherence to assessments about the nature and worth of disparate
qualifications. Yet this goal stands in tension with the very ideology of
'choice' underpinning the development of the new framework. On the
one hand, the NZQA existed (prior to the tertiary education white paper
proposals) as a kind of 'watchdog' over standards – as 'judge and jury'
over *all* qualifications – yet, on the other hand, students were encouraged,
as in any market system, to 'shop around' if they were not satisfied with
one institutional provider, setting their own standards of education in the
process. Student choices about which institution to attend were thus
considered at once both significant and meaningless in determining
educational quality. 'Providers' were expected to compete with one
another to gain student enrolments, potentially.undermining the goal of
upholding standards (where the *number* of students becomes everything):
'quality' here becomes synonymous with 'whatever students prefer' –
for whatever reasons. The NZQA simultaneously supported this equating
of quality with 'student choice' *and* some notion of externally determined
standards (their own Framework) which would, at times, discredit
students' judgements about educational quality.

On the NZQA view of education, the connection between standards
and commitment to educational excellence through the process of

teaching is severed. Students, as consumers of education, choose the institution that best suits their 'needs', and, if they are not happy, look elsewhere. Teachers are made invisible and disempowered in the process. They are held responsible for their failure to hold on to students, and yet they are also divested of any effective responsibility for determining the standards against which student choices about quality might be assessed. This model rests upon an intolerably narrow view of the social world, and of human value and potential. There is, as Codd (1995: 14) notes, 'very little recognition given to the fundamental question that should guide the whole educational enterprise: what kind of human beings do we want our students to become?'. The extension of neoliberal thought into almost all spheres of human life has become so pervasive that it is easy to forget what other philosophical and political positions might have to offer. Critical approaches to education (including, among many other possibilities, Freirean, feminist, Marxist, and various post-structuralist pedagogies), while influential among educational theorists in the tertiary sector, appear to be utterly invisible for those who wield the greatest power over educational decision-making processes. The battle to give recognition to conceptions of education other than those which fall within a narrow 'market' model of society may become more difficult should the new communications and information technologies develop in tandem with a deepening privatisation agenda. The further privatisation of education also has implications for 'quality control' and the monitoring of educational subjects in virtual learning environments. We address these issues in more detail in Chapter 9.

Endnotes

1   All citations and page numbers in this chapter are drawn from a print-out of the Internet version of the green paper: <http://www.mined.govt.nz/data/NQF/paper/htm>

2   We want to continue placing terms such as 'consumers', 'providers' and the like in quotation marks throughout this chapter to signal our unease with applying them to educational contexts. Allowing such terms to become part of the usual flow of the text (i.e. removing the quotation marks) plays a part, we believe, in normalising and legitimating them as part of our educational discourse.

chapter seven

Agendas for Change: Three Visions of Tertiary Education in the 21st Century

It is not coincidental that several OECD countries – the United Kingdom, Australia and New Zealand among them – have recently been engaged in the process of reviewing their tertiary education systems. As we noted in Chapter 2, it is now widely believed that higher education contributes to economic development in a variety of ways: not only in terms of direct improvements in productivity but also through research and development and, in particular, innovation and so-called 'technology transfer'. Recent work in growth theory has concentrated on the importance of 'human capital' and externalities accruing to higher education[1]. Higher education systems provide scientists, engineers and other skilled professionals, who, in turn, help to determine productivity growth. This renewed emphasis on the relationship between higher education and economic growth follows in the wake of nearly fifty years of theorising concerning advanced western economies. In the late sixties both Daniel Bell (1974) and Alain Touraine (1974) began to talk of 'post-industrial societies' where the axial institutions were deemed to be those responsible for the production of knowledge. These ideas were also developed by Fritz Machlup (1962) and Marc Porat (1977), who attempted to measure the growth and contribution of service industries and particularly information industries to the American economy. In the late 1970s and early 1980s, other thinkers, such as the Japanese sociologist and futurist, Yoneji Masuda (1981), construed the post-industrial society as 'the information society', emphasising the magnitude of the changes by pointing to a shift in the nature of production: knowledge and information, he argued, should be seen as the raw materials for the tertiary, quartenary, and quintennial industries of the future in the same way that coal and iron ore were raw materials for secondary industries during the industrial revolution and thereafter.

Theoretical developments based upon notions of the 'post-industrial society', the 'information society', and more recently, the 'information economy' (and 'information superhighway') have also become part of the neoliberal policy agenda. Beginning in the 1980s the world policy institutions – the World Bank, the International Monetary Fund, and the Organisation for Economic Cooperation and Development – encouraged their member countries to adopt a range of structural adjustment policies. These included the abolition of tariffs and subsidies, a floating exchange system, a commitment to 'free' trade, privatisation of key state assets, restructuring and commercialisation of the remaining public sector, and the adoption of a fiscal austerity programme. The effect of this set of neoliberal monetarist policies has been to reinforce existing trends toward globalisation and internationalisation, dismantling trade barriers and eroding national sovereignty. These policies have also created the ideal conditions in which new mega information, communications and media transnational corporations have grown and flourished. They have contributed to the development of a global finance capitalism. These trends have encouraged national governments to focus attention upon trade and competition as the full realities of what it means to participate successfully in the global economy begin to be realised.

In these changed conditions higher education systems become one of the key touchstones for future development and competition: a crucial arena in which these trends, forces and policies meet and criss-cross one another. This chapter compares two visions of tertiary education: the view broadly embraced by the New Zealand Government and the alternative furnished by the Dearing Committee in the United Kingdom. The first, as we have argued in previous chapters, can be described as a neoliberal market model of tertiary education; that is, a consumer-driven system. The second is neatly encapsulated in the Dearing Committee's notion of 'The Learning Society'. The former, driven by the ideology of the New Right, is narrow in its vision and complacent in its expectation that the market will provide all the answers to educational questions. It seeks to obliterate distinctions between education and training, vocational and academic learning, and universities and other tertiary institutions. There is little recognition of the public service functions of universities (their larger cultural and social functions), and the statutory role of the university as critic and conscience of society is undermined. By contrast, the latter is broad in its vision and is strongly committed to the traditional roles and functions played by universities. At the same time, the more expansive vision of 'The Learning Society' recognises the distinctive features of the current historical moment (including the importance of 'information' as a commodity in contemporary economies) and confronts, in a rigorous and investigative manner, the new expectations and challenges facing tertiary educators in the twenty-first century.

In the Introduction and Chapter 1 we drew attention to the similarities between the green and white papers on tertiary education (Ministry of Education, 1997a and 1998 respectively). Having analysed the latter in some detail in Chapter 1, we return in this chapter to the green paper. A comparative analysis allows concerns raised only briefly in the first chapter to be given more extended treatment here. We see the critical points made in this chapter as equally applicable to both the green paper and the white paper. The chapter falls into four parts: the first two sections sketch some of the key features of the tertiary education review green paper and the Dearing Report, while the third addresses some of the pivotal differences between the two documents. We confine the discussion to four issues: the concept of education, resourcing, globalisation and the role of the humanities. Other themes – the role of the new information technologies in tertiary education, for example – have been investigated at length elsewhere (Peters and Roberts, 1998b) and find some elaboration in the last chapter of this book. The fourth section provides a snapshot of one scenario for the future of higher education in this country. We believe that should New Zealand follow the path set out in the leaked Ministry of Education document – and it is possible to see the white paper as another step in this direction – the result will closely resemble the vision conveyed in an appendix to a third major report on tertiary education: the West Committee's policy discussion paper, 'Review of Higher Education Financing and Policy' (West, 1997). The appendix was produced by Global Alliance Limited (1997) for a review of higher education in Australia, but it could just as easily have served as a blueprint for the fully consumer-driven system envisaged, albeit in only superficial detail, by the authors of the leaked Ministry of Education document. We conclude that both statements should be regarded as serious proposals, heralding a radically different, highly marketised and customised educational future.

New Zealand's Tertiary Education Review Green Paper

The tertiary education review green paper (Ministry of Education, 1997a), one part of a wider review process foreshadowed in the National–New Zealand First Coalition Agreement, was made available for public viewing on 11 September 1997. This followed the release, some weeks earlier, of the leaked Ministry of Education document (Ministry of Education, 1997d). The leaked document quickly found its way into the hands of various educational and media groups and prompted a wave of protests from students and tertiary staff across the country. While the proposed move toward greater privatisation in the educational sector was not unexpected, and indeed had been under way for some years, the scale of the changes signalled in the leaked document surprised many people. Here, it seemed, was the neoliberal model of tertiary education in its purest form to date. Vouchers, long lobbied for by powerful business organisations such as the New Zealand Business Roundtable and many politicians in the National governments of 1990–1993 and 1993–1996 (former Minister of Education, Lockwood Smith, was in favour of them, as was Simon Upton, 1987), would be put in place. Traditional governance arrangements would be greatly altered: under a Crown company-type structure the government would appoint all members of the council, which would be reduced in size. In effect, a 'board of directors' business model would be substituted for the current 'democratic' model of goverance. Both faculty and students would lose representation on councils and the vice-chancellor would no longer be a member. Teaching would be separated from research, and competitive bidding for research funds would be encouraged. Government subsidisation of tertiary fees would diminish, with students paying an increasing proportion of the costs associated with their studies.

The green paper (entitled *A Future Tertiary Education Policy for New Zealand*) echoes the focus on fiscal constraint so dominant in the leaked document, but exhibits a different style in discussing significant areas of tertiary policy. Under the guise of an apparent openness, the government – through the Ministry of Education – sets out policy possibilities (on questions of tuition, research, governance, etc.) in the form of options. While there are variations in the number and range of options in different sections, the general format in each case is the same: one option typically shows a close correspondence with the policy direction signalled in the leaked document while the alternatives are more closely aligned with current policies or practices. With only a few exceptions, then, the changes set out in the leaked document remain *possibilities* in the official version of the green paper.

Many of the key features of the green paper are summarised in the 'Overview' accompanying the document. The tertiary education review, it is noted, is 'being undertaken on the assumption that the limited resourcing currently available to the tertiary sector can be used better' (p. 1). The government's expressed aim, through the Ministry, is to evaluate 'the ways in which existing spending can be made more effective – in both achieving higher participation rates and supporting a high-quality, dynamic, and innovative tertiary sector' (p. 1). It is stressed that the proposals advanced in the green paper do not represent a 'final Government position'; the intention is to inform readers of the government's thinking to date and to foster discussion and debate (pp. 1, 8). The 'overview' notes that the white paper to be ublished in 1998 would be informed by both submissions on the green paper and work in other policy areas, including the Employment Strategy, the National Qualifications Framework (see Ministry of Education, 1997c), the review of student support, the Maori Education Strategy and the Teacher Education Review (see Ministry of Education, 1997d).

Beginning from the proposition that New Zealand's 'greatest asset is its people', the green paper summarises the purposes of tertiary education thus:

Tertiary education is central to New Zealand and New Zealanders successfully meeting the challenges of the future. Tertiary education enables personal and professional growth, and contributes significantly to the richness of our society and the lifestyles of New Zealanders. It is central to the future positioning of New Zealand in the global economy, where the competitive advantage of industry and business will depend more on the knowledge, skills, adaptability, and innovation of our workforce and its leaders (p. 1).

The report identifies three major 'forces' expected to shape demands on tertiary education over the next twenty years. First, there is the question of access and the range of people demanding a variety of courses and learning opportunities. Second, tertiary education will become internationalised, reflecting the need for global standards, encouraging relationships between New Zealand and overseas 'providers' and creating a global market. Third, developments in information technology will break down national and international barriers to tertiary education and alter the way it is delivered (p. 2). In this context, the report delineates the following goals for the tertiary sector (p. 3):

- improving opportunities for participation
- improving the participation and achievement of currently under-represented groups
- encouraging high quality qualifications, programmes, and providers
- encouraging value for the students' and the government's financial contribution.

While acknowledging that the tertiary sector has made 'much progress' since the last major set of reforms in 1989, it is noted that 'further improvements need to be made to ensure high quality, innovation, and responsiveness'. The following current policy issues are identified (pp. 3–4):

- better ways of getting subsidies to students
- the need for incentives to keep costs low
- the need to encourage innovation and responsiveness
- the need for more consistent quality

- the need for better information
- the need for improved governance and accountability of tertiary education institutions.

In terms of indicating future directions for reforms, the Ministry focuses on a 'coherent' approach to questions of resourcing, regulation, ownership and governance (p. 4). The green paper canvasses two major choices concerning the resourcing of tuition: 'to share resources across all students irrespective of age or the amount of tertiary education they have already had'; or, 'to allocate to all students a fixed amount of government subsidy for their tertiary education' (p. 5). The second option – a student entitlement or voucher scheme – appears to be the preferred position (as revealed in the leaked document). In terms of the resourcing of research the report identifies two key issues: first, the question of whether all degree providers, or only postgraduate degree providers, should carry out research activities; second, the question of how resources for research might be allocated (p. 6). The Ministry intends to establish a 'minimum quality requirement' (threshold) for tertiary qualifications, programmes and providers through the NQF (p. 7). On matters of governance and accountability, the Ministry aims to encourage an ownership monitoring regime with mandatory reporting on matters of strategic direction and suitable financial performance indicators. The report countenances smaller councils and the possibility of establishing TEIs as 'Public Tertiary Education Institutions', based on the Companies Act 1993 (p. 7). Private training establishments (PTEs) would receive government funding, thus spreading the tertiary tax dollar even more thinly across the sector.

In short, the key areas of tertiary policy covered by the green paper include tuition, research, resourcing, governance, quality and regulation. The general directions signalled in the document were summarised in a submission by the Association of University Staff of New Zealand (1997):

- to endeavour to increase participation in tertiary education and ensure the quality of that education – without increasing public expenditure
- to encourage the expansion of private provision largely by funding

private training establishments at the same rate as public institutions

- to ensure that the system is more heavily driven by individual student choice
- to extend competition in the tertiary education sector rather than develop coordination and planning
- to decrease each individual student's government tuition subsidy, as student participation increases overall
- to place an overly optimistic belief in the benefits of providing information to students – to improve quality, choice and efficiency
- to move away from representative university councils towards business-focused Ministerial appointees operating under legislation based on the Companies Act 1993
- to treat public education institutions as businesses – their assets to be vested in them, valued and required to make a payment to government by way of a capital charge.

The Dearing Report: A Vision of the Learning Society

Higher education is fundamental to the social, economic and cultural health of the nation. It will contribute not only through the intellectual development of students and by equipping them for work, but also by adding to the world's store of knowledge and understanding, fostering culture for its own sake, and promoting the values that characterise higher education: respect for evidence; respect for individuals and their views; and the search for truth. Equally, part of its task will be to accept a duty of care for the wellbeing of our democratic civilisation, based on respect for the individual and respect by the individual for the conventions and laws which provide the basis of a civilised society.

(Dearing, 1997: 1–2)

Carrying the title 'Higher Education in the Learning Society', the Dearing Report (1997) sets out a detailed vision of education and training in the United Kingdom over the next two decades[2]. The Report begins from the proposition that education is 'life enriching and desirable in its own right ... [and] fundamental to the achievement of an improved quality of life in the UK' (p. 1). The Report speaks of the need to promote 'world class' learning and research, and advocates a compact between 'institutions and their staff, students, government, employers and society in general' in working toward this goal. In summarising the future envisaged by the Committee, the Report notes (p. 1) that higher education in the UK will need to:

* encourage and enable all students – whether they demonstrate the highest intellectual potential or whether they have struggled to reach the threshold of higher education – to achieve beyond their expectations
* safeguard the rigour of its awards, ensuring that UK qualifications meet the needs of UK students and have standing throughout the world
* be at the leading edge of world practice in effective learning and teaching
* undertake research that matches the best in the world and make its benefits available to the nation
* ensure that its support for regional and local communities is at least comparable to that provided by higher education in competitor nations
* sustain a culture which demands disciplined thinking, encourages curiosity, challenges existing ideas and generates new ones
* be part of the conscience of a democratic society, founded on respect for the rights of the individual and the responsibilities of the individual to society as a whole
* be explicit and clear in how it goes about its business, be accountable to students and to society, and seek continuously to improve its own performance.

The Report documents trends in higher education in the United Kingdom over the last thirty years, observing that participation rates have increased substantially in that time. Institutions of higher education have maintained their international standing for research while at the same time becoming more efficient and adapting to the changing 'needs' of students. The Report notes that the recent funding cap on growth in undergraduate student numbers has had a deleterious impact on many staff in higher education and acknowledges concerns that 'short term pressures to reduce costs, in conditions of no growth, may damage the intrinsic quality of the learning experience which underpins the standing of UK awards' (p. 2). Several areas for potential improvement in the higher education sector are signalled. These include ensuring comparability in quality standards, improving collaboration between institutions, and maintaining high standards of teaching as well as good quality research (p. 2).

The Report also identifies a number of international trends – increased competition from developing countries with a strong commitment to education and training, the growing importance of knowledge in the new economic order, and probable changes to modes of delivery following the development of new information technologies – all of which can be expected to have a significant bearing on higher education over the next two decades. The challenge facing higher education is to respond to these changes while continuing traditional contributions to culture, citizenship and the values of a civilised society (p. 2). A learning society which synthesises these aims has four main purposes:

- to inspire and enable individuals to develop their capabilities to the highest potential levels throughout life, so that they grow intellectually, are well equipped for work, can contribute effectively to society and achieve personal fulfilment
- to increase knowledge and understanding for their own sake and to foster their application to the benefit of the economy and society
- to serve the needs of an adaptable, sustainable, knowledge-based economy at local, regional and national levels
- to play a major role in shaping a democratic, civilised, inclusive society (p. 3).

The Report predicts that demand for higher education in the United Kingdom will continue to grow and makes a large number of recommendations. These include:

- increasing participation rates for under-represented groups
- placing greater emphasis on enhancing the quality of teaching in higher education
- developing clear outcomes statements for different programmes of study
- boosting research funding via a range of government initiatives
- providing stronger government support for work in the arts and the humanities

- encouraging interdisciplinary and collaborative academic activities
- providing all students with access to networked desktop and portable computers within the next decade
- reviewing pay, conditions of service and policies of staff development
- according further education colleges priority in sub-degree provisions and halting the growth of degree level qualifications in these institutions
- indexing government support for student living costs against movements in prices and earnings
- increasing, over the long term, public spending on higher education in line with the growth in Gross Domestic Product
- removing disincentives for part-time learning
- making government contributions to tuition costs contingent upon income
- implementing a system requiring students to make a flat rate contribution of around 25% of the average cost of higher education tuition (subject to a range of constraints)
- considering alternative approaches to national accounting to allow the repayable part of loans and grants to students to be treated differently
- establishing a UK-wide independent advisory committee for assessing the state of higher education after five years (and subsequently every ten years).

The authors of the Report admit that some of their recommendations will require substantial developmental work before they can be implemented, and express their concern to ensure that organisations are not overburdened in having to complete too many tasks at once. There is, however, 'an immediate short-term problem with the funding of higher education' (p. 18). If this is not addressed by the government, the Report claims, 'there is a real danger that some institutions will be severely damaged and that others will take unilateral action, for example through the introduction of supplementary fees, which make it impossible for our long-term vision to be realised' (p. 19). The Report draws attention to the need to reward staff in higher education for their achievements, while also encouraging institutions of higher education to continue responding to national and international challenges. The summary of recommendations concludes on an optimistic note:

We know, from all the contacts we have had in our work, that the value and importance of higher education is widely recognised. We also know that those within higher education are committed to its wellbeing and are willing to embrace change. If all that good will, energy and professionalism can be focused on the developments proposed in this report, we are convinced that UK higher education will match the best in the world over the next 20 years (p. 19).

A Critical Comparison

The differences between the Dearing Report and the New Zealand tertiary education review green paper are evident not only in the scope of the reviews and their terms of reference, but also in terms of their recognition of the wider social, cultural and historical context(s) for higher education. The Dearing review was wide in its scope and was committed to a democratic policy process. The New Zealand tertiary education review (of which the green paper is a part), by contrast, has been largely an officials-driven process. Consultation has been sporadic and often at the behest of 'stakeholders' (this is the Ministry's term). The green paper only briefly mentions 'The Future Context'. The overwhelming concerns are those driven by the logic of efficiency: by the desire to extract greater value from the government's investment in higher education. Some of the principles on which the Dearing Committee based its deliberations are similar to those underpinning the green paper. There is talk, in both cases, about maximising participation, enhancing student choice, maintaining degree standards, improving the effectiveness of teaching and learning, being responsive to employment needs, and promoting fairness in student support. However, the Dearing Committee was concerned not only with 'cost-effectiveness' but also questions pertaining to intellectual culture, tradition, the spirit of critical inquiry, the importance of the humanities, the contribution that higher education makes to moral and spiritual life and the upholding of democracy. These dimensions of higher education barely warrant a mention in the green paper. While there are many important differences between the two documents, we have selected four for more detailed discussion below.

The Concept of Education

The Dearing Report and the green paper are underpinned by quite different concepts of education. The former, whatever one might say about its vision, at least makes a 'philosophical' attempt to place education at the centre of its policy proposals. In the Dearing Report, education is fundamental to the fabric of a new society – and not simply an adjunct to the economy. The society of the future for the Dearing Committee is one committed to learning. The Dearing Report explores, in a rigorous manner, the relationship between learning and social, cultural and economic wellbeing. The green paper, on the other hand, is informed by what we see as an impoverished view of education. As earlier chapters in this book have argued, there has been a relentless move in recent years to make the New Zealand tertiary education system conform to the rules of the market. The green paper does not disrupt this trend. Education, in a marketised system, becomes a *commodity* to be sold, traded and purchased. 'Education', in this view, cannot be distinguished from any other service or product in the marketplace – it has an exchange value like everything else. The notion of education becoming a *public* good disappears here; education becomes fully privatised and individualised in a marketised, consumer-driven system.

Of course, once a market model has been embraced, all subsequent policy questions – concerning, for instance, the resourcing of tuition, research, governance and accountability – have ready answers. These answers are based on the principle of individual consumers making continuous choices among competing providers, products and services with a view to maximising their own interests. A market model cannot address or answer questions that go beyond the logic of individual self-interest. The economic sphere within which this model operates is narrow: questions about the externalities of higher education are avoided. Similarly, traditional questions about the cultural, social and spiritual dimensions of education and the intrinsic benefits of learning (for both individuals and groups) disappear. There is, in a fully consumer-driven system, no longer any need to draw distinctions between different modes or forms of education – e.g. 'vocational' as distinguished from 'academic' – as all activity within the tertiary sphere can ultimately be reduced to a series of transactions between 'providers' and 'consumers'. In all cases, the implied contract is the same: students pay fees for courses, while institutions (or other tertiary organisations) discharge their obligations in providing what the students have paid for. There is no substantive difference between 'education' and 'training' in such circumstances; these words simply provide different ways of describing (perhaps marketing) the exchange process.

Resourcing

Governments in many Western countries often claim that they face resourcing demands for the tertiary sector which cannot or ought not to be satisfied entirely from public expenditure. There are a number of ways of responding to this dilemma. It might be argued that tertiary education can be fully funded via taxation. The question is whether it is politically viable to do so and, related to this, whether such a system is efficient and just. The notion of covering all tertiary education costs through taxation is not supported in either the Dearing Report or the green paper, where two rather different directions are signalled. One route – implied in the green paper and made explicit in the earlier leaked document – involves the introduction of parallel forms of privatisation in the state sector. One dimension of this change is the move toward funding individuals through vouchers (or entitlements) rather than bulk-funding institutions. In this way the system becomes more fully consumer-oriented: tax dollars are shifted from traditional publicly funded institutions to students, and, indirectly, to a range of new private education and training establishments. Consistent with this process, the green paper talks of the need for providing incentives to allow private educational establishments and organisations to flourish.

We might expect to see further contracting out of educational services and a push to make the resourcing of research more dependent on external agencies. Both of these appear as real possibilities in the leaked document and neither are ruled out by the green paper. The white paper makes this move to a contractual environment quite explicit, and there has been some support for greater contestability by members of the New Zealand academic community. Boston (1997a; 1997b), for example, favours a mix of student-driven funding and competitive bidding (with a stronger emphasis on the latter) for research monies. Against the radical transformation implied by the green paper, he argues a case for maintaining a modified version of the present bulk-funding regime for tertiary education. Changes, he suggests, might include 'a reduction in the number of funding categories, the introduction of multi-year funding arrangements, ... opportunities for private providers to have greater access to public funds', and the abandonment of 'study-right/non-study-right funding distinctions' (p. 23).

In the Dearing Report, the overall aim is to preserve the nature of public institutions. Universities are seen as having a cultural heritage, a public-service function, and a spiritual dimension. These features of higher education, the Report suggests, should be explicitly recognised, actively maintained and continuously enhanced. The Report speaks of the need to encourage cooperation, rather than competition, between state institutions, businesses and community groups. Limited privatisation – in the service of upholding a rich educational, cultural and spiritual life within a learning society, rather than as an end in itself – is favoured. Entitlement systems are not excluded from consideration, but if the other recommendations of the Dearing Report were to be enacted, the overall context for the introduction of vouchers would differ markedly from the marketised environment of which such schemes would be a part in New Zealand. In the United Kingdom, voucher schemes would (if the Dearing Committee's findings were taken seriously) be subject to, rather than inherently at odds with, a range of other traditional values and practices in higher education.

Globalisation

A clear difference between the two documents is evident on the issue of globalisation. The green paper contains nothing more than occasional references to living in a rapidly changing world and to positioning New Zealand within the global economy; yet the neoliberal policy paradigm represents a commitment to internationalisation of education as a trading commodity and export. Discussion of global issues in the green paper is couched within the language of competition. Various forms of regulation (of quality, competition and ownership monitoring, for example) will still be present, but pressures to seek additional funding from a range of sources will increase for many institutions and organisations. It seems likely that overseas educational institutions and corporations will increasingly vie with local 'providers' for student dollars. The white paper positively encourages this form of overseas investment by allowing government funding for all private education organisations meeting quality assurance criteria. Given such circumstances, the danger of eroding cultural traditions and resources (including intellectual property) in Aotearoa/New Zealand become very real. Already New Zealand is a signatory to the General Agreement on Trade in Services (GATS). The parameters within which such agreements operate are, as Jane Kelsey (1997) has demonstrated, disturbingly narrow:

> There is no place in this new paradigm for the nation-building function of universities; no virtue in an educated population of graduates and academics who are committed to the society which invested in them; no inherent value in education and knowledge which is not highly priced in today's commercial market; no purpose in academic contributions to research, policy, legislation and public debate; no need for expert analysis and public critique which is free from party political and commercial-vested interest; no obligation to comply with the Treaty. These become casualties of the global educational marketplace (pp. 85–86).

'Taken to its logical conclusion,' Kelsey continues, the GATS could produce:

> ... a global education system run by trans-national education corporations with branches in numerous countries, using uniform computerised teaching modules, based on one dominant value-structure and perspective, serviced by a small mobile staff who move freely between countries, which compete with each other for the education market in each country within which they operate (pp. 86–87).

The Dearing Report recognises that if the United Kingdom is to participate successfully in increasingly competitive international markets, then it must invest both in the education and training of its graduates and in its research base. This acknowledgement is offset, however, by a commitment to maintaining and enhancing the United Kingdom's distinctive cultural heritage and identity within the world order. Higher education is seen as a major contributor to local, regional and economic growth and regeneration. While recognising the fact that higher education is an important 'export' in its own right, the Dearing Report also wants to protect the defining elements of its own national system of higher education. The Dearing Committee is, in other words, cautious about opening the system up to full international competition. As the report notes,

> Through scholarship and research higher education provides a national resource of knowledge and expertise for the benefit of our international competitiveness and quality of life, and provides a basis for responding to economic and social change through innovation and lifelong learning (p. xx).

The Role of the Humanities

In the green paper there is no explicit recognition of the role of the humanities and arts, or indeed, of the importance of research per se[3] (this weakness has not been remedied in the white paper). The discussion is limited to issues of resourcing and questions about whether all degree 'providers' should carry out research. In terms of the current funding system for research, the arts and humanities in New Zealand have suffered in comparison to the sciences and technology which together are seen as providing the engine for economic growth. Only through the recent establishment of the Marsden Fund have the humanities found a state-funded avenue for supporting large-scale research projects. Competition for Marsden grants is intense, with only about a tenth of those submitted receiving support. The current funding categories in the science policy regime exclude funding for humanities research. Under the severely restricted view of education implied by a market model, both the intrinsic and the instrumental benefits of the arts and humanities in post-industrial societies tend to be ignored.

By comparison, underlying the Dearing Report is an explicit recognition of the role of the arts and humanities in contributing both to economic growth and cultural development. The third appendix to the Report (a paper entitled 'The Need to Invest in Research in Humanities and Arts') recognises, for instance, that the humanities and arts enhance cultural, civic and social experiences while also contributing to the aesthetic quality of life. The paper argues that research in the humanities and arts has been unduly neglected, and that such research contributes to national prosperity and a higher quality of life. Study in the humanities is seen as leading to lifelong benefits for individuals, an enhancement of the mind, and greater access to national and international culture. Humanities graduates, the paper suggests, actively contribute to the construction and preservation of a culturally rich society.

In addition, the paper identifies a number of direct economic benefits – particularly in the rapidly expanding tourism, heritage and leisure industries – associated with work in the humanities. The humanities and arts contribute directly to the maintenance and transmission of different cultural traditions through research in and management of libraries, galleries, museums and national monuments. Graduates in the arts and humanities play a significant part in preserving and interpreting heritage in all its forms: 'from buildings and the landscape to books, manuscripts, paintings, sculpture, music and other media'. The paper argues that such graduates will provide the 'research and administrative base for a range of increasing opportunities for leisure, in museums, galleries, libraries, theatres, television and film production companies and concert halls'. The arts and the humanities are also important in the teaching and learning of English, computation linguistics and translation work. They already have a very significant and direct role to play in the publishing industry and will, in the future, contribute to the major export business represented by education and training (estimated to be worth £7 billion per year in the UK).

The University: Hallowed or Hollowed-Out?

While there are many other critical contrasts between the Dearing Report and New Zealand's tertiary review green paper, the points of difference identified and discussed above should give some indication of what might be at stake for higher education in the two countries. The Dearing Report acknowledges that in the United Kingdom, as elsewhere in the Western world, universities must adapt to changing circumstances, keep up with advancements in technology, and align (some of) their teaching and research functions with the expressed needs of employers and industry groups. The Report also recognises, however, that a university is more than a commercial enterprise. There is a sensitivity to – indeed, an overt emphasis upon – the longstanding traditions of scholarship within the humanities, the role of the university in promoting social criticism and debate, and the value of higher education for cultural enrichment. The green paper is premised upon a view of education tied to the imperatives of the market. If the vision of higher education implied by the green paper (and subsequently reinforced by the white paper) becomes a reality, research and teaching in the humanities will only survive if it can be reconfigured along utilitarian lines. With a decline in real terms in state spending on universities, the impediments to learning 'for its own sake' will be substantial. Higher education will become a terrain for vigorous international competition as 'providers' of all kinds seek to secure student dollars.

It has been necessary to speak of an *implied* vision for higher education in the green paper, for, unlike the Dearing Report with its well developed notion of 'The Learning Society', the New Zealand document is lacking in detail on many pivotal policy areas. (The white paper is even more sparing in its attention to crucial issues facing the tertiary sector.) In considering how such a skeletal framework for a fully consumer-driven, marketised system of tertiary education might be fleshed out in practice, we believe much might be gained from examining a policy document produced for the Australian review of higher education. The document in question is an appendix to the West Committee's policy discussion paper 'Review of Higher Education Financing and Policy', released in late November 1997. In our view, the appendix brings (if unintentionally) many of the elements of a neoliberal view of education into clear focus. It conveys what we regard as a deeply distressing vision of higher education – a vision so vivid that critique does not seem necessary. The appendix, in short, serves as *its own critique* – at least when viewed alongside the alternative vision developed in the Dearing Report – and will be summarised below as an example of what the future might hold for New Zealand if current policy trends continue. The appendix spells out the end of the era of state planning – in essence the end of a public tertiary education system – and argues that the emerging system will be consumer driven, much more diversified, and part of the global information economy. In an almost total antithesis to the values of the existing system, the system emerging under the dual pressures of the international market and the new communications and information technologies will be one in which highly specialised, internationally-oriented, privatised, university corporations compete to deliver flexible programmes anywhere in the world. Our comments on the appendix will be preceded by a brief overview of the main discussion paper in the West review of higher education.

The discussion paper itself is unexceptional in many ways. It begins with a preface by Roderick West, the Chair of the Higher Education Review, who asserts two 'certainties': first, 'the twenty-first century will mark the era of tertiary education and lifelong education for everybody' and, second, there are 'extraordinary possibilities in the provision of education through ever expanding technological advance'. These two elements dictate the approach to financing and policy. The paper spells out a vision for 'learning for life', a seamless tertiary education environment with commitments to building a culture of learning, civic values, scholarship, preparing graduates, advancing knowledge and skills, 'developing the industry', and equity. The paper then lists the principles on which the future should be built:

- enhancing access – a commitment to universal access
- maximising study options by fostering a direct relationship between the student and provider and emphasising student choice
- promoting outcome-based assessment of quality and accountability to students and the taxpayer
- maximising the benefits of research in terms of a national strategy
- cost-effectiveness of public funding and orientation to the community's needs
- fair levels of private contribution.

In the context of identifying forces for change the paper directs its attention to the 'digital revolution'. The changes wrought by the digital revolution will be so pervasive, the paper maintains, that universities will be forced to rethink fundamentally every aspect of the way in which they provide their services. The increasingly competitive environment that the new technologies will bring will encourage universities to respond to the following questions:

- How can they protect their student numbers against local and international competition?
- Can they afford to develop individual courses and course materials when better quality and less expensive materials could be developed by cooperative action?
- Can they afford to build and maintain expensive support services, such as library services, when better and cheaper services could be provided through collective action?
- Can they afford to continue to invest in large-scale 'bricks and mortar' infrastructure ... when new technologies offer cheaper and less expensive means of communicating information to large numbers of people?
- Should they seek to meet all educational needs of students ... or should they focus their energies on areas of greatest expertise, and, therefore, advantage?

The paper goes on to discuss the strengths and weaknesses of the current system before identifying issues and options for the future. The paper expresses the Committee's strong preference for a demand driven approach to tertiary education policy and financing; this means, of course, a student-centred funding model where students will have access to a 'lifetime entitlement' and to income contingent loans. A student-centred funding model is seen to offer greater flexibility, encourage high quality learning and promote equity. This would occur in a largely deregulated environment for providers where greater incentives are provided for more private investment. The Committee also indicates that current university governance structures are not appropriate for a more competitive environment.

The real vision for the discussion paper is provided in the first of the commissioned papers: 'Australian Higher Education in the Era of Mass Customisation' (Appendix 11) by Global Alliance Limited. Global Alliance Limited (GAL) is a Tokyo-based investment bank established in 1995. GAL specialises in providing investment and corporate advisory services, mainly to Japanese and Taiwanese companies, and especially in relation to the information technology sector. GAL has investments on its own account in Internet service providers and related companies.

Its vision is stark and uncompromising: the GAL report proclaims both the end of 'the era of homogeneity' under state planning and the beginning of another era which will be consumer-oriented, more diversified and exposed to international competition. The remnants of an era of state planning show that while costs of production are world competitive, productivity incentives are poor and capital management requires reform. The existing providers are protected in the Australian domestic market but not for too much longer.

The report identifies the following forces for change: a reduction in public subsidies and increasing fees, the associated shift of power to the consumer, increasing international competitive exposure, and changes in the technology of production and consumption. Computers will lower costs of marketing and the provision of customer services while at the same time promoting greater access to learning and enhancing the quality of the learning experience. Back-end systems will be automated and learning systems will increasingly apply computer technologies to allow courses to be delivered over the Web. The effects of these forces will lead to 'the hollowing out of the university'. The report is worth quoting at some length here:

> The vertically integrated university is a product of brand image, government policy, history and historical economies of scale in support services. If government policy is no longer biased in favour of this form, and technology liberates providers from one location, then we would expect to see new forms arising such as multiple outlet vertically integrate specialist schools and web based universities .... Specialist service providers, such as testing companies and courseware developers will arise, as will superstar teachers who are not tied to any one university. Many universities will become marketing and production coordinators or systems integrators. They will no longer all be vertically integrated education version of the 1929 Ford assembly plant in Detroit (p. 12).

The overall result of the effects of these combined forces of changes will be an increased segmentation of markets, together with further specialisation and customisation in the provision of educational programmes. The new university system will take the form of one of a series of possible business models: a low-cost producer university, the Asian middle-class web university, the 'Harvard in Australia' university, or a world specialist school university.

Concluding Remarks

GAL's report provides the naked neoliberal underbelly for the West Committee's more muted and 'humanist' student-centred funding model. It is a vision that in all its starkness spells out 'the new world order' of global competition for national systems of higher education. It certainly seems consistent with the principles and preferred options underlying New Zealand's green and white papers. Criticisms can be made of both the substance of the green paper and the process associated with its production. The Dearing Report is the product of a very comprehensive and systematic review of higher education policies in the United Kingdom, undertaken by an independent committee of high calibre, over a reasonably lengthy period of time. The Dearing Committee's work was very well funded. By comparison, the New Zealand's tertiary review green paper was prepared within six months by a handful of staff in the Ministry of Education, and was not nearly as ambitious in its scope, research orientation, or consultation with specialists in the higher education sector. The contrasts between the two reports can be explained in part by the significant differences in the size and resources of the two countries. It might be argued that it would be very difficult in New Zealand to mount a review of similar magnitude to that conducted by the Dearing Committee; yet the limits of the green paper (and white paper) are also deeply ideological in nature. Decisions about tertiary education in New Zealand must be seen in the light of a wider set of policy reforms: in particular, the aggressive programme of privatisation mounted by successive governments over the past decade, underpinned by an economic philosophy of market liberalism and an ethic of competitive individualism. More extensive dialogue with the groups most affected by possible changes in tertiary education *was* possible, and could have contributed to a much more thorough treatment of many policy issues glossed over in the green paper.

The GAL scenario is both technologically determined and market-driven. Local or national markets, the GAL authors would have us believe, must give way to international competition. Such assumptions must be contested. Political sovereignty allows us to elect or reject governments on the basis of their economic and social policies. The concept of 'The Learning Society' certainly captures the commitment to higher and adult education, and the need for 'perpetual retraining' that lies at the heart of visions of the 'postindustrial' or 'knowledge society'. The concept also fulfils ideological purposes: it may simply indicate a softer and more human face to a neoliberal paradigm of globalisation that threatens to turn universities into service and training centres for the world's transnational corporations. At a cultural level, 'The Learning Society' does seem to encapsulate a desire both to preserve a heritage and to respect the institutional autonomy of universities. Yet in the final analysis, if the notion of 'The Learning Society' is predicated upon globalisation as a form of world economic integration, then the autonomy of the cultural sphere will be eroded and statements as to its preservation will amount merely to pious wishes.

Endnotes

[1] See the appendix on externalities in higher education in Dearing (1997). For a critical examination of human capital theory and education, see Fitzsimons and Peters (1994).

[2] All page numbers in references to the Dearing Report are from a printout of the Internet version of the document:
<http://www.leeds.ac.uk/educol/ncihe/docsinde.htm>

[3] For further discussion of the humanities and tertiary education reform in New Zealand, see Humanities Society of New Zealand (1997) and Opie (1995).

chapter eight

The Crisis of the University and the Future of Scholarly Life

The terms 'education' and 'crisis' often seem to go together. From the perceived crisis in the teaching of science and technology in the West (and in the United States in particular) following the launching of Sputnik by the Russians in the late 1950s, through perpetual shortages of funds and the under- or over-supply of teachers, to claims that standards are slipping and morals declining, educational institutions seem to have experienced serious difficulties for much of the present century.

Higher education has been especially prone to 'crisis talk', as witnessed by the titles of numerous books on the subject over the years. A sampling from the past decade can easily create the impression of a very dire situation indeed: *The Closing of the American Mind* (Bloom, 1988); *Profscam: Professors and the Demise of Higher Education* (Sykes, 1988); *The Moral Collapse of the University: Professionalism, Purity, and Alienation* (Wilshire, 1990); *Killing the Spirit* (Smith, 1990); *Illiberal Education: The Politics of Race and Sex on Campus* (D'Souza, 1991); *Education Without Impact: How our Universities Fail the Young* (Douglas, 1992); *Higher Education under Fire* (Berube and Nelson, 1995); *Why our Universities are Failing: Crisis in the*

Clever Country (Maslen and Slattery, 1994); *The University in Ruins* (Readings, 1996); *The Twilight of Common Dreams: Why America is Wracked by Culture Wars* (Gitlin, 1995); and *Will Teach for Food: Academic Labor in Crisis* (Nelson, 1997).

Financial constraints have almost always been perceived as an impediment to the full development of higher educational programmes, and to this day the question of money – how to avoid spending too much of it, and how to acquire more – remains uppermost in many minds when references to crises the tertiary sector are made. But over the last ten years, the prevailing concern with fiscal matters has been joined by talk of crises in the humanities, scholarly publishing, the nature of university teaching, conditions of employment, the scope and purpose of the curriculum, and the governance of institutions. In countries dominated by economic and social policies grounded in neoliberal political assumptions, a new language has been invented to describe a series of moves designed to change institutional academic profiles and seriously erode conditions of work. Thus, sackings and redundancies have been dressed up as 'career change opportunities', enforced early retirements have been accompanied by 'golden handshakes' that might better have been described as 'cold shoves', and the casualisation of academic labour has been portrayed in terms of a healthy 'flexibility' in industrial relations.

This chapter addresses some of the implications of neoliberal policies for academic and student life. We advance a series of predictions based on a critical reading of key Ministry of Education policy documents and reflections on trends in tertiary education reform to date. We concentrate on three related themes: the emergence of the perpetually choosing student; changes in conditions of work for university employees; and the reconfiguration of academic priorities in the age of the market. The chapter concludes with a call for collective action against further marketisation in the tertiary sector.

The Perpetually Choosing Student (in a Competitive World)

If the current programme of marketisation in tertiary education continues apace, a new version of the goliards (wandering scholars) of old will emerge: students will become roving consumers, continually seeking out the best value for their educational dollars. The goal of fostering student choice – sometimes stated explicitly, sometimes dressed up in the language of 'needs' or 'consumer preferences' – has, as we have noted in earlier chapters, become a key element in the New Zealand government's educational reform programme. Institutions, should they survive at all, will be seen less as repositories of knowledge and more as providers of services. Academics, likewise, will no longer be seen as (merely) bearers of intellectual wisdom but as sellers of products. For many involved in educational enterprises, there will be a loss of a strong sense of scholarly and disciplinary traditions. These will be replaced, to an increasing degree, by a focus on the 'here and now', by a desire for the 'quick fix' or the 'packaged solution'. Indeed, there are already signs – prevalent in both popular youth culture and the ideology of the New Right – of an emerging distaste (perhaps even a repugnance) for things past. Students' relationships with their peers (as well as their teachers) will change. Those who wish to foster a spirit of cooperation, camaraderie and collectivity will find stiff resistance in the competitive and individualistic climate of a marketised system.

The five key policy documents discussed in earlier chapters (Ministry of Education, 1997a, 1997b, 1997c, 1997d, 1998) all give evidence of a move toward a more competitive tertiary environment. There is a widespread belief among government officials that greater competition between tertiary institutions and organisations leads directly to both cost reductions and improvements in educational quality. The leaked Ministry of Education document (1997d) is unequivocal on this point:

> Increasing the level of competition between tertiary providers by allowing private providers to compete for resources on an equal basis to public providers should place downward pressure on prices. This competition would also be enhanced by requiring information from providers so that students have more information on which to compare course costs (p. 4).

Increased competition would 'enhance the quality and relevance of tertiary education'. The aim would be to set up a position of what the Ministry calls 'competitive neutrality', where students would be given an entitlement (tertiary education voucher) to use as they see fit. This, Ministry of Education officials believe, would encourage institutions to 'more readily respond to the educational needs of students through diversification and specialisation' (p. 4).

The reference to 'needs' finds expression elsewhere. The green paper on qualifications reform (Ministry of Education, 1997b), for example, argues that students and employers should play a major role in determining what counts as quality in certificates, degrees and diplomas. Wishing to avoid a process in which decisions about quality rest entirely or predominantly with 'providers' (institutions and other tertiary education organisations), the Ministry 'focuses on the value of qualifications to users' (p. 18). Qualifications, it is stressed, 'need to match employers' and labour market requirements as closely as possible, and be accessible to the widest possible range of students' (p. 4). This is because '[m]ore people with higher and more relevant skills and knowledge are critical to our economic and social success' (p. 8). A National Qualifications Framework, it is believed, will play a vital role in an education system 'which will serve employers' and students' needs into the twenty-first century' (p. 8). The rationale behind this thinking is clear:

> If New Zealand is to prosper, we must be internationally competitive. We must produce goods and services which not only measure up against imports, but which achieve their share of world markets. With limited economic power and physical resources, we must look to the skills and knowledge of our people to feed innovation and improvements in productivity. In a world marked by rapid technological change, intellectual skills will increasingly command a premium over manual ones (p. 8)[1].

To some extent this transformation in the concept of quality reflects a wider move, in New Zealand and elsewhere, to (supposedly) 'student-centred' curricula and systems of learning. The universities, more than any other institutions in the tertiary sector, have often been singled out as lacking in their attention to student needs. Traces of this line of thinking can be detected in numerous statements by business leaders, politicians, bureaucrats, and newspaper commentators on university teaching. The following passage from a recent OECD report on tertiary education in New Zealand encapsulates some of the concerns commonly expressed. Arguing that a strong research culture ought not to override the importance of undergraduate teaching in universities, the authors of the report call for deeper contemplation on:

> ... the fundamentals of student learning; the kinds of things undergraduates need to know and be able to do as citizens, economic actors and individuals (as distinct, for example, from the latest trend or fashion in conceptions of the subject); the relationships among the different subjects or topics students are studying both horizontally and vertically; contemporary and likely future uses and applications of what is being learned; and the conditions in which learning is occurring.
>
> (OECD, 1997a: 29)

On the basis of their observations, the OECD investigators conclude that neither the universities themselves nor the quality assurance procedures in the New Zealand tertiary education system allow sufficient attention to be paid to this 'broad repertoire of student-centred needs' (p. 29). Later in the report it is noted that improvements in quality – 'an appropriate goal' – ought to be 'geared to client needs and expectations' (p. 37). For the OECD evaluators, the primary 'client' in tertiary transactions is the student, but the 'needs' of other groups – e.g. employers – also need to be taken into account. While drawing attention to a number of problematic elements of the reform process in New Zealand, the OECD reviewers nonetheless express broad support for a 'demand (or consumer) driven' system of education.

With successive (or sudden) moves toward full privatisation of the tertiary sector, the reality of growing debt levels will begin to bite. The leaked Ministry of Education document (1997d) foreshadows further cuts in government spending on tertiary education:

> Under the resourcing system proposed, it will not be possible to ensure that students receive a subsidy of 75% of costs for all courses they take because of the need to limit the total student entitlement as the primary means of rationing resources (p. 6).

The government is convinced that greater competition between tertiary 'providers' will force institutions to make the efficiency gains necessary to keep fees at reasonable levels. Ministry of Education officials assert (without evidence) that the increasing involvement of private organisations in tertiary education has already improved student decisions (1997d: 3). The argument is that a reduction in the funds paid directly from the government to tertiary institutions will maintain tuition fees at competitive rates. The overt call for entitlements (vouchers) in the leaked document is advanced in more veiled terms in the tertiary education review green paper with an expressed preference that resources 'follow students'. In the white paper the veil is lifted and an entitlement system is again explicitly supported. Such a system is favoured because at present, tertiary education institutions have 'relatively weak incentives to minimise tuition costs'. Current research funding arrangements, with their 'poor accountability and inadequate quality assurance', also require revision (Ministry of Education, 1997a, Overview: 4)[2]. A similar position on the benefits of privatisation in the tertiary sector has been advanced by the Education Forum (1998).

Concerns over mounting student debt will be magnified by the insecurity of the employment market, with short-term, part-time, contract-based, 'flexible' positions taking the place of permanent, secure, award-based jobs. Students will become increasingly reliant upon their parents or other 'benefactors' (philanthropy is making something of a comeback as the state progressively reduces its commitment to welfare of all kinds) in obtaining tertiary qualifications. This dependency will bring its own problems, not least of which will be a simmering culture of resentment as students compare their own difficult financial situation with the prosperity and generous state provisions enjoyed by those responsible for the new order.

We might expect to see (further) changes in patterns of course selection. Utilitarian criteria (based on prospects for income generation at the completion of a programme) will be uppermost in many minds. The idea of pursuing knowledge for its own sake, or of engaging in a programme of study given a passion for learning in a particular subject area, will seem quaint – if it is remembered at all. The Minister of Education observes in his Foreword to the white paper that post-compulsory education and training will become increasingly necessary 'to secure career paths and quality of life and to achieve an equitable, cohesive, and culturally dynamic society in which all members can fully participate' (Creech, 1998: 2). In the tertiary education review green paper a similar claim is made: tertiary education, he says, 'plays a vital role in the intellectual advancement and fulfilment of individuals, in the development of creative, socially cohesive communities, and in the pursuit of learning for personal interest' (Creech, 1997b: 3). Yet, neither the white paper nor the green paper have much to say about how or why these benefits might be nurtured and enhanced. The notion of supporting study in the humanities and the arts as part of a wider process of national cultural enrichment is utterly out of place with the heavy emphasis on meeting the 'needs' of employers and international economic competition[3]. In a system driven by these imperatives, students with limited financial resources will often be, in effect, forced to abandon areas of study and human endeavour to which they might otherwise make a major contribution. In such cases, student choices might be considered 'autonomous', but could hardly be deemed 'free'. Wealthy students or, to be more precise, students willing to accept assistance from their wealthy families, will be less constrained, but may choose to follow profitable degree paths anyway given the overwhelming pressure to conceive all human activity in commercial terms.

Academics will also be increasingly encouraged, perhaps 'forced', to alter courses and teaching styles to better respond to perceived student needs. As we have noted in earlier chapters, talk of 'needs' has been a prominent feature of the policy landscape in New Zealand over the past decade. The (mis)use of this term, however, dates to much earlier than this, as the work of educational philosophers such as Richard Dearden in the 1960s showed. In New Zealand, references to 'needs' can now be found at all levels of the policy-making and policy-implementation process. Statements about serving the needs of particular groups appear in curriculum documents, school charters and political speeches. What counts as a 'need' in such discourses might better be termed an 'expressed (and sometimes justified) *want*'. The connection with the language of 'choice' is clear (and circular): 'needs' are *generated* by the choices 'consumers' (citizens) make about what is important to them. In choosing between competing on-line 'providers' of education, then, students will take their personal 'needs' into account, but these 'needs' are themselves simply choices about what matters to them (at that time, given their goals and aspirations). What matters to them will, however, be determined in (large) part by what they have previously encountered or experienced, what they presently know, who they work and/or live with, and so on. Preferences, including those expressed in choices about courses in cyberspace, thus have the *appearance* of being both 'free' and based on 'need', yet the very idea that such choices *could* be free and needs-based is itself the reflection of an ideological position and a corresponding set of material practices (Roberts, 1997d).

Changing Conditions of Work

We predict that over the next few years an increase in the 'casualisation' and exploitation of academic labour in universities and other tertiary institutions will become evident. This process, already established in countries such as the United States (see Shumar, 1997; Nelson, 1997) and well under way in New Zealand, involves the widespread use of fixed-term lecturing appointments and the development of a growing army of tutors in poorly paid, teaching-only jobs. In the longer term, *all* university employees may move on to short-term contracts. Tenure, once seen as an essential if university employees were to exercise academic freedom without fear of losing their jobs, is now often portrayed as inimical to the spirit of the times. Flexible specialisation, the dominant regime of capitalist production in the latter part of this century, positively demands an easily disposable, infinitely malleable, unsettled, non-unionised workforce.

Criticisms of tenure are often dressed up in the language of accountability. Employees should, supporters of the new regime claim, be accountable to those who pay their wages. The fact that in the case of public universities it is taxpayers who must ultimately foot (much of) the bill simply adds grist to the critics' mill. In the white paper readers are reminded of the need to protect the investment made by taxpayers and students in tertiary education (Ministry of Education, 1998: 55). Similarly, in the tertiary education review green paper we are told that 'no government will have unlimited resources' and that '[g]reater public spending on tertiary education would need to be considered in relation to where the tax burden falls' (Ministry of Education, 1997a: 14–15). Few would disagree that care needs to be taken in decisions about how money devoted to tertiary education is to spent. Yet such statements also serve as subtle expressions of a view conveyed in rather less moderate terms by many Treasury officials and influential business people. Tenure and other forms of permanent employment, it is argued, allow people to 'relax', 'slack off' and say or do outrageous things without fear of being sacked. What is needed, the critics suggest, is 'a more commercial set of operating arrangements' (Ministry of Education, 1997d: 4), with greater 'flexibility' and 'accountability'. 'Flexible' working conditions, it is believed, allow productive workers, high achievers, and innovative thinkers to flourish while also leaving room for the easy removal of 'dead wood' and 'trouble-makers' from the system. The rules here are very much those of the business world. Those who fail to espouse the new rhetoric, refuse to be 'team players', or show a lack of 'corporate spirit' can be dropped just as quickly and painlessly as others who show the *wrong kind* of team spirit (e.g. forming a union) or become a little too fond of fiscal responsibility (when it shows others – in positions of greater power – to be imprudent or fraudulent).

The move toward (increasingly) 'flexible' conditions of employment will be accompanied by a transformation in the nature of academic work. The 'cult of efficiency', variations of which have long been present on the New Zealand educational policy scene (McKenzie, 1997), will reassert itself and provide a major part of the motivation for virtualising learning (cf. Luke, 1997a). At the same time, 'niche marketing', the provision of unique services or products to more specialised groups of customers, will become part of the language of higher education. A movement in this direction is clearly signalled in the green paper on teacher education (Ministry of Education, 1997c):

Schools of the future will need to be increasingly responsive to the needs of individual students and local communities. Information technologies, including distance learning, with the capability of supporting individualised learning programmes, will have a major impact on the structure and management of classrooms and schools in the future. To meet the demands of change, the organisation of schools, classes, teachers and the school day will need to become more flexible and diverse, with individual students accessing programmes of study in a number of different ways.

(Creech, 1997c: 3)

High-risk ventures targeted at small groups will flourish or flounder depending on the whims of the relevant 'customers' (students), the 'needs' of employers, and the level of state or corporate support. Ministry of Education officials have acknowledged that increased competition could create 'ownership risk' if (some) tertiary institutions cannot gain the necessary student enrolments. This, the leaked document notes, 'may force the Government to consider the future viability of some providers' (Ministry of Education, 1997d: 5). Efficiency will be defined almost exclusively in terms of the imperative to generate revenue, and the goal will be to maximise net (dollar) returns on committed funds. The risks associated with further privatisation are worth it, the Ministry of Education seems to believe, even if both staff and students in some tertiary institutions may have to suffer from time to time. Staff can be held accountable for their failures by noting that they simply did not adapt adequately to a changing tertiary market, while students, with increased autonomy (under the favoured voucher system), can also be expected to carry greater responsibility for their 'purchasing' decisions (cf. Ministry of Education, 1997d: 5).

Reconfiguring Academic Priorities in the Age of the Market

Over time we might expect to see new symbolic economies (Luke, 1997b) at work in decisions over promotion, appointment and salaries in universities. At present, public universities employ a complex system, combining both scholarly and commercial criteria. Promotion forms in most major universities typically ask candidates to advance their case on the basis of contributions to three major areas: research and publication, teaching, and other contributions (to one's department, the university, and the wider community). Considerable emphasis is (theoretically at least) still placed on the quality of one's scholarship and the ability to convey what one has learned to others. These features of academic life have been present, in one form or another, from the earliest days of the university. Over the last few decades, however, new criteria for assessing academic performance have emerged. The bureaucratisation of the university has brought with it an increasing emphasis – particularly at senior levels – on administration, and the processes through which academic value has been measured have, for much of the second half of the twentieth century, been driven by a technocratic mode of rationality. In more recent years, this technocratic thinking has been extended to include 'performance indicators' built on the logic of revenue generation. The signs of this process at work have been many, but one of the most telling is the trend – evident in most countries of the Western world – of recruiting staff on the basis of their demonstrated ability to win contestable research funding from outside agencies. In many fields of study, advertisements for professorial appointments routinely carry some reference to this aspect of academic performance, and in some places – particularly in North American universities – experience in successful grant writing is listed as 'desirable' if not essential for positions at lower levels in the academic hierarchy as well.

It might be predicted that over the next decade this 'grant-writing culture' will become a more deeply entrenched (and almost universal) part of university life. Inculcating a system of competitive bidding for research funds under the proposed new arrangements in the white paper will contribute to the growing commercial ethos in many universities. Some of the reasons for making research resourcing available on a constestable basis are set out in the earlier green paper on tertiary education:

> Contestable funding would allow the proposals of greatest quality to be effectively resourced. This would provide a greater level of accountability and would encourage research of higher quality. It would also allow greater concentration of resources on key areas of research, and specific research targets could be assured.
>
> (Ministry of Education, 1997a: 33)

There is an admission in the green paper that contestability carries risks for 'providers', students and the government. This concern is not addressed in the white paper. In the green paper it is noted that if a contestable regime was adopted, 'assurances for academic freedom in research would need to be maintained' (p. 33). The white paper pays only lip-service to the notion of academic freedom, and does not mention it at all in relation to the question of research funding. Instead, renewed emphasis is placed on the importance of 'strategically-focused

research portfolios' (Ministry of Education, 1998: 32). The leaked
Ministry of Education document (1997d) favours a linking of research
resourcing to degree programmes, but with 'clearer accountability
mechanisms' and a greater emphasis on 'student-led resourcing'. It is
suggested that research resourcing should be separate from tuition
resourcing, allowing degree programmes to attract a higher level of
overall funding than non-degree programmes (pp. 10–11).

   To date, then, the New Zealand Government has resisted the urge to
make all research funding contestable. Yet, in a situation where academics
are required to teach more (for less) than ever before, and complete an
ever-increasing range of administrative tasks, finding time for research
becomes more and more difficult. Gaining additional support for research
through external agencies can often become crucial if a project is to be
completed. If the total government funding for university activities is
insufficient – if academics have neither the time nor the resources to
discharge all their professional duties to the best of their abilities –
research becomes an 'extra': a luxury, more easily won by some than
others. Those most likely to win the necessary financial support to
enable their research activities to proceed are business and management
experts, applied scientists and technologists. Of the limited range of
contestable pools of research money currently available, only one – the
Marsden Fund – has been set up to allow 'blue sky' projects to
proceed[4]. Researchers in agricultural domains, on the other hand, have
a wide variety of funding sources to which they might turn in seeking
support for their work.

   Whether research funding becomes fully contestable or not, the
bureaucratisation of intellectual activity is likely to continue to increase
– at least for the short term. In the longer term, virtual universities may
see some of the bureaucratic elements of contemporary academic life
being broken down (see Peters and Roberts, 1998b). In the meantime,
'busy work' of all kinds will escalate. The endless process of filling out
forms, not only for research grants, but also for annual performance
reviews, course reports, salary and status advancement, teaching
evaluations, etc., will eat away at time that otherwise might be devoted
to scholarship and teaching. A growing proportion of academic time will
be spent struggling to establish the *conditions* for undertaking research
– that is, securing (sufficient) funding to allow a project to proceed –

rather than actually *engaging* in research and scholarly activities. While this will be debilitating, exhausting and frustrating for many, others will thrive in the new environment. The green paper on qualifications reform (Ministry of Education, 1997b) makes much of the need for qualifications to become 'portable', and some people will sell and trade their skills to good effect in generating income for themselves or their organisations in a highly competitive educational 'market'. Similarly, just as businesses have developed around the industry of creating CVs for job hunters, 'grant-writing professionals' may begin to emerge as a new entrepreneurial class within (and outside) universities.

In an environment where academics are increasingly expected to generate their own income, many scholars will be forced to change the focus of their research. Indeed, whole fields of study could disappear or become domains for only part-time academic activity. Even within the surviving areas of study, some scholars are likely to receive greater support than others. Personal politics will become vital in securing a living wage. There has always – in the West at least – been a dramatic imbalance in the level of support available to scholars on the Right as compared with those who position themselves on the Left. While popular critics of political correctness in the humanities complain about 'tenured radicals' gaining research funding and jobs in universities (see, for instance, Kimball, 1990; Kerr, 1997), any support for work of an even vaguely leftist character pales into insignificance when viewed alongside the financial resources at the disposal of the Right. As Messer-Davidow (1993) reports, all the most well known right-wing critics of the university in recent years – Bloom (1988), Kimball (1990), and D'Souza (1991) among them – were supported by enormous grants from conservative 'think tanks' and foundations (see Roberts, 1998b).

Several ways of generating extra revenue are now in evidence in public universities. For academics these include internal research funds, popular authorship (in magazines and newspapers where a fee is paid for all article-length contributions), media presentations, external granting agencies, and consultancies of various kinds (for government, industry, corporations, unions and private organisations). For institutions, full-fee-paying students from other countries provide an important source of income. Many universities ensure that should any potentially profitable scientific or medical discoveries be made by their employees, the institution will retain some or all rights to use the findings for commercial gain. In fact, most universities have a commercial 'arm' – e.g. 'Uniservices' at the University of Auckland in New Zealand – responsible for taking a 'cut' on almost all funded research activities by academics. There are now, in effect, often two parallel institutions running alongside each other on most university campuses, one of which retains some traditional scholarly functions, the other of which is driven exclusively by commercial goals (thus we find 'Monash International' existing alongside Monash University in Melbourne, Australia).

If government funding of universities continues to decline (in real terms), the pressure to make money in non-traditional ways will show a corresponding increase. Funding for research projects – or even for jobs – in the humanities may not dry up altogether, but the prospects for paid employment in positions encouraging genuinely open, critical inquiry are likely to diminish. Research with a direct, quantifiable, and predictable (financial) 'payoff' will prosper, while work in other areas could become more like a form of 'leisure' activity. While a few foundations for supporting research in the humanities may continue to exist, the funding agencies with the most money at their disposal will almost certainly set tight limits around what comes to count as 'worthwhile' (permissible) work. Much of the scholarly work currently undertaken by scholars in the humanities and social sciences will be denigrated as 'esoteric', 'useless', 'left-wing', etc. (cf. Kerr, 1997) and declared utterly unsuitable for funding. In this respect, Jean François Lyotard's comments on the decline in financial support for philosophy are highly apposite:

> It has become an enviable rarity these days to obtain a salary in exchange for the kind of discourse that is commonly called philosophy. As the twentieth century draws to a close, the statesmen and families who run French secondary school system seem to want to have nothing to do with it. For according to the spirit of the times, which is theirs, to do is to produce – that is, to reproduce with a surplus value. Those who teach philosophy are thus condemned to decimation or worse, while those who have studied remain unemployed or give themselves up as hostages to other professions.
>
> (Lyotard, 1993: 70)

In the United States, there has been much debate in recent times over the ethics of encouraging students to go on to complete doctoral degrees when employment prospects for academics in some fields of study are minimal. While tutors are not expected (or paid) to engage in research, many do – some in the hope that their temporary role as teachers and markers will eventually lead to a continuing, full-time academic appointment. These efforts could be misplaced. Indeed, as Shumar (1997) has argued, the number of part-time tutors and lecturers with more impressive records – in both teaching and research – than some of their more senior, full-time counterparts on continuing appointments is increasing. Ironically, these achievements can work *against* part-timers when they apply for jobs: if the institutional embarrassment of having slothful older members of faculty alongside un(der)employed, underpaid, highly productive younger staff is not sufficient to rule an applicant out, he or she might be sidelined for having a research agenda already in place. Many excellent young scholars find themselves in a 'lose-lose' situation. If the burdens of a very heavy teaching load have prevented them from publishing, they might be regarded as 'hacks'. On the other hand if, despite financial and workload obstacles, they have established a good record of publishing in international journals, reasons can still be found for eliminating them:

> ... [Y]oung faculty, trying to get ahead in a tight job market, who publish books and articles in an effort to bolster their credentials may hurt themselves in this hiring process because their having extensive credits makes it harder for the department to recast them in terms of department needs and wishes. With a record of work behind them, that imagination is eclipsed.
>
> (Shumar, 1997: 54)

The situation in New Zealand is perhaps not quite this desperate (yet), but it would not be inaccurate to say that tutors, in particular, have been subjected to steadily worsening working conditions at a time when their prospects for full-time academic work appear increasingly grim. This has set up an insidious cycle of exploitation. Aware of the unfavourable comparison between part-time university tutoring and other forms of work, some graduates nonetheless subject themselves to low wages, long hours and sporadic employment in the hope, however distant this may be, that their exploitative experience of teaching and marking will assist their quest for a full-time academic job. Decisions to get involved in part-time university tutoring work may be guided, in part, by a sober recognition of wider changes in the world of work, where demand for graduates with broad educational experiences and critical minds is being superseded by the scramble for specialists, technocrats and managers.

As Rob Crozier (1997), Executive Director of AUSNZ, points out, 'academia no longer provides the opportunities it once did and the young undergraduate should do some number crunching before committing to graduate study' (p. 7). Working through some cost-benefit figures in contemplating a career produces some startling results which do not augur well for future employment prospects in universities. Crozier calculates that the total cost (to the individual) in getting to a point where one might begin to take up an academic career is close to a quarter of a million (New Zealand) dollars. At a starting salary of around $42,000 (from which approximately $2,850 will be deducted in beginning to pay back a student loan), the financial incentives for pursuing a career in a university are hardly compelling. When coupled with ever-worsening conditions of employment, problems in recruiting staff emerge as a real possibility. This difficulty will, on present predictions, become especially acute from about 2003, when a demographic upturn will see increasing numbers of school leavers entering the tertiary education scene (Crozier, 1997: 7).

What is to be Done?

If the possible developments outlined in the preceding pages come into being, the traditional scholarly mission of the university will be seriously undermined. While such a scenario is deeply worrying for many academics, it cannot be assumed that this concern will be shared by all or even most New Zealanders. Indeed, it must be acknowledged that some people *within* New Zealand universities are likely to be unperturbed by, or actively supportive of, moves toward further marketisation in the tertiary sector. Contributing to the university's role as 'critic and conscience of society' has never been a high priority for all academics.

New Zealand has a long history of anti-intellectualism. This probably has its roots in a variant of the pioneering mentality – a mindset grounded not on academic achievement but the ability to 'do anything with a piece of no. 8 wire' – and has resurfaced at different moments in New Zealand's educational history. Bruce Jesson, one of our most astute social commentators, has this to say:

> Although the New Zealand [free market] transformation has been recent, the reasons for the colossal failure on the part of our intellectuals are not at all recent but go back to this country's colonial origins. Like many frontier societies, New Zealand has not provided a friendly environment to culture or to thought. Early settlers of a cultured background complained about the barbarism of the frontier, and while we are now far from frontier days, many of the colonial attitudes prevail, for instance the way the words 'intellectual' and 'wanker' tend to be combined.
>
> (1997:11)

Butterworth and Tarling (1994: 52–53) detect elements of an anti-intellectual attitude in the policies and practices of the fourth Labour government. More recently, university-bashing has become a favourite pastime for prominent representatives of major business and commercial organisations. Roger Kerr (1997), Executive Director of the New Zealand Business Roundtable, has been especially forthright in his criticisms of intellectual activity – particularly within humanities departments – in universities. When the widespread propensity to be suspicious of or actively hostile toward intellectual activities is viewed alongside the marketisation of what used to be 'a life of the mind', the prospects for maintaining a commitment to the scholarly ideals on which the university (as an historical institution rather than in New Zealand in particular) was founded appear rather grim.

Why should it worry us if traditional scholarly life is abandoned? It would certainly be a mistake to view the history of the university – as an international institution – through rose-coloured spectacles. Sexism, racism, ageism, Eurocentrism and homophobia have all been present in different sectors of the university world, and have at times been manifested in course programmes, reading materials, appointments and promotion decisions. For much of its history, the university has been available as an educational option for only the most privileged – i.e. wealthiest – students. 'Time served' models of advancement and 'old boys/old girls' networks have often prevented younger, harder working, more productive scholars from receiving the recognition they deserved. The gulf between theory and practice has sometimes been too wide, and some academics have been reluctant to offer their knowledge, skills and commitment to causes, concerns and endeavours beyond the confines of specialist teaching and research. Education, against overwhelming evidence to the contrary, has often been viewed as a neutral terrain, allowing oppressive, interest-serving policies and practices to prevail when the rhetoric of the university suggests they ought not to.

Some of the books listed at the beginning of this chapter give evidence of how such oppressive practices have worked in a variety of contexts. Carey Nelson's edited collection, *Will Teach for Food: Academic Labor in Crisis* (1997), demonstrates that teaching assistants at Yale University in the United States have been systematically exploited. In a tight academic employment market, senior students have often been willing to work long hours for low wages. University administrators have sometimes either explicitly endorsed such situations or felt no need to resist them. Establishing legal grounds on which to contest exploitative working conditions (as Yale students did) provides one way of addressing a distressing situation, but the moral issues at stake in such conflicts also demand attention. Bruce Wilshire (1990), in another of the 'crisis' books listed earlier, argues that some of the moral principles and practices on which the university was founded have been neglected with the professionalisation of academic life. Sykes (1988), from a rather different point of view, documents cases of academics on full-time salaries doing as little teaching as possible while drawing extra income from lucrative consultancy contracts. Other volumes (e.g. Berube and Nelson, 1995) provide examples of sexism, racism and Eurocentrism in the curriculum and draw attention to the forgotten voices of women, ethnic minorities and Third World writers in traditional 'Great Books' programmes. D'Souza (1991), by contrast, shows that some attempts to make the curriculum more inclusive and to encourage diversity on university campuses have themselves become racist and sexist.

Acknowledging a less than perfect past does not, however, mean the university is barely worth saving! Indeed, the battle to retain some traditional features of university life should, we believe, be fought with the utmost vigour and urgency. While '-isms' of all sorts (sexism, racism, etc.) have been present at times in universities, other values have been upheld by the academy on many occasions. These include: tolerance, a respect for the value of knowledge, a commitment to rigour and scholarship, a spirit of investigation and critique, a willingness to put ideas to the test and to change where appropriate, a belief in the value of collegiality and democracy in matters of governance, and the promotion of academic freedom. Many academics see themselves as members of an international scholarly community, place considerable stock on peer review, and value open debate, discussion and dialogue through publication, conferences, seminars and correspondence. The integration of teaching and research, one of the distinguishing features of the university, is cherished by most.

When tertiary education is defined purely as a form of (self-interested) private investment, goals such as promoting a love of learning, fostering public debate and enhancing democratic citizenship disappear from the agenda. These ideals must be defended. Although it is now highly unfashionable, collective action seems to us to be fundamental if any effective challenge is to be mounted against further marketisation in higher education. Forming alliances (e.g. through unions) on a national and international scale with others committed to similar scholarly ideals will be essential if technocrats and business élites are not to gain a stranglehold over university policies. This could involve various forms of protest action: marches, occupations, letters and visits to MPs, strikes of various kinds, refusing to complete seemingly pointless bureaucratic tasks demanded in the new environment of performance indicators and perpetual evaluation, and working to rule (i.e. for the 37.5 or 40 hours per week indicated on academic pay packets, rather than the 50 to 60 hours per week often required to meet an average range of teaching, research and administration obligations). Making the most of the new information technologies to gain support from colleagues overseas will be pivotal.

An important dimension of the struggle against the marketisation of education is upholding the right to live a scholarly life (Roberts, 1997d). Protecting the process of study, and the need for intellectual activity, will not be easy in a system geared toward the commodification of all knowledge and learning. Yet academics should be well placed to mount this form of resistance. As Jesson observes,

> It isn't, of course, essential to go outside Anglo-American culture in order to develop a critical perspective of developments in our society in general, and of our educational institutions in particular. It is only necessary to go outside the dominant finance culture. In a situation where knowledge is losing its value and gaining a price, *the role of the intellectual is to defend the role of the intellectual.* It may seem as though this amounts to stating the things that we have always thought obvious. But defending the taken-for-granted is sometimes the most difficult thing to do, and at the same time the most valuable.
>
> (1997: 14, emphasis added)

Maintaining a commitment to scholarship and academic rigour through adopting what might, in Freirean terms, be termed an investigative, curious, probing, questioning, dialogical, *critical* approach toward the act of study (Freire, 1985) rubs against the grain of a market system built on the process of *consumption*. To consume – and market liberals are quite happy to speak of students as consumers – is, precisely, to avoid reflection, contemplation, and considered critique. To consume is, in a pedagogically significant sense, to act without a great deal of thought. Consumers know what they want (or *believe* they know what they want). In the neoliberal educational marketplace consumers enter into contracts with providers, who become obliged to supply what is wanted. The product or service is 'devoured' hungrily. The consumer's eagerness springs from the desire to put the qualification or course (or whatever else has been 'purchased') to work in serving his or her own interests over others and in positioning him- or herself to be successful in the competitive world of the market. Adopting a scholarly stance, however, demands a position of uncertainty (cf. Lyotard, 1988: xvi), a willingness to challenge and be challenged. Influential supporters of further marketisation (e.g. Myers, 1996b) believe only the ideas of the 'New Right' are worthy of serious consideration; the alternatives can be dismissed as 'Old Wrong' ideas. Combating such blatantly self-serving, one-sided attitudes is surely a battle worth fighting. If the integrity of university education is to be maintained, encouraging an inquisitive, critical openness to views other than the (overwhelmingly) dominant ideology of market liberalism will be essential[5].

Endnotes

[1]   All quotations from the green paper on qualifications reform are from a print-out of the Internet version of the document: http://www.minedu.govt.nz/data/NQF/paper/htm

[2]   The Tertiary Education Review green paper was published in two parts (with separate page numbering). The main document of 96 pages is accompanied by a brief 'Overview' of eight pages. If a quotation is from the latter, this will be noted. Otherwise, all page numbers refer to the main document.

[3]   For a more extended analysis of the Dearing Report and the Tertiary Education Review green paper, see Chapter 7.

[4]   'Blue sky' investigative activities are those without an immediate or obvious quantifiable payoff for government or other funding bodies. They are forms of research which might be said to carry intrinsic rather than extrinsic benefits, and are driven by intellectual curiosity and a spirit of inquiry. The term is usually employed by government officials rather than academics.

[5]   The ideas advanced in this chapter are developed in greater detail in Roberts (1999a; 1999b; 1999c).

chapter nine

The Virtual University?
Higher Education in Cyberspace

The last decade has witnessed a remarkable growth in the computing industry. Computers have become faster, smaller, and more powerful with each passing year. Software systems of all kinds – wordprocessing, spreadsheets, graphics programmes, games, and so on – have become more complicated and colourful (read: 'memory hungry') as each new version is produced. Computer monitors have improved, speakers and CD-ROMs have been added, 'mice' have come out of closets and now move incessantly across padded surfaces at computer workstations, and a host of peripheral devices – printers, zip drives, scanners, etc. – have become seemingly indispensable for contemporary computing purposes. Computing is, as the often cited example of Bill Gates' personal fortune demonstrates, very big business indeed.

If the personal computer might be said to have truly arrived in the 1980s, it was not until the early 1990s that systems for linking computers across the globe began to flourish. While the Internet has a history dating back some decades, the idea of building a vast international web of connected sites has only gained popular momentum in the last few years. Estimates of the total number of Internet users on the planet vary widely, but many believe the figure now exceeds 100 million people. The Internet has been hailed by some as one of the most significant technological developments of the twentieth century; a new era in communicative relationships has been initiated. The possibility of breaking down old geographical barriers brings the concept of a 'global village' – predicted by McLuhan and other visionaries – to life. The Internet, it seems, will usher in new ways of meeting people, doing business, conducting relationships, earning a living, and providing entertainment. Some suggest it heralds the arrival of a new dawn not just in the history of technology but in human evolution: with global connectivity, we might expect to see ontological, epistemological, ethical, and political changes of enormous import.

A burgeoning literature on the social, cultural and educational dimensions of computing and the new information technologies has developed. A growing proportion of this material is available in electronic form. Several key areas for discussion and analysis have emerged. These include the changing face of scholarly publishing (the emergence of electronic journals and virtual libraries); issues of copyright and intellectual property in the era of the Internet; questions about what being human might mean as cyborgs (once the product of science fiction) become a reality; the emergence of 'virtual communities'; new (hypertextual) modes of reading and writing in cyberspace; the politics of the global village; the history and philosophy of technology; and possibilities for alternative systems of teaching and learning in the (so-called) information age[1].

This chapter falls into two major parts. The first section considers some of the forms 'virtual' learning and scholarship might take in university settings. We argue that technological innovations need to be *contextualised* if they are to be understood. The second section assesses the extent to which, and ways in which, these new developments have been identified and discussed in recent education policy statements in New Zealand. The key document for those concerned with higher education in New Zealand – the tertiary education white paper (Ministry of Education, 1998) – has virtually nothing to say about the new information technologies. This stands in marked contrast to the Dearing Report, which deals with these issues at length in developing a detailed vision of 'The Learning Society'. We situate what *has* been said about the new technologies within the wider framework of neoliberal social policy change in New Zealand, and analyse the latest phase in the reform process in the light of prophetic comments from Jean Francois Lyotard on the changing role of the state in postmodern societies.

Learning and Scholarship in Virtual Universities

Many of the proposed and enacted developments in 'virtual' systems of teaching and learning are extensions of practices already in place. Among the myriad forms virtual learning might take, consider the following possibilities:

1. *An Extramural (or 'Correspondence School') Model.* This would be similar in many respects to learning via traditional university courses. There might be a standard programme of study, with a range of topics to be covered, set texts to be read, and assignments to be completed. Academics or tutors would have responsibility for developing the course content and marking written work. Instruction would, however, be carried out through correspondence rather than in a face-to-face manner, and communication would be via electronic media rather than via the postal system. Course readings would be downloadable from the Internet. Assignments would be submitted via e-mail attachments or linked to students' Internet home pages. All correspondence (with the possible exception of formal print-outs of final grades) would be conducted through the medium of e-mail.

2. *A Simulation Model.* The aim here would be reproduce, as closely as possible, a 'real life' learning environment via virtual reality technologies. Students would attach themselves to the appropriate equipment, or (in the future) perhaps enter a room, which would allow them to experience the same sensations they might find in the world outside. This sort of approach might be particularly suitable for learning in scientific and applied fields, where students can acquire the necessary skills for a practical or technical task without the expense and/or danger associated with the 'real thing'. Chemical reactions could be simulated, features of the natural environment could be replicated, emergency scenarios could be played out, and so on. The technology has already found an application in driver instruction and aircraft simulation exercises, among other areas.

3. *A Video-Conferencing Model.* Video-conferencing was introduced with much fanfare some years ago. It was claimed that this system of linking people via cameras, connecting cables or satellites, and screens would revolutionise communication within the business and

educational sectors. For a variety of reasons (including financial constraints, inflated expectations and misunderstandings about what video-conferencing could deliver, difficulties in establishing links within the necessary localities, and a lag in perceptions about what counts as feasible or desirable for communication purposes), the technology in practice has failed to live up to the initial hype. The timing for the technology may have been 'wrong'. As virtual systems of various kinds begin to take off (if they do) over the next two decades, video-conferencing could re-emerge as an important part of academic communication and tertiary learning. The major advantage of video-conferencing over the two approaches noted above is that learning can occur on a 'real time', 'live' basis, allowing for a certain kind of face-to-face contact (even if bodies are located in different parts of a country or the globe) as well as the communication of voices and other sounds.

4. *An Interactive Model.* This would be similar in many respects to the system listed under the previous heading. Video-conferencing would be used here, but with a new element added: the joint reading, writing and discussion of textual materials (and graphics and sound) through simultaneous Internet hook-ups. There are thus possibilities for 'live' joint-authorship of articles, reports, etc. without the requirement that two or more academics be sitting in the same office, be housed in the same university, or even live in the same country.

These possible developments constitute alternatives to traditional (face-to-face, classroom-based) learning, but they tell us very little about the *organisation* of tertiary education in the future. This is the key from a policy point of view, for an examination of organisational questions demands consideration of the *context* which shapes and limits teaching and learning situations. We thus need to ask not just 'What might be possible (as far as virtual technologies are concerned)?', but 'What is *likely* or probable, given current trends in social, economic and educational policy?' We believe it is unlikely that existing universities will become 'redundant' in the short term. Nor will large numbers of university staff in all subject areas lose their jobs overnight. In some domains of study (as noted below) there will be staff *increases*. But in the longer term, both the physical spaces occupied by university buildings and the work undertaken by people within them will be put under pressure. The quest for 'efficiency' – whether dressed up in the Treasury language of better serving 'consumer' preferences or couched within the discourse of performativity – will make traditional forms of university organisation seem very expensive and 'inefficient' by comparison with on-line systems of education.

We ought not, however, to underestimate the willingness of students, employers and parents – as well as academics – to draw distinctions between different organisations and institutions involved in tertiary education. Whether the current system, with its proliferation of 'providers' and heavy emphasis on maximising 'choice', properly *prepares* students to make good (carefully considered, well informed) decisions is quite another matter. The concern for quality and reputation – driven in some cases by self-interest (projected financial gains), in others by a desire to work with the 'best' people in a particular area of study – is still uppermost in many minds. With so many programmes on offer, the tertiary education environment can be quite bewildering. In the absence of a firm commitment from the government to a well funded public education system, many are likely to fall back on institutions with 'proven' records of achievement. The advantage such institutions have accrued from the reputations they have built up over time may, of course, diminish with succeeding generations. The 'traditional' universities most likely to survive and flourish in the next century, we suggest, will be those with generous endowment funds and a willingness to make some concessions to the spirit of 'cyberspatial' times.

If the imperative is one of saving money, the options for virtual learning noted earlier are likely to have mixed appeal. The major savings in any attempt to virtualise learning at the tertiary level are likely to come through decreases in salary budgets (for both academics and support staff) and plant costs (including initial outlays for buildings and equipment, maintenance, ongoing leasing or rental costs, and taxes on fixed assets). Expenses associated with printing and posting are also not insignificant, and as more and more reading material becomes available through the Internet expenditure on books, serials and other library acquisitions will come under increasing scrutiny. Against potential savings in these areas, additional costs in setting up and maintaining the new systems must be taken into account.   Bills to telecommunications companies will inevitably rise, costs associated with almost all aspects of computing (including hardware, software, peripherals, and networking costs) will increase, and money must be invested in further technical support for staff and students learning to make use of the new technologies. The extent to which savings from virtualisation might exceed increases in expenditure in some areas depends, to a significant extent, on what remains of a genuine commitment to *high quality* tertiary education. The experience of some institutions overseas suggests that, contrary to common perception, running a high-quality virtual university is *more* expensive than operating a tertiary institution in the traditional manner (see, for example, Luke, 1997a).

Systems based on the technology of video-conferencing (the third and fourth approaches identified earlier) allow educators to construct a learning environment which is substantially similar to a university classroom situation. The major contrast is that where in a traditional lecture, tutorial or laboratory all participants occupy the same room, in a video-conferencing learning environment teachers and students occupy different geographical spaces. For those who believe that traditional pedagogical relationships (those requiring face-to-face contact between lecturers and students) involve the interplay of a range of subtle, interpersonal – perhaps even unconscious or 'erotic' – dynamics, the separation of bodies in the learning situation is highly significant. It could be argued that something (of pedagogical importance) will be *lost* from a learning situation when direct interaction between human actors in the same physical space disappears. Indeed, one commentator (Chambers, 1998) has suggested that if the liberating potential of the new technologies is to be realised, a return, via computers, to the Oxford style of tuition must be made. The mass customisation of learning, envisaged by groups such as Global Alliance Ltd, removes the *educational* component from the instructional process and replaces it with a transmission model. Such a model calls into question the status of teaching as a profession demanding not merely 'how to' skills but also a deep knowledge of a subject and an understanding of human interaction and the nature of learning. Of course, some responsibility for the effective integration of virtual technologies with good pedagogical practice must rest with individual teachers. As Gunn (1998: 136) wryly observes, 'any teacher who can be successfully replaced by a computer should be'. It is important, however, to see such 'failures' on the part of individual teachers in their wider political context. The proletarianisation of teachers' work is an established trend in many Western countries, including New Zealand. The new technologies could exacerbate this trend (Jesson, 1998), and where there is a lack of governmental commitment to teaching as a profession the potential for mass customisation in learning is greater.

There has been much debate – in education, literacy studies, sociology, and philosophy, among other domains of study – over the nature of technology. We are persuaded by arguments that no technology is ever neutral (see further, Roberts, 1997f). This applies as much to the technologies of the computing era – including networking via the Internet – as any others. Technologies are always embedded in, and shaped by social contexts. They are defined not by their electronic components, but by the processes, practices, ideas and relations associated with their development and use. Computing, in its myriad forms, is a thoroughly political activity – from the moment of assembly to the application of advanced software packages for entertainment, educational, commercial or surveillance purposes. Computers are built, at least in part, by human beings (and even if robots could assemble all components necessary for a complete computer system, someone would still have to first construct the robot, or the robot responsible for constructing other robots). The workers employed in most computer building operations receive low wages, toil for long hours and endure poor working conditions. The same is true of most software companies. Bill Gates may be a multi-billionaire, but the people who allow several thousand units of Microsoft products to be sold each week by packaging the goods on the factory floor are hardly likely to reach exalted financial heights. Internet traffic travels along network paths established, owned and controlled by telecommunications giants, few of whom are renowned for their commitment to social justice, the preservation of the natural environment or the notion of education as a public good.

The importance of contextualising developments arising from the new technologies finds ample illustration in debates over the future of scholarly publishing. We believe the Internet holds much promise in addressing elements of what is widely perceived as a 'crisis' in scholarly publishing, but there are also real dangers in making the move to electronic environments. The reasons for favouring electronic journals over conventional print periodicals are, we think, compelling and have been discussed at length elsewhere (see, for example, Peters and Lankshear, 1996; Roberts, 1996d, 1998c). In recent years the costs of sustaining comprehensive collections of print serials have become unsustainable in all but the most generously endowed universities. With annual subscriptions for many periodicals running into the hundreds of dollars (thousands in some cases), and with the number of new journals continuing to rise, severe pressure has been placed on both library space and university budgets in trying to maintain existing collections and cover new developments in most disciplines. The delays associated with publication in print journals are frequently excessive – a lag of two years between the original production of an article and its appearance in print is not unusual – and the need to visit a library for each new issue of a journal also wastes time that might otherwise be spent reading the article(s) of interest in each issue.

Electronic journals can save time at all steps in the publication process, from the initial submission of manuscripts through the reviewing process to the release of a paper for public viewing. While there is some debate over the exact level of savings, the weight of opinion in the literature suggests that costs can be substantially lowered (Odlyzko, 1997). Electronic journals do not take up space on library shelves. The quality of computer hardware, the type of software employed, transmission bandwidth, and questions of access become more significant. Electronic journals exhibiting similar characteristics to print periodicals – with collections of peer-reviewed articles, most around 5,000 words, housed together in discrete issues – will be joined by a host of other publications and new forms of scholarly discourse. Already there are (on the Internet) numerous discussion groups, academic forums of all kinds, and multiple collections of material in particular subject areas. Hypertext links allow readers of electronic publications to jump immediately to another book or article of related interest. Sound and images are increasingly being woven with textual material, reconfiguring the nature of 'reading' in cyberspace and promoting new routes through which to encounter ideas. In the future, multimedia presentations are likely to be conveyed not just through computers but via a range of systems in home and work environments. Talk of finding large television-like screens in every room of a house (for the fortunate few at present) with integrated Internet and broadcasting functions is commonplace, but, on a more radical note, it is not difficult to imagine multimedia devices appearing in cars, buses, trains, street corners, public buildings of all kinds – perhaps even on, or *in*, bodies. Such developments obviously have a potentially chilling edge to them and evoke images of 'big brother' surveillance systems, but do not seem far-fetched given what has occurred to date.

With the emergence of the Internet and electronic journals, scholarly publishing could increasingly shift back into the hands of academics. As print periodicals have proliferated over recent decades, publishing has become a multi-million dollar business. Large publishing companies now exert considerable power over academic decisions, and authors have only limited rights to redistribute their own work. Copyright for most established international journals is usually retained by the publisher, not the author. This produces a situation in which authors have no effective control over the distribution and circulation of their own ideas once they have been published – or even submitted – to a print journal. Authors must seek permission from a journal publisher to reproduce their work elsewhere and are sometimes even required to pay fees to the publisher before permission will be granted. With the move from the printing press to electronic publishing, the production process changes. While large publishing firms are already beginning to produce electronic versions of existing print journals, these are almost always available on a subscription basis only. Against this commercial model, numerous journals are now accessible, free of charge, to anyone with access to the Internet. Those who produce such journals incur some costs, but these are – depending on the nature of the journal – typically much lower than those associated with print journals. Readers too must pay Internet user charges but, again, these are far lower than subscription costs for printed academic journals.

With increasing acceptance of the move toward electronic publishing, the idea of journals being 'sponsored' by a university, a department, or a professional organisation has gained ground. This shifts the publication process – which is, after all, intended to provide a means through which ideas and findings can be disseminated to the international academic community – back into the hands of those more directly involved in writing and reading scholarly articles. It represents something of a return to the old scholarly societies model of publication, from which the professional journal emerged. Publication in the print journals of the modern era has become a complicated commercial transaction; the move back into academic hands reinforces the notion of peer-reviewed publication promoting a distinctive form of *scholarly* exchange.

This, in our view, represents a positive development for academics. If the marketisation of education continues, however, scholarly publishing will face new difficulties. Maintaining the integrity of published scholarly work could, if the logic of the market seeps into every pore of academic activity, simply come to seem largely *irrelevant*. Peer-reviewed publication, with the exchange of ideas and findings between academic specialists, has no significant place in a system geared toward making money. While commercial publishing houses certainly have an interest in making a profit (or at least staying financially viable), most authors of academic articles receive nothing for their efforts. There is, at best, a form of indirect compensation through an academic salary, payment of which is conditional upon the proper discharging of professional obligations – including publication and research. If electronic publication becomes the norm rather than the exception in producing academic journals, the profit element will become even less significant. There may be some extra money in electronic publishing for telecommunications companies, computer dealers and software manufacturers. But for those who sponsor and produce the journals, the main financial consideration will be to maintain costs at a reasonable level. Authors will continue to have no financial interest in the publication of their work.

The primary motivations in setting up, producing and contributing to electronic academic journals will be scholarly in nature: a commitment to debate and the open exchange of ideas; the desire to test the quality of one's work in the international community through peer review; a love of one's subject and a willingness to share this with others; a fascination for the process of investigation and art of writing; an interest in maintaining the highest standards of academic rigour; and so on. Other motivating factors – the drive for recognition, or status, or advancement – may enter into publishing decisions, but other activities are far more likely to provide a route through which these rewards might be obtained. Publishing articles for scholarly reasons will, if market forces take an even stronger hold over academic minds and bodies, come to seem 'quaint', old-fashioned, perhaps even *pointless*. Unless there is a direct or easily foreseeable practical, technical or commercial gain to be made in disseminating one's ideas or findings through electronic journals, the logic of the market would suggest there is little point in bothering to invest professional energy in this domain of academic activity. We now consider whether such a pessimistic reading might be justified given recent policy trends in New Zealand.

Information Technologies and Tertiary Education Reform in NZ

In Chapter 7 we noted that over the last two years, the United Kingdom, Australia and New Zealand have all undertaken significant reviews of their tertiary education systems. In each case, government officials associated with the review processes have stressed, as they almost always do, that financial resources for expansion in the tertiary sector are strictly limited. Money for further and higher education is, it seems, in perpetually short supply. On the one hand, governments are keen, for a variety of reasons (including the desire to lower unemployment statistics), to increase participation rates in tertiary education. On the other hand, any new developments in the sector are expected to proceed in a climate of continuing fiscal constraint. In contemplating how both imperatives might be met, higher education authorities have increasingly turned to the new information technologies as a means of enhancing participation while reducing costs. This 'turn to technology' is not, however, merely a money-saving exercise. It reflects and perpetuates deep changes in the nature of the knowledge, the concept of education, and the role of the state in postmodern societies. Some countries have been quicker to recognise these changes than others.

In the tertiary education white paper there are scattered references to the importance of adapting to and exploiting new technologies (e.g. Creech, 1998: 2; Ministry of Education, 1998: 2, 3), but such statements are not supported with any surrounding discussion of the issues involved in moving to new virtual environments for learning. The only policy initiative to even touch on this area in the white paper is the proposal for a public database, available in electronic form, with information on career and training options. In the tertiary education review green paper (Ministry of Education, 1997a), a few short statements on information technology can be found. In his Foreword to the document, Minister of Education Wyatt Creech claims:

... [T]he development of information technology will greatly extend the range of learning opportunities for all New Zealanders. This will break down the barriers of time and location which historically have prevented people from learning. It will change how learning occurs as well as when it occurs.

(Creech, 1997b: 3)

A few pages later, under the heading 'Goals for Tertiary Education', the green paper states:

Information technology, in particular the growth of the Internet, will continue to provide new and diverse forms of education delivery. This is likely to introduce a new range of providers – including international ones – for students to choose from, and so reduce the costs of tertiary provision.

(Ministry of Education, 1997a: 8)

Apart from one other brief reference to information technologies and the internationalisation of the tertiary sector (p. 68), this is all the green paper has to say on the issue.

Information technology figures rather more prominently in the green paper on teacher education (Ministry of Education, 1997c), published some weeks after the tertiary education review green paper. In his Foreword to the teacher education document, Wyatt Creech claims that teachers will need to be able to respond to 'advances in technology and consequent changes in the mix of skills valued in the wider world of employment' if they are to become 'proficient managers of change' (Creech, 1997c: 3). Creech observes:

Schools of the future will need to be increasingly responsive to the needs of individual students and local communities. Information technologies, including distance learning, with the capability of supporting individualised learning programmes, will have a major impact on the structure and management of classrooms in the future. To meet the demands of change, the organisation of schools, classes, teachers and the school day will need to become more flexible and diverse, with individual students accessing programmes of study in a number of different ways.

(Creech, 1997c: 3)

The document, in tandem with many other policy statements from the New Zealand Government and particularly the Ministry of Education in recent years, makes much of the fact that we live in a 'rapidly changing world' (see Roberts, 1997d). In this case, however, more attention is paid to the role of information and communication technologies in the process of change. The new technologies, the green paper claims, have led to 'fundamental and irrevocable' changes in the world of work: '[h]igh value is now placed on flexibility, innovation and adaptation to change, rather than the acquisition of one static set of skills and knowledge'. This, it is believed, will necessarily have an impact on the nature of teaching and learning. The green paper continues:

> While the traditional objectives of mass education – basic literacy, numeracy and fact-based knowledge – remain essential, the method of achieving these objectives has changed. Students are now more able to access and process information for themselves, and to communicate widely. In this way, information and communications networked tools provide greater opportunities for students to engage in self-directed learning.
>
> (Ministry of Education, 1997c: 20)

The need for all teachers to obtain an understanding of (and actively work with) the new technologies is seen as paramount. Advances in this area are, it is claimed, 'changing the nature, practice and philosophies of teaching and learning' (p. 31). The green paper speaks of information and communication technologies providing 'alternative routes to knowledge, directly challenging the traditional role of teachers as conveyers of knowledge'. Retaining existing approaches to the organisation of learning 'simply delays the inevitable' (p. 20). Extending the tone of urgency, the green paper proposes that in addition to the functional competencies specified in the unit standards for pre-service teacher education developed by the Teacher Education Advisory Group, trainees should 'acquire skills in the uses of information technology for aiding the teaching and learning process'. Ideally, functional competence in this (new) area should be 'practised and developed during the practicum as well as through the provider-based programmes' (p. 31).

As we have observed in earlier chapters, by comparison with major policy documents on higher education in other countries – particularly the Dearing Report – New Zealand's green and white papers on tertiary education are positively emaciated. They are thin on detail in almost every area of tertiary education policy, having very little to say about teaching practices, the process of research, the nature and purpose of a university, the role of the humanities, and so on. The Dearing Report, at over 1,700 pages in length, gives all of these areas – and the question of what role the new information technologies might play in universities of the future – the attention they deserve in a major review of tertiary education.

The tertiary education white paper is driven, more than anything else, by questions about money. In essence, the government wishes to extract what it sees as better value (both in dollar and 'quality' terms) from the education budget and, consistent with other reforms over the past thirteen years, believes the market provides the best model for this. Given this overriding concern, however, the neglect of information technology issues appears to be an error in judgement. Developments in 'virtual' teaching and learning technologies at the tertiary level have been seen by some as the saviour of an ailing system. The new information technologies, many believe, have arrived at precisely the right time to enhance access to higher education, improve scholarly communication, allow innovative teaching to flourish, and (of greatest importance for bureaucrats and politicians) rescue the universities from their desperate financial plight.

It is important to contextualise these potential developments. The information age ushers in changes in the role of state and the emergence of new (sometimes uneasy or even contradictory) alliances of power. Among other defining features, this moment witnesses a diffusion of social responsibilities into the private (or philanthropic) sphere and an *apparent* reduction in the regulatory life of bureaucracies and institutions of all kinds. Accompanying these trends, however, is the need (desire) for greater control over individual subjects who negotiate the fresh pathways of competitive consumption in a computerised world. This process has been accelerated in the last decade as computers have become more sophisticated and widespread within the realms of commerce, education and the home. Its origins lie, however, in the shift from mechanical and electrical technological systems to new *language-based* technologies. This shift has prompted a change in the status of knowledge: 'information' has become a (increasingly *the*) major medium of exchange. Knowledge and learning have become *commodities*, with information being the chief currency through which participants buy, sell and trade in the educational domain (Lyotard; 1984; 1993).

This is not merely an epistemological transformation – a change in ways of knowing, understanding or interpreting the world – but a fundamental shift in the nature of economic, social and cultural life. The still-evolving reality of late (postmodern) capitalism precipitates new roles for all 'players' in the social system. Individuals find themselves renegotiating their conditions of work (or facing unemployment); educational institutions scramble to meet new demands linked to the language of 'performativity'; and (many) families struggle to cope as 'flexible' working hours, un(der)employment and lower real wages bite into already strained household budgets. The state, too, must reconfigure its place within the new order. In an essay on the new technologies first published in 1982 (and later included in his *Political Writings*), Lyotard observes:

> As for state control, the technologies of language touch its domain in regard to all aspects of its responsibility for the Idea of being-together: the multiplication of organizations for management and administration (ministers, agencies, missions); the constitution of memories (files, archives, etc.); the relationship to the new media; and so forth. The important fact is this: in handling language, the new technologies directly handle the social bond, being-together. They make it more independent of traditional regulation by institutions, and more directly affected by knowledge, technology, and the marketplace.
>
> (Lyotard, 1993: 17)

Several trends in the reconstruction of New Zealand's social sphere mirror developments signalled in Lyotard's insightful comments. First, as we noted in Chapter 4, challenges to the regulatory authority of institutions are now commonplace. The heavy emphasis on meeting the 'needs' of 'consumers' undermines the authority teachers, university lecturers and other education professionals used to have over matters of educational standards and quality. Students, employers, government ministers and parents are increasingly asserting the right to question the quality of university programmes. Thus, when a group of students at

Victoria University expressed their grievances about a course programme via the threat of legal action, rather than through internal university procedures (alone), this was seen by many as an important precedent in the new 'contractual' environment for tertiary teaching.

Much of the discourse on the new information technologies concentrates on need for new skills and competencies. We hear a great deal of talk, for example, about developing 'computer literacy'. This concept, like many others (e.g. 'critical literacy' and 'empowerment') has been reduced to a technocratic shadow of its former self, and now seems to imply nothing more than the ability to operate computer hardware systems and software packages (see further, Roberts, 1999d). The focus is very much on knowing *how* rather than knowing *why*. Questions about the contexts – political, cultural, educational, etc. – within which computers are used tend to be pushed into the background. The emphasis is not merely on skills but (supposedly) *'relevant'* skills: that is, those deemed necessary by students, employers and funding bodies (including the government) for competitive advancement.

The language of skills, evident in all of the policy papers discussed above but particularly prominent in the document on teacher education, mirrors trends set in earlier Ministry statements. 'Upskilling' the population has been seen as a key goal for educational reform at all levels of the system. *The New Zealand Curriculum Framework* (Ministry of Education, 1993) – the document on which all subsequent school curricula have been based – is saturated with talk of 'skills'. Learning is understood in terms of eight groupings of 'essential skills': communication skills, numeracy skills, information skills, problem-solving skills, self-management and competitive skills, social and cooperative skills, physical skills, and work and study skills. At the tertiary level, the industry training strategy has been built on the assumption that education ought to be more closely tied to the development of skills necessary for effective employment. The idea has been to 'skill New Zealand' (Education and Training Support Agency, 1993): to build a nation of lifelong learners, committed to the concept and practice of perpetual training in order to stay competitive in a rapidly changing world.

The rhetoric of upskilling and perpetual training finds renewed emphasis in the green paper on teacher education, where it is argued that teachers will need to maintain 'a deep and flexible understanding of the subject they teach' if they are to meet individualised student learning needs (increasingly built on a platform of on-line access to information). 'In this context,' the Ministry notes, 'the ability of teachers to manage their own career-long learning is the key.' Both pre-service and in-service teacher education programmes are seen as important in meeting this objective, the former (in degree or degree-equivalent form) providing confirmation of a teacher's 'cognitive ability' to do the job well, the latter servicing ongoing professional development requirements for those committed to high quality teaching. It is envisaged that the Internet might provide an effective way of linking schools – particularly in remote and rural areas – for in-service education.

Neoliberal political thought suggests there should be a 'thinning' of the state, with minimal government intervention, in order to allow rational, self-interested individuals to make independent decisions in the marketplace. (The 'marketplace' here is multifaceted, and includes domains such as education and health as well as the commercial sphere.) If the theory works well in practice, individuals should prosper or perish on the basis of their own efforts, the state having interfered only in the sense of setting (and where necessary reinforcing) the rules for the competition. The New Zealand experience has shown that while some 'withering' of the state has occurred – with, for example, the sale of state assets and cuts to welfare – there has also been a strengthening of bureaucratic power in strategic areas (e.g. in economic forecasting, social policy formulation, the control of qualifications, etc.). In the educational arena, the past decade has witnessed the removal of some important buffering policy bodies – notably, the old education boards and the University Grants Committee. The key financial planning wing of government – the Treasury – has, by contrast, enjoyed healthy staffing levels, with generous salaries, conditions and bonuses for its employees (Young, 1997: A5) and considerable latitude for 'getting it wrong' (frequently, in economic predictions) without fear of sackings.

The development of new 'memory' systems, another feature of the postmodern moment identified by Lyotard, is also in full swing in New Zealand. In recent years extensive archives of information about individuals have been assembled in government departments and commercial organisations. Computerisation has allowed systems of information storage, retrieval and transmission to become more sophisticated, efficient and widespread. The practice of 'information sharing' between different bureaucratic wings of the state apparatus has become official government policy. The boundary between the state and the business world has become increasingly blurred in this process. A classic example of the intertwining of the two spheres was provided some years ago when banks 'encouraged' their customers to give over their Inland Revenue Department numbers in exchange for a lower withholding tax rate. These developments have raised new concerns about surveillance and the regulation of citizens in an information economy. Such concerns also apply to changes in the education sector.

In Chapter 6 we discussed the relationship between the universities and the New Zealand Qualifications Authority. We argued that while bureaucratic bodies such as the NZQA are in some senses out of step with the government's neoliberal ideology, the qualifications green paper of 1997 was, in general, consistent with an agenda of further marketisation in the New Zealand education system. With the arrival of the new information technologies, the dovetailing of qualifications reforms with other steps in the marketisation process becomes not only possible but, in a certain sense, inevitable. The technologising of education at the school level is already under way, even if the supporting policy literature and resources for schools have been slow in developing. This process has been made explicit since at least the sudden appearance of 'Technology' as a new core subject in the school curriculum, and has continued to gain momentum in succeeding years. The process has been helped along, to a not inconsiderable degree, by the open enthusiasm of key Ministers in the National and National–New Zealand First Coalition Cabinets. Maurice Williamson has been a prominent advocate of computerisation, and his interest in the information superhighway has had a significant bearing on a number of new policy developments.

If current trends in the global politics of computerisation continue, and if the new reforms signalled in the qualifications green paper become cemented as official policy, we might begin to detect a shift in the balance of power, or at least the rules of the game (with a designation of major roles to new players), in the educational sector. The encroachment of corporates (including computer companies) into schools – via, for example, the scheme to exchange supermarket dockets for Macintosh desktops some years ago – has attracted relatively little debate in the popular press. Academics have also been rather quiet on this issue, if the absence of any sustained discussion in the major education journals (and journals in related areas) is anything to go by. Certainly the widely-held view among members of the public appears to be that such developments are either harmless or highly desirable. The fact that such rampant commercialism has been greeted with a minimum of fuss (or with clear approval) may simply reflect the tiredness levels of those who have repeatedly raised concerns – usually to no avail – about similar processes in the past. Alternatively, what we could be witnessing is one more step in the extension of corporatist hegemony over all spheres of social life. The educational domain is crucial in this corporatisation process, for it provides a huge 'captive market' of people whose minds might (as Plato argued more than two thousand years ago in the *Republic*) be regarded as especially malleable. The promotion of neoliberal thought as a precondition for the acceptance of New Right economic and social policies will ultimately have to begin in childhood, and 'computers for the kids' programmes might (but not under all circumstances) provide one means toward this end.

It is not the case that the new information technologies are inherently dangerous, or that (all) programmes to put computers on classroom desks must be seen as undesirable. Arguably, we must, as educationists (whether in school or tertiary settings), 'move with the times', and grasp the new possibilities for changing modes of reading, writing, publishing, and learning in the information age. The danger lies in seeing computerisation as a *necessarily* positive process with benefits for all. It is vital that we maintain a critical posture when examining the new information technologies and their implications for education (Roberts, 1997e). Computing developments across the globe need to be *politicised* if the risk of lapsing into either a technocratic approach or a position of passive acceptance is to be avoided.

In this respect, the work of people such as Tim Luke is very helpful. In a provocative essay entitled 'Going to cyberschool in the virtual university', Luke (1996) argues that the major players in the computer market (e.g. Microsoft) are, in subtle and not-so-subtle ways, beginning to dictate the future of education. Such corporate giants tell those eager to listen (and many in the educational world are) that almost every aspect of social life is becoming digitised, that we must move quickly (in both our adoption of new technologies and our thinking) to keep up with such changes, and *then*, in one and same marketing movement, provide – at considerable cost to consumers, and with considerable gains for people such as Bill Gates – the hardware and software ('absolutely') necessary for this transition.

In this context, it is not difficult to imagine the NZQA becoming a relatively minor player in the educational market (if the corporates take over completely, in a fully privatised system). Alternatively, if 'arrangements' between government bodies and corporate providers of digital services become more explicit and widespread, the NZQA, or some other bureaucratic organisation with a similar designated function, could become a significant regulatory force in the social system – one which nonetheless (of necessity in a marketised world) must not be seen as too intrusive by 'consumers' in the educational marketplace. The notion of maintaining some distance from the day-to-day workings of assessment processes and judgements about educational quality is clearly envisaged in the qualifications green paper (Ministry of Education, 1997b), where it is proposed that the NZQA will play a role as 'overall guardian' in the qualifications system. The NZQA would have 'an overview role; it would not focus on the detail of courses and teaching' (Ministry of Education, 1997b: 7).

A particularly distressing scenario would involve the increasing employment of new technologies for surveillance purposes, where ultimately every movement of every citizen might be monitored. A clear link between government agencies and major corporate entities has been made with the practice of 'information sharing'. The amount of data on each New Zealand citizen stored in the infamous and mysterious 'Wanganui computer' – or others like it – is a matter for continuing speculation. Cameras keep a watchful eye on people as they shop, drive and walk the streets. An idea for running a surveillance camera continuously in a pre-school classroom was recently hailed by some as an important innovation (in making sure teachers do not abuse children), and some employers now regard the digital recording of employee actions as an inalienable right.

'Information sharing' of a different kind is signalled in the qualifications green paper. References to building databases of credit information can be found at selected points in the document. Such references have a close relationship to the emphasis on portability and the need for a common currency. The following passage effectively conveys the government's plans:

> A common 'currency' for parts of qualifications (outcomes, level and credit) would be expected to facilitate providers' decisions on credit transfer, leading to improved portability, but would not be a *guarantee* of portability. It is further proposed that the NZQA should maintain a database of education providers' agreements for credit transfer, and this information should be publicly available through *KiwiCareers*. This would mean that students could know in advance if providers already had arrangements which recognised each other's programmes and their components. This could assist students' choices of programmes and providers in many cases.
>
> (Ministry of Education, 1997b: 22–23)

Such proposals, also given support in the tertiary education white paper (Ministry of Education, 1998), seem harmless enough, and we see the desire to make databases of this kind available to the public as laudable. But if this move toward gathering large amounts of data about qualifications is coupled with an attempt to collate, through increasingly sophisticated electronic means, more and more information about *individuals* (or groups, organisations, institutions, etc.), the process begins to take on a slightly different face. While such a scenario may seem far-fetched, it needs to be considered alongside other mechanisms for maintaining detailed records (both visual and written) on individuals and groups in New Zealand society, and elsewhere in the world, already in place. Once a 'common currency' for exchanging information about qualifications and assessment has been established, as mooted in the qualifications green paper, it is conceivable that the entire educational history of each New Zealand citizen – including not just the certificates, degrees or diplomas they have gained, but a host of other details as well – could be recorded in a huge NZQA-administered database. How *much* detail might be regarded as necessary by officials in the NZQA, the Ministry of Education or other wings of government would be a matter for considerable debate and would depend on other developments in social policy over the next decade. This is a speculative, and perhaps rather unduly pessimistic, portrait of educational policy in the future.

Still, the possibility of appearing to 'set the educational subject free' (to wander the marketplace, making continuous consumer-style choices about 'providers' and qualifications) while at the same time watching over his or her every move is not an entirely unrealistic scenario. A critical reading of the qualifications green paper (or the tertiary education white paper) need not presuppose that such developments are part of a carefully crafted plan; but while we may want to grant policy makers the benefit of the doubt, there is nevertheless some merit in contemplating alternative educational futures – some of which are horrific indeed.

Concluding Comments

When Cardinal John Henry Newman published the first version of *The Idea of a University* in 1873 (Newman, 1996), it would have been difficult to imagine how much the world would change in little more than a century. While there is still much in Newman's classic account of relevance to the contemporary age, it is perhaps now necessary to talk of 'the idea of the *electronic* university' (Landow, 1996). We believe further changes in tertiary education under the influence of new developments in information technologies and systems of communication are inevitable. These will be accompanied by a new logic of legitimation and a substantial transformation in the nature of scholarly life for both students and staff in the tertiary sector. Electronic networks will allow academics to reclaim some control over the circulation of their own ideas, yet at the same time our thoughts and actions could be increasingly shaped and regulated by sophisticated (computer-based) mechanisms of surveillance. Corporates will increasingly encroach into every area of social life (including education), and distinctions between government and commercial activity will continue to break down.

The New Zealand Government is only just beginning to 'wake up' to the potential of the new information technologies for furthering a neoliberal agenda inaugurated more than a decade ago. The almost complete absence of any discussion of information technology issues in the green and white papers on tertiary education is remedied, to some extent, in the teacher education green paper. There are also other initiatives under way via the Foresight Project and the Information Technology Advisory Group. We do well, however, to examine these documents (and others) in the context of wider changes in social and educational policy. Talk by the Ministry of Education of enhancing learning and training through flexible delivery systems using information and communication technologies can, on one level, be seen as a somewhat belated but important recognition of changing global realities. The promotion of a lifelong learning system, in which networked computers will obviously play an important role, is to be applauded. Similarly, the development of comprehensive databases on different qualifications can assist students in gaining the necessary information for making sound educational decisions.

These positive features must, however, be balanced with a sober examination of the potential dangers attending a synthesis of neoliberal social reform and the new information technologies. Unless academics, students and other interested groups can mobilise effectively to resist the tide of recent changes, further privatisation of the tertiary education sector in New Zealand seems inevitable. This will involve a complex set of relations between the state, students and tertiary education 'providers'. Following a trend that started with the abolition of the University Grants Committee almost a decade ago, further steps toward a 'board of directors' style of governance will – if the indicative legislation in the white paper (Ministry of Education, 1998) is supported in Parliament – be put in place in New Zealand universities. It is clear that the government has no desire to protect traditional systems of governance. Universities, like almost all other organisations in a neoliberal policy environment, will increasingly be expected to operate like businesses and follow the rules of the market. On the one hand, then, privatisation will be actively encouraged; declining state support for public institutions of higher education (and particularly universities) will see to this, even if the rhetoric is to the contrary. On the other hand, regulation of any remaining public institutions will – despite some appearances to the contrary – be tightened. This might, as Bryan Gould, Vice-Chancellor of the University of Waikato, puts it, be seen as 'an unattractive combination of market pressures and government control' (1997: 9).

This awkward synthesis, when viewed alongside the parallel development of 'virtual' universities (making maximum use of the new information technologies) will dramatically change the face of tertiary education. The new information technologies do have the potential to liberate many teachers and learners from the tyrannies of time and distance. The withdrawal of the state from people's lives could furnish new freedoms and foster modes of intellectual independence commensurate with the bold and adventurous technological spirit of our times. At the same time, further computerisation may also provide the means for more sophisticated and oppressive forms of state regulation – through continuous monitoring of the movements and thoughts of citizens – while reducing tertiary education to nothing more than a contractual exchange between self-interested consumers and 'providers' in a competitive marketplace.

Resisting these negative possibilities may involve harnessing computer networks for 'subversive' purposes. There is already a strong 'anti-establishment' attitude in many sections of the Internet community, but the forms of protest flowing from this sometimes lack structure and theoretical substance. Anarchy rather than informed resistance seems to prevail in many cases. This is, of course, part of what Internet enthusiasts love about the new medium: it is, or *seems* to be, a terrain largely without rules, policed more by users themselves via the informal codes that collectively construct a kind of 'netiquette' than by regulations imposed by others. Indeed, freedom of speech is perhaps the most cherished of Internet values, as demonstrated by the outcries surrounding government attempts to control access to offensive and sexually explicit materials. Nonetheless, even if resistance without rules is common practice, access to the Internet opens up new opportunities for organised struggle. Disenfranchised (academic and other) groups can communicate with their peers at a speed and on a scale hitherto unimagined. The breaking down of (some) geographical barriers to communication in the cyberspatial age provides one of the keys to a new form of *international* politics. The New Zealand Government's slow response to changes already well established elsewhere provides some hope that there may still be time to realise the more positive vision of a tertiary education future: one in which the new information technologies are dynamically integrated with critical, democratic and innovative traditions in teaching, learning and research.

Endnote

1   For an overview of some key books on the information age and an indication of what this vast and wide-ranging literature has to offer, see Cox (1998).

Bibliography

Alliez, E. (1997), Questionnaire on Deleuze. *Theory, Culture and Society, 14* (2), 81–87.

Association of University Staff of New Zealand (1995). Tertiary Action Group's consultation with stakeholders – response to discussion papers 1–3, Oct. 2.

Association of University Staff of New Zealand (1997). Submission on *A future tertiary education policy for New Zealand: Tertiary education review* (green paper). Wellington.

Association of University Staff of New Zealand (1998). *Bulletin.* December.

Association of University Staff (Victoria University of Wellington) (1996). Response to Victoria University of Wellington Council working party discussion document on governance. Wellington.

Barker, A. (1995). Standards-based assessment: The vision and the broader factors. In R. Peddie & B. Tuck (Eds) *Setting the standards: Issues in assessment for national qualifications.* Palmerston North: Dunmore Press.

Barnett, R. (1994). *The limits of competence: Knowledge, higher education and society.* Buckingham: The Society for Research into Higher Education & Open University Press.

Barradori, G. (1994). *The American philosopher* (R. Crocitto, Trans.). Chicago & London: Chicago University Press.

Barry, A. Osborne, T. & Rose, N. (Eds) (1996). *Foucault and political reason: Liberalism, neo-liberalism and rationalities of government.* London: UCL Press.

Bell, D. (1974). *The coming of postindustrial society: A venture in social forecasting.* Harmondsworth: Penguin.

Berube, M. & Nelson, C. (Eds) (1995). *Higher education under fire: Politics, economics, and the crisis of the humanities.* New York: Routledge.

Bloom, A. (1988). *The closing of the American mind.* Harmondsworth: Penguin.

Bok, D.C. (1982). *Beyond the ivory tower: Social responsibilities of the modern university.* Cambridge, Mass.: Harvard University Press.

Bollard, A. & Mayes, D. (1993). Corporatization and privatization in New Zealand. In T. Clarkes & C. Pitelis (Eds) *The political economy of privatization* (pp. 308–336). London & New York: Routledge.

Bollard, A. (1994). In J. Williams (Ed.) *The political economy of reform.* Washington D.C.: Institute for International Economics.

Boston, J. (1988). *The future of New Zealand universities: An exploration of some of the *issues raised by the reports of the Watts Committee and the Treasury.* Wellington: Victoria University Press, for the Institute of Policy Studies.

Boston, J. (1995). *The state under contract.* Wellington: Bridget Williams.

Boston, J. (1997a). The tertiary education review: Issues and implications. Paper prepared for a staff seminar at the University of Auckland, 23 October.

Boston, J. (1997b). The tertiary education review: A critical appraisal. Paper prepared for the NZUSA annual conference, University of Canterbury, 30 August.

Boston, J. Martin, J., Pallot, J. & Walsh, P. (Eds) (1991). *Reshaping the state: New Zealand's bureaucratic revolution.* Auckland, Oxford University Press.

Boston, J. Martin, J., Pallot, J. & Walsh, P. (Eds) (1996). *Public management: The New Zealand model.* Auckland: Oxford University Press.

Buchanan, J. (1986). *Liberty, market and the state: Political economy in the 1980s,* Brighton, Sussex: Wheatsheaf Books.

Burchell, G., Gordon, C. & Miller, P. (1991). (Eds) *The Foucault effect: Studies in governmentality, with two lectures and an interview with Michel Foucault.* Hemel Hempstead: Harvester Wheatsheaf.

Burge, K. (1997). Quest for excellence: NZQA chief answers exam criticisms. *New Zealand Herald,* 3 March, A17.

Bushnell, P. & Scott, G. (1988). An economic perspective. In J. Martin, & J. Harper (Eds) *Devolution and accountability* (pp. 19–36). New Zealand Institute of Public Administration Studies in Public Administration No. 34, Proceedings of the 1988 Conference. Wellington: Government Printer.

Butterworth, R. & Tarling, N. (1994). *A shakeup anyway: Government and the universities in New Zealand in a decade of reform.* Auckland: Auckland University Press.

Carnoy, M. (1995). Structural adjustment and the changing face of education. *International Labour Review,* 653–673.

Chambers, M. (1998). In quest of appropriate applications of digital multimedia for purposes of higher learning. In M. Peters & P. Roberts (Eds) *Virtual technologies and tertiary education* (pp. 171–195). Palmerston North: Dunmore Press.

Chapman, J. (1995). The NZQA qualifications framework – university autonomy under threat. Paper circulated to Association of University Staff members, 29 August.

Clark, T. & Royle, N. (1995). Editorial audit. In Clark & Royle (Eds) *The university in ruins: Essays on the crisis in the concept of the modern university.* Special issue, *Oxford Literary Review,* 15, 3–14. (See essays by Readings, B., Hindess, B. and Hunter, I.)

Codd, J. (1993a). Equity and choice: The paradox of New Zealand educational reform. *Curriculum Studies, 1* (1), 75–90.

Codd, J. (1993b). Neo-liberal education policy and the ideology of choice. *Educational Philosophy and Theory, 24* (2), 31–48.

Codd, J. (1994). Designing a framework for university qualifications: A question of standards. Paper presented at the annual conference of the New Zealand Association for Research in Education, Christchurch, December 2–4.

Codd, J. (1995). NZQA and the politics of centralism. Paper presented at the annual conference of the New Zealand Association for Research in Education, Palmerston North, December 7–10.

Codd, J. (1996). Higher education and the qualifications framework: A question of standards. *Delta: Policy and Practice in Education, 48* (1), 57–66.

Codd, J. (1997). Knowledge, qualifications and higher education: A critical view. In K. Morris Matthews & M. Olssen (Eds) *Education policy in New Zealand: The 1990s and beyond.* Palmerston North: Dunmore Press.

Codd, J. (1998). The price of freedom. *New Zealand Education Review*, 2 Dec., 11.

Cox, R. (1998). Drawing sea serpents: The publishing wars on personal computing and the Information Age. *First Monday: The Peer-Reviewed Journal on the Internet, 3* (5). http://www.firstmonday.dk/issues/issue3_5/cox/index.html

Combined Chaplaincies at Victoria University of Wellington (1995). *The university, ethics and society – Tertiary Christian studies.* Wellington: Victoria University of Wellington.

Creech, W. (1997a). Foreword. In Ministry of Education, *A future qualifications policy for New Zealand* (green paper). Wellington.
<http://www.minedu.govt.nz/data/NQF/paper/htm>

Creech, W. (1997b). Foreword. In Ministry of Education, *A future tertiary education policy for New Zealand: Tertiary education review* (green paper). Wellington.
<http:/www.minedu.govt.nz/data/NQF/paper/htm>

Creech, W. (1997c). Foreword. In Ministry of Education, *Quality teachers for quality learning: A review of teacher education* (green paper). Wellington: Ministry of Education.
<http:/www.minedu.govt.nz/data/NQF/paper/htm>

Creech, W. (1998). Foreword by the Minister of Education. In Ministry of Education, *Tertiary education in New Zealand: Policy directions for the 21st century* (white paper). Wellington: Ministry of Education.

Crocombe, G. Enright, M. & Porter, M. (1991). *Upgrading New Zealand's competitive advantage.* Auckland: Oxford University Press.

Crozier, R. (1997). Demographic guinea pigs. *New Zealand Education Review*, 16 April, 7 ("Tertiary education special supplement").

Cunningham, S. *et al.* (1998). *New media and borderless education: A review of the convergence between global media networks and higher education provision.* Evaluations and Investigations Program, Higher Education Division, DEETYA: Commonwealth of Australia.

Daintith, T. (1994). The legal techniques of privatization. In T. Clarke (Ed.) *International privatization: Strategies and practices* (pp. 43–77). Berlin & New York: Walter de Gruyter.

Dale, R. (1997). The state and the governance of education: An analysis of the restructuring of the state-education relationship. In A. H. Halsey, H. Lauder, P. Brown & A. Stuart-Wells (Eds) *Education: Culture, Economy & Society* (pp. 273–282). Oxford: Oxford University Press.

Dale, R. (1998). Globalisation: A new world for comparative education. In J. Schriewer (Ed.) *Discourse and comparative education.* Berlin: Peter Lang. (Pre-published copy of manuscript.)

Dale, R. & Jesson, J. (1992). Mainstreaming education: The role of the state services commission. *New Zealand Annual Review of Education, 2,* 7–34.

Dale, R. & Robertson, S. (1997). "Resiting" the nation, "reshaping" the state. In K. Morris Matthews & M. Olssen (Eds) *Education policy in New Zealand: The 1990s and beyond.* Palmerston North: Dunmore Press.

Davidson, A. (1997). Structures and strategies of discourse: Remarks towards a history of Foucault's philosophy of language. In A. Davidson (Ed.) *Foucault and his interlocutors.* Chicago & London: The University of Chicago Press.

Dearing, R. (Chair) (1997). *Higher education in the learning society.* Report of the National Committee of Inquiry into Higher Education (United Kingdom). <http://www.leEdsac.uk/educol/ncihe/docsinde.htm>

Delanty, G. (1998). The idea of the university in the global era: From knowledge as an end to the end of knowledge. *Social Epistemology, 12* (1), 3–26.

Deleuze, G. (1992). Postscript on the societies of control. *October, 59,* 3–7. <ftp://etext.archive.umich.edu/pub/Politics/Spunk/anarchy_texts/misc/Spunk962.txt>

Department of Education (1988a). *Report of the working group on post-compulsory education and training* (Hawke Report). Wellington: Department of Education.

Department of Education (1988b). *Administering for excellence: Report of the taskforce to review educational administration* (Picot Report). Wellington: Government Printer.

Department of Education (1988c). *Tomorrow's schools: The reform of education administration in New Zealand,* Minister of Education, the Rt. Hon. David Lange. Wellington: Government Printer.

Department of Education (1989a). *Learning for life: Education and training beyond the age of 15.* Wellington: Department of Education.

Department of Education (1989b). *Learning for life II: Policy decisions.* Wellington: Department of Education.

Derrida, J. (1983). The principle of reason: The university in the eyes of its pupils. *Diacritics,* Fall, 3–20.

Derrida, J. (1994). Of the humanities and the philosophical discipline: the right to philosophy from the cosmopolitical point of view, *Surfaces, 4.* <http://tornade.ere.umontreal.ca/~guedon/Surfaces/vol4/derrida.html>

Douglas, G.H. (1992). *Education without impact: How our universities fail the young.* New York: Birch Lane Press.

Douglas, I. (1997). Globalisation and the end of the state? *New Political Economy, 2* (1), 165–77.

Douglas, R. (1993). *Unfinished business.* Auckland: Random House.

Doyle, J. (1997). Qualified solutions. *New Zealand Education Review,* 16 April, 7–8 ("Tertiary education special supplement").

Drucker, P. (1993). *Post-capitalist society*. New York: Harper.

D'Souza, D. (1991). *Illiberal education: The politics of race and sex on campus*. New York: The Free Press.

Duncan, I. & Bollard, A. (1992). *Corporatization and privatization: Lessons from New Zealand*. Auckland: Oxford University Press.

Durie, M. (1988). Social policy perspectives. In J. Martin & J. Harper (Eds) *Devolution and accountability*. New Zealand Institute of Public Administration Studies in Public Administration No. 34, Proceedings of the 1988 Conference (pp. 8–18). Wellington: Government Printer.

Dyke, C. (1993). Extralogical excavations: Philosophy in an age of shovelry. In J. Caputo & M. Yount (Eds) *Foucault and the critique of institutions*. Pennsylvania: Pennsylvania State University Press.

Easton, B. (1995). The commercialisation of tertiary education. In J. Marshall (Ed.) *The economics of education*. Faculty of Education: University of Auckland.

Education Forum (1998). *Policy directions for tertiary education*. Auckland: Education Forum.

Education and Training Support Agency (1993). *Skill New Zealand: lifelong education and training*. Wellington: New Zealand Qualifications Authority.

Elam, D. (1994). *Feminism and deconstruction*. London & New York: Routledge.

Elley, W. (1995). What is wrong with standards-based assessment? In R. Peddie & B. Tuck (Eds) *Setting the standards: Issues in assessment for national qualifications*. Palmerston North: Dunmore Press.

Elley, W. (1996). Unresolved issues in fitting academic courses into the qualifications framework. *Delta: Policy and Practice in Education, 48* (1), 67–76.

Evans, J. (1997). Economic globalisation: The need for a social dimension. Trade Union Advisory Committee (TUAC-OECD).

Farrands, C. (1996). The globalisation of knowledge and the politics of global intellectual property: Power, governance and technology. In E. Kofman & G. Youngs (Eds) *Globalisation: Theory and practice*. London & New York: Pinter.

Fitzsimons, P. (1995). The management of tertiary educational institutions in New Zealand. *Journal of Education Policy, 10* (2), 173–187.

Fitzsimons, P. (1996). Electronic networks and education in the postmodern condition. Paper presented at the Philosophy of Education Society of Australasia conference, Brisbane, October.

Fitzsimons, P. (1997). Human capital theory and participation in tertiary education in New Zealand. In K. Morris Matthews & M. Olssen (Eds) *Education policy in New Zealand: The 1990s and beyond*. Palmerston North: Dunmore Press.

Fitzsimons, P. & Peters, M. (1994). Human capital theory and the industry training strategy in New Zealand. *Journal of Education Policy, 9* (2), 245–266.

Foray, D. & Lundvall, B-Å (1996). The knowledge-based economy: From the economics of knowledge to the learning economy. In OECD, *Employment and growth in the knowledge-*

based economy. Paris: The Organisation.

Foucault, M. (1970). *The order of things*. London: Tavistock.

Foucault, M. (1994). La philosophie analytique de la politique. In D. Defert & F. Ewald, with J. Lagrange (Eds) *Dits et écrits, 1954–1988, v. 3*, Paris.

Francis, D. (1996). *Changes to the governance/ownership structures of New Zealand universities*. Futures Management, Lincoln University.

Freire, P. (1985). *The politics of education*. London: MacMillan.

Fritzman, J.M. (1995). From pragmatism to the differend. In M. Peters (Ed.) *Education and the postmodern condition*. Westport, Connecticut: Bergin and Garvey.

Gee, J., Hull, G. & Lankshear, C. (1996). *The new work order*. Sydney: Allen and Unwin.

Gitlin, T. (1995). *The twilight of common dreams: Why America is wracked by culture wars*. New York: Metropolitan Books.

Global Alliance Limited (1997). Australian higher education in the era of mass customisation. Appendix 11 in R. West (Chair) *Review of higher education financing and policy*. Interim Report of the Higher Education Review committee (Australia).

Goedegebuure, L.C.J. (Ed) (1992). *Higher education policy in international comparative perspective*. Enschede, Centre for Higher Education Policy Studies.

Gordon, L. (1995). Human capital theory and the death of democracy: Tertiary education policy in New Zealand. In M. Olssen & K. Morris Matthews (Eds) *Education, democracy and reform*. Auckland: NZARE/RUME.

Gould, B. (1997). The way forward for universities and the tertiary sector: A view on the Tertiary Education Review 1997. [On behalf of the New Zealand Vice-Chancellors' Committee].

Guha, R. (Ed.) (1982–92). *Subaltern studies*. Delhi, Oxford University Press, v 1–7.

Guha, R. & Spivak, G.C. (1988). (Eds) *Selected subaltern studies*. New York: Oxford University Press.

Gunn, C. (1998). Virtual technologies in higher education: Vision or reality? In M. Peters & P. Roberts (Eds) *Virtual technologies and tertiary education* (pp. 134–145). Palmerston North: Dunmore Press.

Habermas, Jürgen (1987). The idea of the university-learning processes. *New German Critique*, 41, Spring–Summer, 3–22.

Hall, C. (1995a). University qualifications and the NZ national qualifications framework: Obstacles and a way forward. In R. Peddie & B. Tuck (Eds) *Setting the standards: Issues in assessment for national qualifications*. Palmerston North: Dunmore Press.

Hall, C. (1995b). Why universities do not want unit standards. *NZVCC Newsletter*, July.

Harris, P. (1989). The international politics of privatisation. In *Private power or public interest? Widening the debate on privatisation* (pp. 21–35). NZPSA, Palmerston North: Dunmore Press.

Haynes, B. & Fitzsimons, P. (1997). The politics of teacher competence. Paper presented at the Philosophy of Education Society of Australasia conference, Sydney, July.

Heing, J., Hamnett, C. & Feigenbaum, H. (1988). The politics of privatisation: A comparative perspective. *Governance, 1* (4), 442–468.

Hindess, B. (1995). Great expectations: Freedom and authority in the idea of the modern university. *Oxford Literary Review, 17,* 29–50.

Hood, C. (1990). De-Sir Humphreyfying the Westminister model of bureaucracy. *Governance, 3* (2), 205–214.

Hood, D. (1995). Address at the Principals' Forum 1995, Training Centre, National Archives, Wellington, 15 September.

Hood, D. (1999). NZQA demotion. *New Zealand Education Review,* 15 January, 6.

Humanities Society of New Zealand (1997). Submission to the Tertiary Education Review (Draft), Wellington.

Hunter, I. (1994). *Rethinking the school: Subjectivity, bureaucracy, criticism.* St Leonards, N.S.W.: Allen & Unwin.

Hunter, I. The regimen of reason: Kant's defence of the Philosophy faculty. *Oxford Literary Review, 17,* 50–86.

Irwin, M. (1995). The national qualifications framework. Address to the Principals' Forum 1995, Training Centre, National Archives, Wellington, 15 September.

Jesson, B. (1997). Foreword: The role of the intellectual is to defend the role of the intellectual. In M. Peters (Ed.) *Cultural politics and the university in Aotearoa/New Zealand.* Palmerston North: Dunmore Press.

Jesson, J. (1998). Virtual technologies and academic labour: More questions than answers. In M. Peters & P. Roberts (Eds) *Virtual technologies and tertiary education* (pp. 93–110). Palmerston North: Dunmore Press.

Kant, Immanuel, *The conflict of the faculties* (Trans. M. Gregor). New York: Abaris Books, 1979 [orig. 1798], p. 23. Cited in Jacques Derrida 'Mochlos; or The Conflict of the Faculties' (Trans. R. Rand & A. Wygant). In Richard Rand (Ed.) (1992) *Logomachia: The conflict of the faculties,* Lincoln & London: University of Nebraska Press.

Kelsey, J. (1993). *Rolling back the state: Privatisation of power in Aotearoa/New Zealand.* Wellington: Bridget Williams Books.

Kelsey, J. (1995). *The New Zealand experiment: A world model for structural adjustment?* Auckland: Auckland University Press/Bridget Williams Books.

Kelsey, J. (1997). The globalisation of tertiary education: Implications of GATS. In M. Peters (Ed) *Cultural politics and the university in Aotearoa/New Zealand.* Palmerston North: Dunmore Press.

Kelsey, J. (1998). White paper on education shows muddled thinking rather than vision. *New Zealand Herald,* 3 December, A19.

Kerr, C. (1994). *Higher education cannot escape history: Issues for the twenty-first century.* New York: State University of New York Press.

Kerr, R. (1997). Upgrading New Zealand's human resources. Address at a gathering of the New Zealand Institute of Personnel Management (Auckland branch), Auckland, 17 September. <http://www.nzbr.org.nz >

Kimball, R. (1990). *Tenured radicals.* New York: Harper Perennial.

Kofman, E. & Youngs, G. (Eds) (1996). *Globalisation: theory and practice*. London & New York: Pinter.

Kohn, P. & Mortimer, K.P. (1983). Selecting effective trustees. *Change Magazine, 15* (5), 30–37.

Landow, G.P. (1996). Newman and the idea of an electronic university. In J.H. Newman, *The idea of a university* (F.M. Turner, Ed.) (pp. 39–361). New Haven and London: Yale University Press.

Le Grand, J. & Robinson, R. (1984). Privatisation and the welfare state: An introduction. In J. Le Grand, and R. Robinson (Eds) *Privatisation and the welfare state*. London: Allen and Unwin.

Lee, A. & Green, B. (1997). Pedagogy and disciplinarity in the "new university". *UTS Review, 3* (1), 1–25.

Lefebvre, H. (1991). *The production of space*. Oxford: Blackwell.

Luke, T. (1996). The politics of cyberschooling at the virtual university. Paper presented at the symposium on "The Virtual University", University of Melbourne. <http://www.edfac.unimelb.edu.au/virtu/luke.htm>

Luke, T. (1997a). Discourse and discipline in the digital domain: The political economy of the virtual university. Keynote address at the conference on "Virtual technologies in tertiary education: A vision for New Zealand?", sponsored by the Association of University Staff of New Zealand, Auckland, October.

Luke, T. (1997b). Thinking about cultural politics in the university: Professional correctness or political correctness? In M. Peters (Ed.) *Cultural politics and the university in Aotearoa/New Zealand*. Palmerston North: Dunmore Press.

Lyotard, J.-F. (1984). *The Postmodern Condition: A report on knowledge* (Trans. G. Bennington & B. Massumi). Minneapolis: University of Minnesota Press.

Lyotard, J.-F. (1988). *The differend: Phrases in dispute* (Trans. G. Van Den Abbeele). Minneapolis: University of Minnesota Press.

Lyotard, J.-F. (1993). *Political writings* (Trans. B. Readings & P. Griemas, B. Readings, Ed.). Minneapolis: University of Minnesota Press.

Maani, S.A. (1997). *Investing in minds: The economics of higher education in New Zealand*. Wellington: Institute of Policy Studies, Victoria University of Wellington.

Machlup, F. (1962). *The production and distribution of knowledge in the United States*. Princeton: Princeton University Press.

Mahoney, D. (1994). Government and the universities: The "new" mutuality in Australian higher education. *Journal of Higher Education, 65* (2), 123–146.

Maling, J. (1998). *Future directions for teacher education at the University of Otago* (Maling Report). University of Otago.

Marginson, S. (1996). Comments on the discussion paper by the Victoria University of Wellington working paper on governance. Wellington: Unpublished paper.

Marshall, J. (1995). Skills, information and quality for the autonomous chooser. In M. Olssen & K. Morris Matthews (Eds) *Education, democracy and reform*. Auckland:

NZARE/RUME.

Marshall, J. (1996). The autonomous chooser and "reforms" in education. *Studies in Philosophy and Education, 15,* 89–96.

Maslen, G. & Slattery, L. (1994). *Why our universities are failing: Crisis in the clever country.* Melbourne: Wilkinson Books.

Masuda, Y. (1981). *The information society as post-industrial society.* Washington, DC: World Future Society.

Matheson, D. (1997). NZQA advice discarded by schools. *New Zealand Education Review,* 16 April, 5.

McCormick, R. & Meiners, R.E. (1988). University governance: A property rights perspective. *Journal of Law and Economics, 31,* 423–442.

McKenzie, D. (1997). The cult of efficiency and miseducation: Issues of assessment in New Zealand schools. In K. Morris Matthews & M. Olssen (Eds) *Education policy in New Zealand: The 1990s and beyond.* Palmerston North: Dunmore Press.

McLean, J. (1996). The contracting state. In M. Peters, W. Hope, J. Marshall & S. Webster (Eds) *Critical theory, poststructuralism & the social context* (pp. 212–229). Palmerston North, NZ: The Dunmore Press.

Messer-Davidow, E. (1993). Manufacturing the attack on higher education. *Social Text, 36,* 40–80.

Messer-Davidow, E., Shunway, D. R. & Sylvan, D. L. (Eds) (1993). *Knowledges: Historical and critical studies in disciplinarity.* Charlottesville & London: University Press of Virginia.

Ministry of Education (1993). *The New Zealand curriculum framework.* Wellington: Learning Media.

Ministry of Education (1994). *Report of the ministerial consultative group* (Todd Report). Wellington: Ministry of Education.

Ministry of Education (1997a). *A future tertiary education policy for New Zealand: Tertiary education review* (green paper). Wellington: Ministry of Education.
<http://www.minedu.govt.nz/data/NQF/paper/htm>

Ministry of Education (1997b). *A future qualifications policy for New Zealand* (green paper). Wellington: Ministry of Education.
<http://www.minedu.govt.nz/data/NQF/paper/htm>

Ministry of Education (1997c). *Quality teachers for quality learning: A review of teacher education* (green paper). Wellington: Ministry of Education.
<http://www.minedu.govt.nz/data/NQF/paper/htm>

Ministry of Education (1997d). Tertiary education review: Proposals and key decisions. Wellington. (Draft document dated 17 July 1997, leaked to the media.)

Ministry of Education (1998). *Tertiary education in New Zealand: Policy directions for the 21st century* (white paper). Wellington: Ministry of Education.

Ministry of Maori Affairs (1988). *He tirohanga rangapu: Partnership perspectives.* Wellington: Government Printer.

Ministry of Research, Science and Technology (1998). *Building tomorrow's success: Guidelines for thinking beyond today. The Foresight Project.* MoRST: Wellington. <http://www.morst.govt.nz/foresight/front.html>

Myers, D. (1993) Schooling for the 21st century. Address at the "Successful schools – successful business" conference, 13 March. <http://www.nzbr.org.nz>

Myers, D. (1996a) Why not simply the best? Address at a gathering of the Canterbury Manufacturers Association, 27 February. <http://www.nzbr.org.nz>

Myers, D. (1996b). Education: the way the world should be. Address at the Independent Schools Council annual conference, 18 May.

Nandy, A. (1988). *Science, hegemony and violence: A requiem for modernity.* Delhi, Oxford: Oxford University Press.

Neave, G. & F. A. Van Vught. (Eds) (1991). *Prometheus bound: The changing relationship between government and higher education in Western Europe.* Oxford: Pergamon Press.

Nelson, C. & Gaonkar, D. P. (1996). *Disciplinarity and dissent in cultural studies.* New York: Routledge.

Nelson, C. (Ed.) (1997). *Will teach for food: Academic labour in crisis.* Minneapolis: University of Minnesota Press.

New Zealand Business Roundtable (1987). *Reforming tertiary education in New Zealand.* Wellington: New Zealand Business Roundtable.

New Zealand Business Roundtable (1994). *The funding and regulation of tertiary education.* A Submission to the Minister of Education on the Report of the Ministerial Consultative Group on Funding Growth in Tertiary Education: Wellington.

New Zealand Qualifications Authority (1991). *Designing the framework: A discussion document about restructuring national qualifications.* Wellington: NZ Qualifications Authority.

New Zealand Qualifications Authority (1992a). *Learning to learn: An introduction to the New Zealand qualifications framework.* Wellington: NZ Qualifications Authority.

New Zealand Qualifications Authority (1992b). *The Framework and industry.* Wellington: New Zealand Qualifications Authority.

New Zealand Qualifications Authority (1993a). *Quality management systems for the National Qualifications Framework.* Wellington: New Zealand Qualifications Authority.

New Zealand Qualifications Authority (1993b). *Guidelines, criteria and regulations for the registration of units and qualifications for national certificates and diplomas.* Wellington: New Zealand Qualifications Authority.

New Zealand Qualifications Authority (1993c). *Briefing papers for the incoming government.* Wellington: New Zealand Qualifications Authority.

New Zealand Vice-Chancellors' Committee (1994). *The national qualifications framework and the universities.* Wellington: New Zealand Vice-Chancellors' Committee.

New Zealand Vice-Chancellors' Committee (1997). Submission by the New Zealand Vice-Chancellors' Committee on *A future tertiary education policy for New Zealand: Tertiary Education Review green paper*, Wellington.

Newman, J.H. (1996). *The idea of a university* (F.M. Turner, Ed.). New Haven and London: Yale Univ. Press. (Original work published 1873, final revised ed. 1889).

Nicholson, C. (1989). Postmodernism, feminism, and education: The need for solidarity. *Educational Theory, 39* (3), 197–205.

Nietzsche, F. (1990). *Beyond good and evil* (Trans. Rev. ed., R.J. Hollingdale). Harmondsworth: Penguin.

Nuyen, A.T. (1995). Lyotard and Rorty on the role of the professor. In M. Peters (Ed.) *Education and the postmodern condition*. Westport, Connecticut: Bergin and Garvey.

Odlyzko, A. (1997). The economics of electronic journals. *First Monday: The Peer-Reviewed Journal on the Internet, 2* (8). <http://www.firstmonday.dk/issues/issue2_8/odlyzko/index.html>

Olssen, M. (1997). Reframing educational policy: Choice, Rawlsianism, communitarianism. In K. Morris Matthews & M. Olssen (Eds) *Education policy in New Zealand: The 1990s and beyond*. Palmerston North: Dunmore Press.

Opie, B. (1995). Renderings to Caesar and donations from Constantine: The value(s) of the humanities. In Combined Chaplaincies at Victoria University of Wellington, *The university, ethics and society – Tertiary Christian studies* (pp. 51–76). Wellington: Victoria University of Wellington.

Organisation for Economic Cooperation and Development (OECD) (1996). *Employment and growth in the knowledge-based economy*. Paris: The Organisation.

Organisation for Economic Cooperation and Development (OECD) (1997a). *Thematic review of the first years of tertiary education: New Zealand*. Wellington: Ministry of Education.

Organisation for Economic Cooperation and Development (OECD) (1997b). *Globalisation: What challenges and opportunities for government?* Paris: The Organisation.

O'Rourke, M. (1993). Foreword. In Ministry of Education, *The New Zealand curriculum framework*. Wellington: Learning Media.

Papadopoulos, G. (1994). *Education 1960–1990: The OECD perspective*. Paris: The Organisation.

Paton, H.J. (1948). Translator's preface. In *The moral law* (Kant's *Groundwork of the metaphysic of morals*). London: Hutchinson.

Patterson, G. (1996). *New Zealand universities in an era of challenge and change*. Department of Management Systems, Massey University, Palmerston North: Occasional Paper No. 4.

Patterson, G. (1997). *The university from ancient Greece to the 20th century*. Palmerston North: Dunmore Press.

Peddie, R. & Tuck, B. (Eds) (1995). *Setting the standards: Issues in assessment for national qualifications*. Palmerston North: Dunmore Press.

Peters, M. (1989). Technoscience, rationality and the university: Lyotard on the "postmodern condition". *Educational Theory, 39* (2), 93–105.

Peters, M. (1992). Performance and accountability in "post-industrial society": The crisis of British universities. *Studies in Higher Education, 17* (2), 123–139.

Peters, M. (1993). Welfare and future of community: The New Zealand experiment. In S. Rees, G. Rodley, & F. Stilwell, (Eds) *Beyond the market: Alternatives to economic rationalism* (pp. 171–188). Marrickville, NSW: Pluto Press.

Peters, M. (Ed.) (1994a). *The corporatisation of New Zealand universities.* Special issue of *Access: Critical Perspectives on Cultural and Policy Studies in Education, 13* (1).

Peters, M. (1994b). "Performance", the future of the university and "post-industrial" society. *Educational Philosophy and Theory, 26* (1), 1–22.

Peters, M. (1995). Introduction: Lyotard, education, and the postmodern condition. In M. Peters (Ed.) *Education and the postmodern condition.* Westport, Conn.: Bergin and Garvey.

Peters, M. (1996a). *Poststructuralism, politics and education.* Westport, Conn.: Bergin and Garvey.

Peters, M. (1996b). New Zealand: The failure of social policy. In G. Argyrous & F. Stilwell (Eds) *Economics as a social science: Readings in political economy* (pp. 248–250). Marrickville, NSW: Pluto Press.

Peters, M. (1996c). Cybernetics, cyberspace and the university: Herman Hesse's *Glass Bead Game* and the dream of a universal language. In M. Peters, *Poststructuralism, politics and education.* Westport, Conn.: Bergin & Garvey.

Peters, M. (1996d). Cybernetics, cyberspace and the politics of university reform. *Australian Journal of Education, 40* (2), 162–176.

Peters, M. (1997a). Neo-liberalism, privatisation and the university in New Zealand: The democratic alternative. In K. Morris Matthews & M. Olssen (Eds) *Education policy in New Zealand: The 1990s and beyond.* Palmerston North: Dunmore Press.

Peters, M. (1997b). Hallowed or hollowed-out halls. *NZ Education Review,* 10 Dec, 9.

Peters, M. (Ed.) (1997c). *Cultural politics and the university.* Palmerston North: Dunmore Press.

Peters, M. (1998). Ownership and governance: The privatisation of New Zealand universities. *Journal of Education Policy, 13* (4).

Peters, M. & Lankshear, C. (1996). Critical literacy and digital texts. *Educational Theory, 46* (1), 51–70.

Peters, M. & Marshall, J. (1996). *Individualism and community: Education and social policy in the postmodern condition.* London: Falmer Press.

Peters, M., Marshall, J. & Parr, B. (1993). The marketisation of tertiary education in New Zealand. *Australian Universities Review, 36* (2), 34–39.

Peters, M. & Roberts, P. (1998a). Agendas for change: Universities in the 21st century, *New Zealand Annual Review of Education, 7,* 5–28.

Peters, M. & Roberts, P. (Eds) (1998b). *Virtual technologies and tertiary education.*

Palmerston North: Dunmore Press.

Peters, M. & Roberts, P. (1999). Globalisation and the crisis in the concept of the modern university. *Australian Universities Review, 42*.

Peters, M. & Roberts, P. (2000 in press). Universities, futurology and globalisation. *Discourse: Studies in the Cultural Politics of Education, 21*.

Pitelis, C. & Clarke, T. (1993). Introduction: The political economy of privatization. In T. Clarkes, & C. Pitelis, (Eds) *The Political Economy of Privatization* (pp. 1–30). London & New York: Routledge.

Pollitt, C. (1989). Editorial, *Public Administration, 67* (1).

Porat, M. (1977). *The information economy: Definition and measurement*. Washington, DC: U.S. Department of Commerce.

Porter, M. (1990). *The competitive advantage of nations*. New York: Free Press.

Public Policy Group. (1996). The working party on university governance discussion paper: A brief response, Victoria University of Wellington.

Readings, B. (1993). For a heteronomous cultural politics: The university, culture and the state. *Oxford Literary Review, 15*.

Readings, B. (1995). Towards a heteronomous politics of education. In M. Peters (Ed.) *Education and the postmodern condition*. Westport, Conn.: Bergin & Garvey.

Readings, B. (1996). *The university in ruins*. Cambridge, Mass.: Harvard University Press.

Rhodes, R. (1996). The new governance: Governing without government. *Political Studies, XLIV*, 652–667.

Rivers, J. (1997). Conflict, closed attitudes hamper NZQA. *New Zealand Education Review*, 21 May, 1.

Roberts, P. (1995). Defining literacy: Paradise, nightmare or red herring? *British Journal of Educational Studies, 43* (4), 412–432.

Roberts, P. (1996a). Structure, direction and rigour in liberating education. *Oxford Review of Education, 22* (3), 295–316.

Roberts, P. (1996b). Critical literacy, breadth of perspective, and universities: Applying insights from Freire. *Studies in Higher Education, 21* (2), 149–163.

Roberts, P. (1996c). Defending Freirean intervention. *Educational Theory, 46* (3), 335–352.

Roberts, P. (1996d). A new academic medium? Scholarly publication and the promise of cyberspace, *Sites: The South Pacific Journal of Cultural Studies, 33*, 68–86.

Roberts, P. (1997a). Qualifications policies and the marketisation of education: A critical reading of the green paper. *Access: Critical Perspectives on Cultural and Policy Studies in Education, 16* (2), 31–47.

Roberts, P. (1997b). A critique of the NZQA policy reforms. In K. Morris Matthews & M. Olssen (Eds) *Education policy in New Zealand: The 1990s and beyond*. Palmerston North: Dunmore Press.

Roberts, P. (1997c). Paulo Freire and political correctness. *Educational Philosophy and Theory, 29* (2), 83–101.

Roberts, P. (1997d). Scholarly life in virtual universities. Keynote address at the conference on "Virtual Technologies in Tertiary Education: A Vision for New Zealand?", sponsored by the Association of University Staff of New Zealand, Auckland, 11 October.

Roberts, P. (1997e). Literacies in cyberspace. *SET: Research Information for Teachers* (Special issue on language and literacy), July, item 4.

Roberts, P. (1997f). The consequences and value of literacy: A critical reappraisal. *Journal of Educational Thought, 31* (1), 45–67.

Roberts, P. (1998a). Rereading Lyotard: Knowledge, commodification and higher education. *Electronic Journal of Sociology, 3* (1). <http://www.sociology.org/vol003.003/roberts.article.1998.html>

Roberts, P. (1998b). The politics of curriculum reform in New Zealand. *Curriculum Studies, 6* (1), 29–46.

Roberts, P. (1998c). The crisis in scholarly publishing: Exploring electronic solutions. *Access: Critical Perspectives on Cultural and Policy Studies in Education, 17* (1), 1–16.

Roberts, P. (1999a). The future of the university: Reflections from New Zealand. *International Review of Education, 45* (1), 65–85.

Roberts, P. (1999b in press). The transformation of higher education in New Zealand. In H. Smaller & D. Cooke (Eds) *Laboring in Academe*. Toronto.

Roberts, P. (1999c in press). Nietzsche and the limits of academic life. In M. Peters, J. Marshall and P. Smeyers (Eds) *Beyond past and present values: Nietzsche's legacy for education*. Westport, Conn.: Bergin and Garvey.

Roberts, P. (1999d in press). Knowledge, information and literacy: A critique of two recent policy initiatives. *International Review of Education, 45.*

Roberts, P. & Peters, M. (1998). Information technologies and tertiary education in New Zealand. *First Monday: The Peer-Reviewed Journal on the Internet, 3* (12). <http://www.firstmonday.dk/>

Roberts, P. & Peters, M. (1999). A critique of the tertiary education white paper. *New Zealand Annual Review of Education, 8.*

Roberts, R.H. & Good, J.M.M. (Eds) (1993). *The recovery of rhetoric: Persuasive discourse and disciplinarity in the human sciences*. Charlottesville, Va.: University Press of Virginia.

Rorty, R. (1982). Professionalized philosophy and transcendentalized culture. In *Consequences of pragmatism* (pp. 60–72). Minneapolis: Univ. of Minnesota Press.

Rorty, R. (1990). The dangers of over-philosophication: Reply to Arcilla and Nicholson. *Educational Theory, 40.*

Rorty, R. (1991). Is Derrida a transcendental philosopher? In *Essays on Heidegger and others*. Cambridge: Cambridge University Press.

Royal Commission Social Policy (1998). *The April Report,* 4 v. in 5, Wellington.

Said, E. (1994a). *Culture and imperialism*. New York & London: Vintage.

Said, E. (1994b). *Representations of the intellectual: The 1993 Reith Lectures*. New York: Pantheon Books.

Scott, G. & Smelt, S. (1995). Ownership of universities. A paper presented for consideration by the New Zealand Vice-Chancellors' Committee.

Scott, G., Bushnell, P. & Sallee, N. (1990). Reform of the core public sector: New Zealand experience. *Governance, 3* (2), 138–167.

Self, P. (1993). *Government by the market? The politics of public choice.* London: Macmillan.

Sharp, A. (Ed.) (1994). *Leap into the dark: The changing role of the state in New Zealand since 1984.* Auckland: Auckland University Press.

Shumar, W. (1997). *College for sale: A critique of the commodification of higher education.* London: Falmer Press.

Smith, P. (1990). *Killing the spirit.* New York: Viking.

Soley, L.C. (1995). *Leasing the ivory tower: The corporate takeover of academia.* Boston, Massachusetts: South End Press.

Sosnoski, J.J. (1995). *Modern skeletons in postmodern closets: A cultural studies alternative.* Charlottesville, Va.: University Press of Virginia.

State Services Commission (1992). Governance in tertiary institutions. Paper submitted to the Taskforce on Capital Charging of Tertiary Institutions.

Strange, S. (1996). *The retreat of the state: The diffusion of power in the world economy.* Cambridge: Cambridge University Press.

Sykes, C.J. (1988) *Profscam: Professors and the demise of higher education.* Washington, DC: Regnery Gateway.

Symes, C. & Hopkins, S. (1994). Universities Inc.: *Caveat emptor. Australian Universities' Review, 37* (2), 47–51.

Task Group on Devolution. (1988). *Sharing control, report of the task group on devolution* State Services Commission. Wellington: Government Printer.

Teeple, G. (1995). *Globalization and the decline of social reform.* New Jersey: Humanities Press.

Tertiary Capital Charge Steering Group. (1996). Governance of tertiary education institutions: A discussion paper for the Tertiary Reference Group. Wellington: Unpublished paper.

Thurow, L.C. (1996). *The future of capitalism: How today's economic forces will shape tomorrow's future.* New York: W. Morrow.

He Tirohanga Rangapu: Partnership Perspectives, Wellington, Office of the Minister of Maori Affairs.

Toma, E.F. (1990). Boards of Trustees, agency problems and university output. *Public Choice, 67,* 1–9.

Touraine, A. (1974). *The post-industrial society: Tommorow's social history, classes, conflicts and culture in the programmed society* (Trans. L. Mayhew). London: Wildwood House.

Treasury (1984). *Economic management.* Wellington: Government Printer.

Treasury (1987). *Government management: Brief to the incoming government, vol II: Education issues.* Wellington: Government Printer.

Tuck, B. (1994). Generally fine but occasionally overcast with the possibility of thunder and lightening: A year in the life of the New Zealand Qualifications Authority. In H. Manson (Ed.) *New Zealand annual review of education*. Faculty of Education: Victoria University of Wellington.

Tuck, B. (1995). Issues of objectivity in assessment: a plea for moderation. In R. Peddie & B. Tuck (Eds) *Setting the standards: Issues in assessment for national qualifications*. Palmerston North: Dunmore Press.

Universities Review Committee (1987). *New Zealand's universities: Partners in national development* (Watts Report). Wellington: New Zealand Vice-Chancellors' Committee.

Upton, S. (1987). *The withering of the state*. Wellington: Allen and Unwin.

Van Vught, F. A. (Ed.) (1989). *Governmental strategies and innovation in higher education*. London: Jessica Kingsley.

Van Vught, F. A. (1992). Patterns of governance in higher education: concepts and trends. Paper written for the United Nations Educational, Scientific and Cultural Organisation (UNESCO).

Vattimo, G. (1992), *The Transparent Society* (Trans. D.Webb). Baltimore, John Hopkins University Press.

Victoria University Working Party on Governance (1995). Discussion paper. Wellington: Victoria University of Wellington.

Wallace, D. & Packer, M. (1998). The cultural field in foresight. Humanities Society of New Zealand Knowledge Policy Research Group.

Waters, N. (1995). The role and constitution of university councils. Wellington: Unpublished paper.

West, R. (Chair) (1997). *Review of higher education financing and policy*. Interim Report of the Higher Education Review committee (Australia).

Williams, J. (Ed.) (1994). *The political economy of reform*, Washington, D.C.: Institute for International Economics.

Wilshire, B. (1990). *The moral collapse of the university*. Albany, NY: State University of New York Press.

Wittrock, B. (1993). The modern university: The three transformations. In S. Rothblatt & B. Wittrock (Eds), *The European and American University since 1800: Historical and sociological essays*. Cambridge: Cambridge University Press.

Young, A. (1997). Treasury workers pick up $1.6m in bonuses. *New Zealand Herald*, 29 December, A5.

Index

About the Authors

Michael Peters

Michael Peters is Associate Professor in the School of Education, University of Auckland. His research interests are in the areas of philosophy, education and policy studies. He is the author of a number of books in Bergin and Garvey's *Critical Studies in Education and Culture* series, including: *After the Disciplines: The Emergence of Cultural Studies* (Ed.) (1999); *Wittgenstein: Philosophy, Postmodernism, Pedagogy* (1999), with James Marshall; *Naming the Multiple: Poststructuralism and Education* (Ed.) (1998); *Post–structuralism, Politics and Education* (1996), and; *Education and the Postmodern Condition*, with Foreword by Jean-François Lyotard (Ed.) (1995/97). He is currently Executive Editor of the journal Educational Philosophy and Theory and Co-Editor of the on-line Encyclopedia of Philosophy of Education (http://www.educacao.pro.br/). He has written a number of other books, including: *Individualism and Community: Education and Social Policy in the Postmodern Condition*, with James Marshall (Falmer Press, 1996); Counternarratives, with Henry Giroux, Peter McLaren and Colin Lankshear (Routledge, 1996); *Education Policy* (Elgar, 1999), coeditor with James Marshall; and with Dunmore Press: *Critical Theory, Poststructuralism and the Social Context* (Eds.) (1996); *Cultural Politics and the University* (Ed.) (1997), and; *Virtual Technologies and Tertiary Education* (1998), co-editor with Peter Roberts. He was Academic Vice-President for the New Zealand Association of University Staff in 1997 and Vice-President of the branch at the University of Auckland during the first semester of 1998.

Peter Roberts

Dr Peter Roberts is a Senior Lecturer in the School of Education at the University of Auckland. His major areas of scholarship are educational philosophy and higher education policy. His work has appeared in a wide range of international journals. He has published two other books with Dunmore Press: *Virtual Technologies and Tertiary Education* (co-edited with Michael Peters, 1998) and Paulo Freire, *Politics and Pedagogy: Reflections from Aotearoa–New Zealand* (an edited collection, 1999). He has recently completed another book, *Education, Literacy and Humanization*, to be released by Greenwood Press in 2000.